LETTERS FROM A GENEVA PENSIONNAT

BY FLORA EWING

2015
DOTOS BOOKS
LONDON

Foreword

This book contains about seventy letters written by Flora Ewing during her stay in Switzerland (between September 1913 and October 1914). The appendix includes two extra letters form a later period which are related to the events in the earlier years.

Flora was living in Geneva in Pensionnat Mange at Délices Voltaire, studying, travelling and making new friends.

The original letters have been kept in the family for many years and her daughter Judith David has transferred them into an electronic format.

There are about hundred photographs in the book which show some people and places mentioned in the letters.

This edition is the first publication of the letters and keeps the original orphography.

Publisher

Flora Ewing

Geneva
14th September 1913

Dear Mother,

I got your letter on Friday, with great joy. Mamselle (sic) Albertine, from the other end of the table, grinned audibly at my face, (which, if you had seen, you would never laugh again,) that it would be an awful nuisance to write every week. I am very sorry that my letter was so long in coming but I really couldn't help it and if Mamselle had sent that letter to the post soon after she got it you should have received it at least on Tuesday night. My remark about Olive's dresses was not from envy, but because I was wondering when she could wear them; as for my dresses the difficulty I have with them is that, this one is too grand for one occasion, that too pretty to wear just now, and so I go on, and in consequence I have worn very few dresses yet.

It doesent (sic) matter about that other apron, as I think I can wear one a week quite well (Ginney's). This week's one is not dirty except where I slid down the banister, and that was the first time on, too, but I shall not get my apron in the road again.

I don't care tuppence for my scent bottle, I only wanted to know where it was. I don't know where anything of mine is, with so many people unpacking for me. Did you send the brown mad–cap? Have you got the notice of Simon Peter's funeral yet? If you have I'm glad there's the English Channel between me and the row there will be.

I don't care whether my descriptions sounded jaundiced or

not, I both meant and mean it. Mamselle is nothing more or less than a PIG! with a very big P. I just heartily detest her. She is a big fat heartless creature, she sneers, laughs and is really rude to the girls as well as being unreasonable. I was writing some P.C.s when she came into the room and said, "Let me see your cards," of course I had to hand them over, then she said, "What did you buy them for," so I said because I wanted them. Then she said with a sneer, "So you like coloured cards, do you." I said I did. Then she commenced to criticize them saying this one she thought very comical, what did I get that one for. I was feeling sore about those cards already as some of the girls had been snubbing me before, upon the subject. It's absolutely taken all the pleasure away from the things, and I really have some very pretty ones. The girls are decent enough. I cant think what I put in my last letter to depress you, or how it could depress you if it made you laugh.

We went right to the other end of the lake, on Friday, and visited the Château de Chillion (sic). We were shown all through it. I have enclosed two P.C.s of it. The highly coloured one gives the best idea of its position but doesent (sic) show the mountains at the back. They are simply lovely. I never saw such high ones, some have snow on them. I have seen Mt Blanc, it is simply lovely. When I saw it, it had a lovely pinky light on it. I have nothing much to say this time, but what I have, my fountain pen refuses to put down. I have filled it three times and still it refuses to write.

I feel quite the simple muslin frocked country maiden here among these gaudy and transparent damsels. I have counted as many as ten pieces of jewellery on one girl. Mamselle Albertine has eight rings on, sometimes, all the girls have at least one on, some four, with other items thrown in. I have worn two broches (sic) since I came here, one for my skirt only. It also seems to be the thing to show as much underclothing as possible, in consequence you see blouses like, well, five part holes and one part cloth. It was my pen's fault the paper is in such a mess but it is filled for a fourth time and seems to be right at last.

I have now turned over a new leaf.

You remarked something about eating and habits. Well as to the eating business I never ate so much in my life, before. I have not been so hungry lately as I was at first but I eat plenty. There is not a girl likes the bread much, one of them put the matter very neatly by saying, "You never can get enough of that bread, because if you take a big piece its so full of holes you really can hardly find anything to eat."

I believe I am getting worse instead of better at tennis, at least my serving is. I have too brawny an arm for tennis, because when I hit the ball it goes way out of the court altogether, or else I miss it. As to serving, I either send the ball slash into the net, or nearly knock the fence at the other end down.

You can tell the kid[1] that one of the girls has given me a lot of ripping stamps from her letters which I shall share with her. They will be all new to her. Please tell me when she arrives and I shall send them. This last week seems to have flown. I suppose it is because we have not properly begun lessons, yet, and also Thursday and Friday were holidays. On Thurs. I played tennis and stayed in, and on Frid. we went an all day excursion

---

1 Her sister Dorothy, 5 years younger.

on the lake.

We get ripping food here, everything is beautifully cooked, and of the best, and you can have two helpings if you like. I have been the whole afternoon at this letter and that is all I have done but theres been a thunderstorm and I've got a headache, and the girls have such loud voices and I have no consentration (sic), therefore I was consistently being distracted.

I am the youngest in appearance and in manner too, I believe, here, but I am as tall as most and older than three or four. But the three or four younger are most kindly patronizing and anxious to keep me from falling into evil ways, that's one of the reasons why Olive and I will not get on very well, because she is always either openly or hintingly showing me my faults; we never get together but she starts correcting me, or at tennis she amuses me very much by considering it her duty to encourage me by saying, "That's right, Flora, your getting on," etc, etc. You never see that girl for five minutes but she laughs, she laughs ever and always.

I think French people are absolutely absolutely — —. The other day Mamselle, before starting the lesson, gave us a lecture on how to use the plugs and things in the water closet and, I believe, told us why we were to do such and such thing, and when, etc. Fortunately I could not understand the latter part of her discourse which was, I believe, more interesting than the first. She is awfully cheeky about the girls' clothes. The girl in my room has a lot of clothes she is not allowed to wear. She has a green costume but Mamselle doesent like green, so she was taken into town and had to buy another: the same with a hat, a blouse and a dress. Mam. doesent like dark clothes. She is absolutely like a silly petted child about things she cant forse (sic) you to do, but would like. She says, "Now then, you see, if you had done as I said," or, "You look very hot, its that blouse again." She continually harps on about nothing.

I have read this letter through and I dont see anything to depress you in it, so let me know if it has. The last page is a bit grumbly, certainly, but it means nothing. You must be having a lovely peaceful time there at home with the house to yourselves. I cant get a moments peace anywhere as we are not allowed into our bed–rooms. I find it unpleasantly different from being able to go upstairs at home, and not see anyone for a whole afternoon. I feel much comforted: Marjorie has chosen two of my despised P.Cs to copy for albums or something. All my things, needle book, hanging case for reels etc, and my little button boxes have been very much admired by the girls, also Mam. said, "You have very pretty things (clothes) and must try to keep them nice." That was one of the (cont.) post card.

P.S. The P.C. is for our maid Helen.

THIS OBJECT
IS OUR
DEARLY BELOVED
MADEMOISELLE
MARIE.!

Délices Voltaire
20 Sept. 1913

Dear Mother and Daddy,

I hope you are still enjoying yourselves. Mother mentioned in her letter that it was a little dull. Did you ever hear the story of the man who was greatly bothered with an owl which continually hooted at his window at night so that he couldn't hear the nightingale. He shot the owl, but found the silence much harder to bear than the noise, as the nightingale has stopped too, and was forced to repent his act. Perhaps Dorothy is the nightingale whose voice I (the owl) drown, and now that you are rid of me, Dorothy having nobody to fight with, will be silent also. (Perhaps!!).

The owl is beginning to have rather a good time here. Things arent much different, but I am getting used to things a bit, and I find the time pass very quickly. Each day on looking back seems long, but it seems only yesterday since last Sunday, and yet tomorrow is another. Olive's chum seems inclined to take me under her other wing, and I have no objections to going. She has got a face just like the Madonna's, but is anything but Madonna–like in nature. If there has been any mischief done you can be sure she was not far from the bottom of it. Olive has had a fit of home–sickness at last, but it was jealousy helped it. She got a letter from home, and then we had dancing that evening, and Olive is like me and doesent dance much, and her chum does, and she danced an awful lot with another girl, and hardly spoke to Olive. I noticed she looked funny, and the next I saw was her crying in a corner, and refusing to say what was wrong;

she recovered but hasent (sic) been quite the same since.

We go to church in a Music Hall here, and the people come in any time they like. The Minister stopped his reading today, because the late people disturbed him so, and made a speech at them. Also when the people get tired they get up and go out.

We had tea in a café after spending an afternoon in a museum and then went on the lake in a little motor boat.

When I come home, have either scones or oat cakes waiting for me when I arrive, for I shall see neither here.

You know that fat girl with the languishing eyes I spoke of, well I have had to walk with her these last two days as neither of us can get anyone else, and its awful, we don't want to walk with each other, and simply just don't open our mouths.

I have not got into the yelling habit, nor am I accustomed to it in other people. In fact I have been asked if I *have* a voice and to speak louder, continually. Marjorie is by a long chalk the most ladylike person in this school. Its all very well for Marjorie to stuff you with tales about how Mams. likes you to eat but Mams has a very clever little way of presenting you with a spoonful of stuff which is not very much, and then she says, "Too much, is it?" and takes some of it away. Fountain pens are most obnoxious articles because when you are searching for inspiration and are unconscious of your surroundings, you wake up to find a few blots on your possessions, and know you must have been waving your pen in the air again.

Its funny, but its very convenient, that although we only get butter and jam together on Sunday, I have never, even the very first time, missed the butter. Although at home it was horrid, this type of bread seems better fitted for jam alone. I am getting absolutely gluttonous now. After a meal is finished, I just think over the number of things I could eat more; the result is not pleasing.

We are having both heat and cold here. Cold in the morning and heat when we go out for our daily trot – its nothing more or less than a trot. The girl who has been leading lately, is so afraid anyone will get in front of her that she absolutely runs. I never go out anywhere, church or walk, but I get a stitch in my side with the pace, always.

The only day I can get for writing is Sunday. I believe we can write on Thursday in the winter but not now. I got your letter last Tuesday and the other one on the Friday before. Dorothy's letter was a shock and a convulser, I howled over it. It was a good thing Jeannie was beside her to help her to remember and spell the hens' names.

I expect anything short of chaos would seem orderly after the mess there was. It would take more than all Vienna put together to teach me music. They wont succeed here, I know that much. I am made to play quite a different way, here, and in consequence cant play at all. I have to lift my fingers high into the air when I play, and have all new music and am not allowed to play the old. The only thing this master has inspired my soul with is fear, which only makes me play worse and practise harder. We are not worked very hard yet, I think, and I have been making an exhibition of myself with what we have.

I have only two tooth brushes, perhaps you threw the other one away with the rubbish. Ask Dorothy how many she has, perhaps I left mine there.

I got Kate's[1] letter and she sounded so funny somehow, and

---

1 Her brother Jack's wife.

just as if she wasent (sic) married, her going out to play tennis.

My room–mate is very decent, and doesent care much for talking, either. Mamselle says we suit each other excellently that way. As a matter of fact, my keys are on the table in my room, and in my cupboard, I have been wondering if I could take the key out, because the interfering girl took my racket out and lent it to someone and I don't want her to do it again. Do you know that in all those dresses I have not one pocket, its atrocious. I explained carefully to Mad. how you worked my pink dress and she, as carefully, did it the other way, so I left it at that and sorted it myself after. You can say what you like about my eating but it was not pretense (sic), sometimes I ate a lot of bread and sometimes a little, my appetite was as erratic as the rest of me. Do please give Phyllis[1] a poke and remind her you have an elder daughter. I wrote to her but received no reply. I cant believe I have been here only three Sundays, it seems like three months.

Mamselle remarked that the 'family' was coming to tea to-day, and therefore we are to have tea earlier, as the family is about fifteen strong.

I was reading your first letter over again and noticed that about Olive. I quite agree that she seems older than me in some ways and I think she herself notices it, for she really is most horribly patronizing, sometimes. Somehow I think there is some misunderstanding between us, because sometimes she is quite gracious to me, and others will not hardly look at me, and sometimes I like her very much, and others could scratch her eyes out, or at least give her a good piece of my mind.

---

1 Phyllis Turnbull, her best friend.

The blow which has been threatening for a long time has fallen at last, and I was marched off to the dressmaker with three of my dresses, to start with, and down they have come. However she said, when she heard that I had only begun corsets, that if I left off them, I could have my skirts shorter, so (I could scream just now, there's that fat girl jabbering away about nothing and, not having a gentle voice, she is disturbing all the room!) so I have decided to have my skirts shorter. Mad has done nothing else but peer at my skirts since I came. She has a most piggish way of continually announcing that I am nearly seventeen, everything I do or say, or happens, nearly seventeen, seventeen this, seventeen that. It's bad enough to be going on seventeen, but to have it thrown at you six months too soon is more than human nature can stand. The family has arrived, and the row!! Its all boys except three girls, and the boys are boys indeed! They commenced having a tug–of–war outside the back door and absolutely swarmed around, and I had to wait about fifteen minutes at the head of the stairs, waiting for them to go away before I could come out. I don't think much of your 'charming Swiss youths', and am more than likely to return wholehearted and thankful–hearted. I don't see why, in this outlandish place, girls should put on long dresses soon, and boys of sixteen wear socks! and never dream of long trousers till about twenty–one. Its absolutely comical, the boys here sprout moustaches very early indeed, and the result is not a success with short trousers…

I am enclosing a P.C. to show you the different rooms. The house looks a beautiful country mansion, there in the P.C. but the flats which absolutely surround it are carefully hidden. They have managed that photo very cleverly because it is not nearly so nice as that, the grounds look beautiful there, but they are untidy and look sort of unkempt, a bit.

We sing hyms (sic) at night and its awful!!

There are only two beds in my room. They say its pretty, but I don't see it. The wall paper!!! The floor is polished, and twice I have come bang! onto the floor when walking or dancing over it. The girl in my room leaves a week tomorrow, and I am wondering who I shall get next. I tremble when I think of the undesirables, of which there are many.

We start lessons properly at ten o'clock, but we new girls have an hour with the other pupil teacher who is a most peculiar specimen. She has a broad flat expressionless face. She cant keep order, nobody respects her, she giggles all of a sudden at nothing, has little bursts of temper, also at nothing, is absolutely characterless, has no opinions of her own, absolutely not a scrap of firmness, but wavers and wiggles over her decisions; continually worrys (sic) you to do this or that without need. Even her very walk shows just a weak wiggly nature. <u>She</u> hears our lessons in the morning for Mamselle. We get an old man with twinkly eyes for literature (at least I think its literature, but he talks so fast I understood nothing). We get a young man for, I don't know what, but he lectured us upon Italy, and as he spoke very slowly I understood quite a lot. We also get a conceited funny little creature for History; she absolutely ought to put her hands in a glass case and send them to a museum, she would get more people to look at them then. We don't appreciate them enough.

Did you give Helen her post card?

Olive and Marjorie are so funny when they are writing. Olive will demand in a highly dictorial (sic) voice, "Marjorie, are you remembering such and such a thing." Marjorie replies very humbly that she has not yet done such and such a thing. Olive then replies, "Well, see and remember then," or, "Very well, but don't forget, now." Now and then, Olive comes down off her high horse, being obliged to ask Marjorie how to spell some word which even I could spell, one was, "Please Marjorie is there a 'p' in glimpse?"

They have stopped me reading, very effectually, by simply giving me a French book to read; it isent (sic) even interesting and therefore I always find something very pressing to do when they say I can read.

Do ask somebody to send me a post card because I am going to arrange them on the walls. Mamselle likes you to plaster the walls absolutely, with as many as you like. I am willing to do anything to hide the wall paper.

Its funny but Marjorie is three years younger than the other pupil teacher and has been here only a fortnight, but everybody does what Marjorie wants instantly and never dreams of disobeying, and yet she never scolds or anything. Olive says her father is coming to fetch her as soon as we come back from the mountains, and, really, it is not worth waiting the full time as I wont get any more lessons, so can I come home then with them? It would be ripping because from what little I saw of Mr Reavell[1] I like him very much.

Time's up now so I must stop. Hurry up and write, jog anybody's elbow, Phyllis, Cathie, Ray, anybody, to write to me.

With much love to both,

I am your loving and dutiful! daughter, Flora.

---

1 Marjorie and Olive's father

Phyllis Turnbull

Délices Voltaire

Mesdemoiselles Albertine et Marie

Garden, Délices Voltaire

Dining room, Délices Voltaire

School room, Délices Voltaire

Les Pensionnaires

Délices Voltaire
I am ashamed of this untidy scrawl.
Please forgive me and I wont do it again.
24 Sept 1913

My dear Mother and Daddy,

You will just have to suffer this in pencil as it is written on the boat going to Lausanne, and I have managed at last to break my fountain pen. I was coming dowstairs and I scraped it against the banisters. What I complain of here is the having to write only on Sunday, because during the week I am continually finding something I would like to say, but, always, when I sit down to write on Sunday I find all my news has flown and I have practically to invent things to say. That last sentence is seemingly composed of 'I.s'. Well remembering how bored I was the time we were four hours on the lake I am taking the opportunity to write now. Its simply ripping on the lake today. The sun is shining on us and the water, making us both warm and nice. We are stopping at a little town called Nyon, just now. It is thoroughly picturesque with its painted house fronts and creeper–covered balconies. There is upon the hill an old, grey towered château, it looks very old. I believe it had something to do with Napoleon but what he was doing in Switzerland I don't pretend to know. All along the lake–side are houses (not all along but here and there). It must be lovely to have your garden right on the edge of lake. Its as calm as calm today. There isent scarcely. a ripple on the surface. There is a heat haze hanging round which makes everything blue: blue water, blue sky, and blue haze.

Are you meaning my brown woolen cap or the brown silk mad–cap. I have the woolen cap but havent looked in the list yet to see if you have marked the mad–cap. The tissue paper is all in my box waiting for my return.

It wasent the post cards you paid a penny each for but I should have put another 1 ½ c stamp on that letter but I got it weighed and the girl said it wasent too heavy, in consequence you had to pay twice 1 ½ c. The highly coloured P.C. was only sent to give you an idea of Montreux. It wasent a pretty card. We don't see anything from our school but flats, much less lakes.

You needent worry about me coming back frightfully grown up because just now, at any rate, I am regarded as the school baby. The girls who are younger than me are all older; sort of, in looks. One of them held her sixteenth birthday a day or two ago, but she wears her hair proper up, her skirts proper down, high necks(very) sometimes, and the most super–fine grown up manners. I get most awful scoldings from her sometimes, for what does not concern her at all. I giggle irrelevantly (sic), however, in the middle. I am addressed as 'petite' (little one), and yesterday the under mistress explained carefully to me that I looked much younger than the others although my skirts are quite long now and my hair is up. She simply gasped when I explained that Olive is younger than me. Do I look so very juvenile, please? At home I was accustomed to be called 'A big fat lump', but here it is 'Petite'. As to fads, it wont be that, but a wig, my hair is home–sick and is dying of a broken heart, in other words it has never stopped coming out since Corsock[1], and these last two days its been something awful. This is 'Thonon les Bains' now. We were here for an excursion once, its very pretty. I shall not want to wear all your and my own jewellery when I come home, or at least I don't think so, just now.

The Austrian girl is nothing special, her clothes are smart but not grand. Mamselle has been at me about one of my blouses. She seems to have taken a dislike to it, she doesent like dark things, its my blue alpaca. She tried all sorts of ways to make me take it off without absolutely ordering me, but in vain, then unfortunately something happened. The tape is too high up on the blouse, and in consequence I had to wear a broch (sic), and in consequence the broch tore it, and in consequence Mamselle got her chance and said, "Well, you don't put that blouse on again till its mended", a most unnecessary remark, I think. Well it turned out that this tear was a most fortunate thing as it gave me something to learn how to mend on, you are supposed to tear something every week so as to learn how to mend it at the lesson. I have made not such a bad job of it for a first attempt and have taken the tape off, so now I shall be able to flaunt it once more before Mamselle's astonished eyes.

The food is really ripping, only hasent been so nice lately. We get stewed apples about three times a week. But they are different from home and are nicer, the fruit is whole. The bread is... well, I don't know; I am getting used to it, and am ready to eat anything. I have been punished for my greed, because I have been trying to eat the bread quickly so as to get more, and in consequence my indigestion has come back. Also since

---

1 Her father's home town in Dumfriesshire

I have come here I am horribly pimply, not as bad as Olive, thank goodness, as my pimples come where they are not noticed, but really and truly the bread is indigestible.

I can well believe that 'Poor Lizzie Black[1]' would not in the least need leading from the path of Duty!

(Lausanne) I have been at Lausanne and am in the boat coming home. Lausanne is quite a decent place for nothing special. We just wandered around and did nothing and had dinner and tea. I don't think it will be difficult to make your jams eke out itself. I did not eat much else. I had plenty of butter and jam.

Although you think it and nobody properly realises that I am away for good but you will when school begins again. surprisingly. She is bare faced enough for anything. I shall write for a lot of people in ink

We don't seem to start really properly work until October. I am not learning dancing, German, music and am doubtful about the rest. Dancing and German start later. I have nearly finished my first piece of fancy work (it is fancy work not in the least what was intended). It is a set of mats for the wash–stand. I am going to send them to Jeanny as she was always interested and tried to teach me that fine art. I have had my first singing lessons. If you only heard Olive singing you would never talk of me singing again. She says, if she can get good enough, she'll make it her career. I am getting all kinds of exercises and have to practise for fifteen minutes a day. Its bound to improve my voice a little, which is a consolation. Your underlining of singing, so vigorously, can be taken as anything but complimentary to my voice!

---

1 Her mother's maiden name

You made me giggle when you said my last letter was written in a better spirit, because I had been in a vile temper all day and was kind of at the crisis when I was writing.

These pages are most awfully crushed but they have been in my hand bag.

Mamselle said when she grabbed my pen in an awful fury that a new nib would cost five or six or seven francs, but when she handed it to me today she said, "One franc fifty centimes." I hadent got that however, so she had to do without. She absolutely cleared me out when she made my accounts with me. I still have thirty–five francs yet, which should last me to Christmas, I hope.

The Austrian girl in my room leaves on Tuesday and is packing today, and its awful, the mess in the room and on the landing. There are two new girls coming later, perhaps next week, both German, and as there are two empty beds, one in my room, and one in the room opening off, I expect I shall have two new neighbours, I hope they are decent!

I got your parcel at tea–time today, and am wearing the apron now. It really is most convenient because my other one is horrible! (dirty).

I was walking with a German today, and we had a long discussion about prospective wars. She says that they have no reason to fight and that the children are <u>not</u> collecting for war. She says that they certainly would side against us to help another country, and gave me lists of the countries.

I got a most lovely surprise this morning. The other day I made up my mind to make a definite attempt to find out what had become of Greta Simpson, so I sent a post card to her old address (Bessie McIntosh said she'd gone to Glasgow) but

I thought I'd chance it. Well this morning I got an answer, and so I shall answer her tomorrow and then we shall be all right.

One of the new girls has arrived just now, Sunday morning, don't think much of her, but shall wait and see.

I am going to the English church today with one or two others, so shall at last have a chance of understanding what is said to me, I havent hitherto. You see, with understanding so little, I always forgot to listen.

We have a little Swiss who comes to teach us History of Art (Italy) and when he is lecturing I can understand almost everything he says. I understand very well but cant talk, but really with the talking too, its only the verbs and things like that. I find that I know my words but not how to place them, and their tenses.

Its awful just now, the new girl came into the room just now, and before she came in all was quietness but the moment she came in everybody started showing off. I can tell the minute Olive starts showing off, and shes going it strong, and the voice!! Yesterday I had a headache with the noise and its coming back now. Really I think foreign girls have harder shriller voices than we, and they certainly make the most of them. The girl next to my room has a very shrill voice, and honestly she hardly ever speaks to you, but you think she has got hold of the idea you are very deaf. There is another girl too who has a most fearfully vulgar voice, and absolutely bawls about the place. Olive too has a very loud voice, and when she 'shows off laughs', I could choke her. Now that I have given my opinion so frankly of loud voices, I don't think you need have any fear that I will develop one like those here. The only time I raise my voice is to try and say something that is necessary. Then I have to yell, absolutely. The noise is getting worse and so is my head, everybody is yelling. Now I absolutely had to stop and hold my ears a minute ago. Next time I get started I am absolutely going to throw caution to the winds and ask if they find it absolutely necessary to try and deafen each other, and prevent those who are trying to do their duty and write home, from doing so!

I have been to the English Church, and it was nice enough, but when the man was reciting the commandments he took a big breath, and began in a big voice and gabbled for all he was worth, to the end of his breath, and then took another big gasp and went off again, each time dying down. His sermon was interesting, very, but I thought it was more interesting than improving, and seemed solely to impress upon us that there were such things as angels in the world below, if our eyes were opened to see them. There was absolutely nothing else in it, and I could not see the moral. It was very learned, and he must know a very great deal, but it seemed to me more a lecture. Just fancy, you are only just home from church a minute or two ago, and its two o'clock and weve been home nearly two hours. You cant absolutely imagine how I long for my Sunday afternoons at home, here you cant get away from people and be quiet, but perhaps it is to make me more sociable.

Do you know Mamselle is absolutely uncanny in the way she is continually turning up if you even *think* of doing anything wrong, and to *think* of her is as good as to go and look for her.

I had an awful time this morning: when the gong rang for breakfast I had my hair only just out of plaits, and had it to brush and replait and put up. I absolutely rammed it into plaits, anyhow, rammed it up, and of course it fell down again, and had to be redone, and then I had my bed to put right, but I just hauled the top clothes off, and praying that Mam. would not enter my room, descended, the most awful fright imaginable. Fortunately Mamselle did not appear for breakfast, and I had time to go and redo my hair all over again, and put in pins in various places, and get generally more respectable. In both our two rooms there was an awful scramble, and all because Mam said last night she was very tired and would let us all be late today, and then treacherously had breakfast earlier than she said.

I am not going to spend the whole afternoon over this letter as I usually do, as I have two others to write. Please ask Dorothy to hand that P.C. to Cathie, and tell her to hand it in to McCallums, as they live opposite to her school.

I simply cant understand my watch. Every day I put it fast, and yet its always slow.

At Lausanne we were allowed to buy chocolate, and oh! if you only tasted it, never in my life have I tasted such chocolate. I am going to bring some home, and I shall put it in my big trunk, as I should not be able to keep my hands off it otherwise, and I was only allowed to buy a very little!!!

Perhaps next week I shall be able to send you a photo of all the girls, I have ordered one or two copies.

Ow! Its one whole hour till tea, how shall I hold out!!

Well, goodbye till next Sunday,
with much love to you both.
Flora.

P.S. Please send a photo of the house too; you have some quite decent ones.

Délices Voltaire

Dear Daddy and Mother,

This is another week gone, for which we are devoutly thankful!

This has been what I call a regular English or Scotch day, only it rained harder than it would of at home. I went to church in my oilskin today, and the girls are quite charmed with it, much to my relief. I don't think much of the Pavements of Geneva, because, this morning, as I was daintily tripping along, I tripped daintily into a puddle about seven inches deep and was soaked, stockings and shoes, there being no Sir Walter Raleigh about, with what today would be an oilskin, I suppose.

Fat lucious (sic) pears indeed! If you had seen the thin, tasteless, juiceless article I got at dinner the other day. Pear, indeed! It might have been an uncooked potato, only it was too tough. I put one bit in my pocket, and the girl next me hid another bit, and so I was spared from dying in agonies from indigestion.

If you only saw my face with spots. I have three beauties perched on my chin, others on my cheeks, and more on my forehead. But its not my spots I mind but my hair. Honestly, I have a big big handful of rolls. I get a big one every moring, and you can see the difference horribly plainly. I'm going to demand permission from Mam to wash it twice a month, as you would think I had black hair, its so greasy.

How did your ill assorted party get off? I guess Lois and Mr Harkness would not be difficult to amuse, and Mrs Peebles would wax confidential over the two young men.

Phyllis has not sent her letter yet because, being Phyllis, she locked it up in her writing case, and is at present engaged in picking the lock, having lost the key. I have received Cathie's letter, however, and was obliged to laugh outright when she said she saw the Château de Chllion (sic) on a biscuit tin in a grocers shop, and recognised it at once.

My first thought, when I heard Phyllis' letter had fifteen pages, was, 'I hope she has enough stamps on!'

Have I missed such a very great pleasure in not having seen the Doctor Mackinnon boy, that you have underlined him so vigorously. I have my doubts if he could prefer this bread to any other; but that all depends where he got the other bread; and, at any rate, please remember that a great gluttonous school boy would like anything; and that it is an insult to my eppicure (sic) appetite for my taste to be classed with his!!

Do you know I had to wait till ten o'clock last Wednesday, before I could read my letter, as I had to practise.

Its rather funny, but I hope and suppose that, while I am writing my letter in Geneva, just now, you are writing yours at the same time at home, and, when I get my letter here, you get yours half an hour later, on Wednesday.

I got a most horrible fright this morning. I wanted my school broch (sic) for something, and it was not to be found, although I hunted in my boxes in my drawers, among my papers, under the bed, thought of all my dresses, but it wouldent come to light. At last, I pulled open a drawer, and glared inside it, and my eye fell on my tie box; my thoughts next went to its contents, and, mentally, I rummidged (sic), and, at last, remembered I had used it as a pin for one of my bows, so I have it yet — to lose again....

I have wrapped up the kid's ring, and will send it today. I went directly after breakfast, last Tuesday week, and asked permission to send it, but Mad said, "No, not just now," and then I asked her again, a day or two after, and again she said, "Wait till Sunday," so I waited till Sunday, and, at last, my mind will be at rest.

I have got a story, but its such a silly one, about a little boy who has a cruel aunt and an old grandmother, that I am horribly bored with the thing. (My French reading book). I can speak well enough, in a way, which means I get along somehow, but my verbs are an awful bother — they're frightful.

I got my first dancing lesson last night, and its quite decent. They laugh at my sandals, but they are nicer than the high heels, for all that. We got exercises, mostly, and learned how to curtsy. I can almost do it decently, but it was the nicest when the dancing master went away, and we closed the door upon Mad's watchful eye, and danced to a ripping tune; it's a song, really, which Olivier sings, and which she has graciously consented to lend me, afterwards. It's a most lovely thing, and last night my throat seemed to — I don't know what — and I could sing properly. I havent been able to more than aqueak since I came. I hope I will stay right.

I have got a little Hungarian in my room now; there's nothing like variety, thinks I. I am wondering if the king of Siam has a daughter coming, as I am to have another change after Christmas.

The new inmate of my room is the person who now relieves me of my position as sort of school baby!! She is only newly fifteen, and looks it, every inch. She is little, quiet and gentle, and can talk very little French, and I am now getting punished for trying to show how clever I was and talk German, because now she gabbles away in German at me, and I have to eat humble pie, and say, "I don't know what you are talking about."

My word! I can promise you that that valuable Persian kitten will be dull no longer when Thomas comes home to his own, again. Valuable Persian kitten or no, it will have to skip out lively, I can tell you. Have you heard any news of Tom, yet?

Thanks awfully for the P.C.s. I don't mind even if they are educational; anything to hide the wallpaper. Please, you know those photos of the kittens, and all the rest of the photos Daddy has taken, well, couldent you send a few; you know that nice photo of Dorothy, well, couldent you send a copy of it. It was so ripping: just as I had made up my mind to ask all round for photos, Cathie sent me one in her letter, so that starts the collection, so don't you be behind, but please do send some too.

My word! If you asked or thought our school Madonna was German!!! My word, the Checks (sic) and the Germans are Bosom Enemys (sic). We are quite friendly, but she is Olive's chum, and I never feel quite comfortable when she favours me instead with her company, as Olive is very jealous natured, and stands and glowers at us from a distance...

My pen has another pet on today and refused to work properly although it has been filled twice.

Mamselle says she will buy me another woolen vest, as I have only one, and a pair of boots. Please say that you want me to have long ones, in your next letter, as the girls go about in the most hideous little stubby things.

Mam demanded of me my birth certif., in a voice ferocious, and I had to tremblingly say, "If you please, Mamoiselle, my mother has mislaid it, but will send it as soon as possible." Then Mad became more furious, and said, "Tell your mother to send it AT ONCE!!! At once!" I have had to buy such a lot of things which Mam thinks are necessary but which are not.

She wont let me wear my Sunday shoes, as she says, "People don't wear those sort of things here." I shall wear them all the oftener at home, to make up.

I, very evidently, was not intended to make accounts, as I have not been given the proper powers. My account book was awful this time, and Mam scolded and scolded, and after she had yelled a few nice things at me, and straightened out the muddle a bit, she found I had spent fifteen centimes more money than I had to begin with. That was the climax: she said a few more nice things, and then said she would give me my money franc by franc. Olive also has had trouble today, but she is not so used to being scolded by Mam as me, and so she wept, although the same things were said to us both.. She also seems to have spent more money than she had to spend.

Its so nice now: my correspondence is increasing. I get about three letters a week. I had yours, Cathie's and one from Grandpa this week, but, of course, there is a drawback: it's the having to answer them, and not having enough time. Its funny; at home I hated writing letters, but, here, I long for the time to come when I may unburden my heart. Ahem!

I suppose I must stop for another week, so please remember the photos.

With much love,
your loving
Flora.

Délices Voltaire
12 October 1913

My dear Mother and Daddy,

Heres another week gone and you are another week nearer that dreadful day when I shall invade your peaceful dove cot!!! once more, bringing chaos and confusion with me. Somebody said to me at dinner just now, "Its nine weeks till Christmas," and I just gasped. Really the time passes frightfully quickly. I judge it by my nightgown. I have to put fresh ribbons in every week, and just when I am a little used to the pink, I have to pull them out and put in blue.

My dear mother, you, instead of paying me out for my bad writing by writing me an illegible epistle too, should have heaped coals of fire on my head by making yours copperplate, as an example, but, really, I had a lot of trouble to make it out.

Its atrociously cold here in the morning, but we are always roasted alive, almost, when we go for our promenade. Some of the trees, here, are almost bare, and others are in full plumage still.

I quite agree with you and I alone know how the Ministers' wives manage on £160; not if they sent their daughters to school in Switzerland, especially at Pensionnat Mange. I no sooner get any money but everybody comes flocking round me for it. I thought that 35 francs would last me till Christmas but I don't now, after Mad has most kindly provided me with a drill costume. We do drill in dark blue jerseys and navy blue knickers.

Have you rescued Thomas from the cat home yet? You don't

say, or do you mean to let him languish there for good now, or has he finished languishing now?

What is it you want me to open my eyes and see? The only thing I see here is my extreme ignorance. You can content yourselves with this, that, without any effort on my part, I couldn't help coming home with a little more knowledge in my cranium. I say that in five weeks I have learnt more French than in the five years I spent on it at school, and its true!

I am not keeping a diary, and if I did I shouldent have time to write in it. I have time for nothing here. You will have to be satisfied with my letters as a diary, and I'm sure I put my impressions of the town and people etc very clearly there.

You seem to forget that when I come home my room is to be my drawing room, and, therefore, if that photo of Jack and Kate is not respectable, I shall not have it in my sanctum, which is to be a vision of beauty etc, ahem.

Please do not mention in your letters what you are living on or what you will come to, as I have been imagining you going about with a hunk of cheese in one hand and a hunk of bread in the other — but *bread* and *water*!! Bread and cheese wasent so bad as its very good for you, but bread and water!!...

We don't have fires, stoves or hot bricks here. We have hot air which comes up through a grating in the hall, and which makes the hall frightfully hot and the rooms frightfully cold. I have never been hungry again since I was at Montreux and ate such a huge dinner, but I am always ready for my meals and always eat a lot, and want more. I always say to people that I have never been hungry again after that dinner, but truly it's the last time that I absolutely longed for a meal.

You had better know the worst at once, and its this:

Madmoiselle Albertine said the other day that I was already a little fatter about the face, and I have had a week of stuffing since. They say that everyone fattens here, but I don't see how, the way we are made to walk. Every week we join the boat to some village on the lake, and then we commence to walk! That is besides a promenade every day.

A week ago we crossed the frontier into France which is quite close to us, so now I can say I have stood with one foot in Switzerland and one in France.

Its horribly embarrassing the way everybody admires my things here. Mad said yesterday that I had very pretty things indeed, and she also said the other day that those of the girls who had the smallest wardrobe, always, always have the nicest things, and although my wardrobe is really quite large, it is small in comparison to some, and much prettier. One of the girls who has an unlimited amount of clothes, whenever I put on anything new, regularly comes up and admires it. The last time she said she liked all my things very much, so I told her it was a good thing she liked them, as she'd have to see them for long enough.

I got four letters last week, perhaps it will be five the next, but doubt it, as pretty nearly all who will write to me have done so. I got <u>one</u> letter from Ray and Mary with half inch spaces between the words and inch spaces between the lines. This time I couldn't read your letter till the afternoon. I think, every time I get a letter, it is my turn to practise from half past seven till nine (breakfast in between). Just imagine, at half past five by your time, when you are all sweetly snoring in bed, your daughter is crawling shiveringly out of bed.

I hear Sunday school has started again; has it grown at all?

I think that was the only piece of news I could find in Mary's letter. I am enclosing a photo of us all, but unfortunately its <u>not</u> of us all; the Madonna and several new girls are omitted. Just take the thing in your hand in a good light, examine it carefully and then tell me what it is that I resemble. The first glance at myself brought the word 'mother' to my lips, and afterwards 'Dorothy'. I have it by me now and it is awfully like you.

The Austrian has departed, and I have got a Hungarian, and I don't like her. She is silly, sort of, frankly, I don't know what she is, but I wish I had someone else. I believe she lasts till Christmas only, and then Germany comes to the fore. I suppose that at last, by the time this letter arrives you will have got that awful ring. Really I think the fates were against me ever getting it off. I wrapped it up on Saturday (week) night, and on Sunday night Mad unwrapped it and did it up again, then on Monday morning I put the stamps on, and laid it in the hall to be posted, and on Monday afternoon Mad came in and nearly bit my head off because I had had to put on little stamps as all my big ones were finished. Well, on Tuesday morning she did it up again and told me to steep the stamps. Then I demanded money to post it with, and dident get it till Friday. Then I sent it to the post, and it came back because I had not put on any sealing wax, and even then it wasent going to go unless I stamped it, and I had to borrow a thing with initials, that's why its got A.K. on it. I have had a headache all week and I am sure its with worry.

Do you know since I have come here I am sure I am developing 'second sight'. Please, were you the seventh child? If I think of a thing I see it; if I think of a sound I hear it; if I think of a thing it happens; and just the day before yesterday a girl looked at me, and then opened her mouth to say something, and, mentally, I said what she said to me, in the exact words (it was a question), and we had not been speaking even to each other, and the thing had nothing to do with the present; and, ever so often, I have had warnings not to do a thing, and, when I have done the thing, harm comes. I read a book some time or other about that, and how it could be trained. Fun if I started prophesying for the nation, and gave lectures and exhibitions. Ahem!

We went an excursion on the lake on Friday and had tea on the lake edge, and afterwards our photos taken. There were at this inn, sort of place, four great, huge St Bernards, and, I think, eleven or twelve little puppies all sprawling under and around an old wheelbarrow. They were the sweetest, dirtiest, softest little things, and, after tea, I grabbed handfuls of sugar for them. It was so pretty to see them struggling to get at the sugar.

We get a simply lovely lesson on Fridays here. Its 'History of Art'. We are taking Italy, and its most frightfully interesting, and we are shown pictures of all the places. Also we are getting the French Revolution for History and its much more detailed than we get at home and much more interesting; we get Litterature, I think its about some French authors of Louis XIV time, but really I don't know, as I cant make out a word he says, as he speaks so quick and indistinctly; even the more advanced have difficulty, but the Art–full one speaks slowly and distinctly, and in consequence he adds F.M.E. to the sum of his listeners.

We get the flat uninteresting subjects, like grammar, from the prosaic and uninteresting Mad. I would really like to pay proper attention to her words of wisdom, but I never quite succeed.

We go to a hall for Drill, where there is another Pension which gets Drill with us too. Its decent enough but not very interesting, as yet. It's the dancing lesson that is the cure though. The master is the best dancer in Geneva, has danced in the Ballet, teaches all the Pensions, practically, and, oh, etc, etc. Really, I think a man is very out of place teaching dancing. We got more exercises and are learning to waltz, but its not very much good to me as we do it different at home.

I got Phyllis' letter at last but it wasent fifteen pages, in fact it was only three, but better than nothing.

Mad made us raid our cupboards yesterday and hand out everything belonging to summer and put them away in our trunks, and bring out our winter things. I put on my winter flannels yesterday and they are so lovely and warm. Boo! I have ten minutes to finish this letter in and my pen is giving out.

I have got to the stage where I am beginning to think in French, a little, and where it sounds funny when I hear English. Also I suppose you notice that my spelling is a little worse (if possible) than usual.

I am going to send you money at Christmas and ask you to buy me a few little tartan things, and send them to me, as presents to the girls I want to present with trophies of my favour..

I am getting alarmed now because I am smaller than girls who arent a bit big, and at gym the mistress said, "Oh, youre among the 'Petits'".

What are they going to have at the Junior Choir this year? I suppose it has started once more.

I want to write a P.C. to Helen and have two minutes to write it in, so au revoir (Pardon me).

With much love to you both, and
best wishes for her future
happiness to the Kid,
your loving
daughter,
Flora.

Please, I know my composition is awful, but when you have much to say and little time, you cant help jumbling things in your hurry.

Madmoiselle Marie (right)

Madmoiselle Mange (Marie)

Délices Voltaire
18th Oct. 1913

My dear Mother and Daddy,

Once more I set me down to write my weekly epistle, doesent the time fly? I no sooner get one letter safely posted but I begin all over again.

We keep very early hours here, earlier than Mad thinks. We go to bed at nine (eight at home) and I get up at six (five at home). Mad forbids us to get up before half past six, but that's nothing. Mad does not know that I get up so early, and would be considerably surprised if she did. In fact this morning she took the opportunity to say as much as, "It would be good for Flora to get up at <u>seven</u>!!

I hope and suppose you have received that ring by now. I should love to see that kitten, but I suppose it's the first of the round of nice things that will come, now I'm off the scenes.

The dancing is quite nice and I can almost quite curtsey now. My Sunday shoes I can use for dancing now as they are what all the girls wear. With heels I am as tall as all the girls, pretty nearly.

My hair has stopped pouring out now after the perfect avalanche that fell after it was washed.

My spots almost went away but they have returned.

Thanks so much for the photos. I at last have got the tacks, and they grace the head of my bed, quite the thing. Bye, bye, I now go to practise my singing.

Kate's house sounds palatial, if it weren't for the polished floors I would be off to visit them at once, but I have had enough of polished floors.

I wouldn't mind a lesson or two in Swiss cooking as we do get the most lovely things but unfortunately they don't think to impart the art to us.

I also wonder when I shall wear my pink frock. I will get plenty of oppertunities (sic) later, as the others have all very grand frocks. It also has to be lengthened.

I still eat, but am not hungry. I am just glad when it is meal time and always eat plenty.

It was as I said in my last letter, I only got two letters this week from home and one from Greta Simpson. She also has a brother in Canada, Andrew, the nice one, do you remember him?

Do you know how many times I have changed my dress today, four times, and it is only two o'clock.

Two or three of the girls are complaining that they cant write today, and I am among them I think.

The dancing lesson was ripping last night, and I am beginning to like waltzing. I danced and danced with one girl, and could have gone on more.

The first tragedy after my change of room–mate is that we had no light last night, as she is always the last and wastes an awful lot of candle. I had half left at the end of a fortnight.

I stood again with one foot in France and one in Switzerland. The lesson of History of Art is becoming more enchanting than ever.

Its so funny but every snapshot where I am a fright is most painfully distinct, and those where I am good are so dark you can hardly see me.

I am sending you another photo but you cant tell whether I

am good or bad in it.

Please ask Phyllis to start writing her Christmas letter to me now, so that it will be finished in time, or in case she locks it up again.

What are the Junior Choir going to have this year?

I hope that medal isent broken, it really is a silly thing to send, but Mad refused to let me buy anything, and was furious with me when I put that in my letter. She was so furious that she snatched the letter up and dident give it back till the next day.

How are my chresanthemums doing; tell Dorothy to cut off nearly all the buds or they will not be nice. I suppose the grass wants cutting again. Is Dorothy doing it!

Melle Bailly, my singing teacher, said that some of my notes were quite good, and that I might be able to sing very well, if I worked!!

I have quite decided that I don't like Mad, in fact I detest her horribly.

I have got piles of ideas that will be useful afterwards, and already my habits are reforming (but only a little). I have been puzzled lately to know whether it is that I am cleaner or dirtier than everybody else, certain it is, however, that I wash a great deal oftener. We are only allowed to wash our faces once a day, so that leads to one more act of disobedience, washing in my bedroom.

I am trembling for the struggle that is threatening and will come surely, mainly that of the windows. I am absolutely going to refuse to sleep in my room if that little wretch shuts the window, and she says she will be very ill, sure, if the window is left open; as it is, the window is always shut in the morning, and I would like it open always as the room is not very big, and the kid has such a funny smell, always, which pervades all the room if the windows are shut.

It was a pity Lois and Melville refused to come to supper, but try, try, try again! But isent she about fifty years older than him?

I suppose Dorothy reigns in undisturbed possession of the seat; has she been moved in Sunday School?

So you have seen Alex Pitcairn off the scenes too, have you? I hope you will get over it. You see, its always you who falls in love with the young gentlemen, and I was bored when their praises were sung. Who are you setting on now?

Has Dorothy got an invitation to parties yet? Its about time, isent it.

I hope I shall have more to say next week but really I don't know what has come over me this time, I havent any news at all. I simply cant believe it's a week since I wrote the last letter, I think this week has gone quicker than any.

I am beginning to contaminate the girls already. Today six of us marched off in advance, the pupil teacher not being ready, and upon seeing her looming up in the distance I said, Lets run away, which we promptly did, four of us, and we hurried all the way to Church and got in long before the others, and got seats by ourselves. After the service the irate mistress said she was going to tell Mad, as we had no right to go without a mistress, but we told her it was her fault because she was late, and we had no time to wait for her!! She has not told Mad yet, and we are <u>not</u> waiting.

With much love to both,
I am your loving daughter
Flora.

They all giggled when they saw my letter, its so short.

A ma chére Flora, un petit souvenir de sa Mimi (fragment)

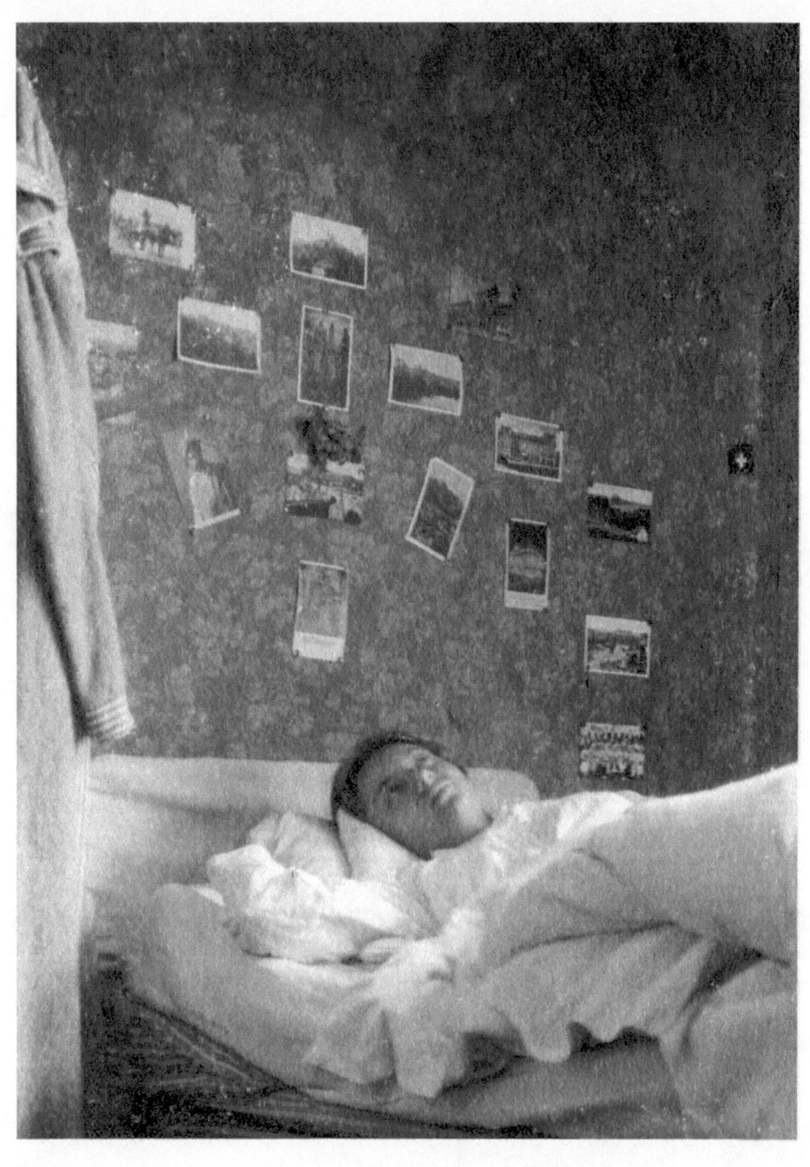

Postcards and photos on bedroom wall at Pensionnat

A ma chére Flora, un petit souvenir de sa Mimi

Délices Voltaire
26 Oct. 1913

My dear Daddy and Mother,

Heres another Sunday; privately, I think there are more Sundays in a month here than at home. Imagine, its nearly two months since I left my bereaved family lamenting. You never tell me if you are having such an easy and good time now, without the work–maker in chief (me), as you were expecting to have.

I have a piece or two of news (for the first time), its this, that, at last, after many years, some of the French rules are beginning to penetrate my brain. Quite naturally, I just gradually began to see them. I think it must have been what Mr Scott called 'unconscious cerebration'. Now that Marjorie has taken us in hand I really do understand what I am learning, and can apply it a little in my dictations. Mad said the other day when she saw I had (only!!) twenty–two mistakes in my dictée that it was not so bad, and it was improved (from thirty–four). She always does say that my dictations are really not bad, certainly not as bad as some. It's a great consolation to me to know that I can talk and spell better than some, which says little and means less. 'There came a loud triumphant sound, the girl, oh where was she? Ask of the maids who washed the dishes, I pray you don't ask <u>me</u>.' (Dinney).

Another piece of news is that Mad thinks that I have perhaps grown a little, and that I certainly will grow a lot more, and in consequence is getting my dresses prepaired (sic). I have some of them longer than my brown costume which is to be let down too. I have just given my party dress, but I am sure it will spoil it as it is so very thin, the stitches will leave a mark.

We also are boiling under winter blouses, woolen vests, etc. I refuse to wear my vest for a long time yet.

I have caught a cold, I don't know how, but Mad thinks she does, and talks appropriately. She says its with having my window open when I am in the room, and also she once caught me dressing with it open. If you catch a cold here, things are made pleasant for you. We are all catching them now, and are blessing the girl who started it. The others are getting asperines (sic) and made to stay in the house but I am supposed to be a big strong lump, and so I get nothing but scoldings, and plenty of them too. It's the biggest sin you can commit here, to catch a cold.

Mad has a lot of the girls on pills, and malts, and forced feeding, as there are <u>some</u> few girls who don't eat. All those that Mad thinks are anemic are forced fed and pill–dosed.

Am I supposed to be anemic, still? As I don't think it, or Mad's sharp eye would have found it out, but then I always get such a colour in the middle of the morning and the evening that she thinks I am as healthy and strong as a young horse, and also my <u>appetite</u>… but, to do me justice, I don't eat anything like what Olive eats, and she's pill–fed. Mad said the pills give energy. Don't I wish shed give me a box or two, as I am every bit as floppy as ever. Its really very mild here but Mad refuses to let us put on light things.

I am most relieved that that's the last of that awful ring. I hope Daddy's parcel arrived whole, and that hes not disgusted with the silk thing I sent him. As she wont let me buy presents, I suppose I shall have to invent something to send to the kid.

This is 1913 and its giving credit to its name, as every day last week Mad read accounts of accidents. Airships seemed to be falling in showers, and such a lot, German. And such a lot of mining disasters, too, all over the world. Whenever Mad tells us something really dreadful, I immediately think of the Daily Sketch with its graphic pictures.

It just struck me a little while ago, that, couldn't you send me a copy perhaps, if there was ever anything very interesting in it, not just mining or airships or things like that, but something important like, Mr Asquith's funeral after being murdered by the suffragettes, or the ruins of Westminster Abbey, or things like that – I hope you will never really have cause to send me a copy of things like that.

I was dreadfully sorry to hear that Mr McFee was dead, as he looked such a nice man, and although I never spoke to him I always liked him very much. Its funny, but its always those big handsome men who go off suddenly. You don't nearly so often hear of a little man.

I thought it would comfort your wearied soul and lightened purse to know that my things were a success. Marjorie caught sight of my green dress when I was examining the length and she pounced upon it with many ohs! and ahs! I know this much, that, when I put it on, I will have to put it off again very quick, and trail round to the dressmaker once again, but I prefer to wait.

I believe it would be as well to send me a little money soon, as I expect I have nearly finished what is left. You can take it from me that I will get a great deal of wear out of my wedding dress[1], as Mad expects us to put our best on for every little concert, I think.

I don't see what you found to laugh at when I said I would send you money to buy things with, as I have got some private funds to draw from, but, if you prefer to send them and deduct my allowance, its all one to me, only don't send expensive things. I only want little things, and half a crown is piles too much. That little broach (sic) you brought from Oban was greatly admired. Are they dear? Also those little poetry books, or little purses, or tiny bags; anything cheap and pretty, if those two vertues (sic) will go together. Thanks awfully much if you will send them. I only want about six, I think, or perhaps ten, and I'll send you a lovely Christmas present, as I have got an idea. You certainly must try to send a few tarten broidered hankeys as that's a lovely idea.

Oh la, the way the ribbon in my white dress is now yellow, and will have to come out. Shall I buy some myself or will you send that pretty blue, that came out of my wedding dress petticoat. It will cost perhaps a shilling to buy more, and only a penny to send it, so which is it to be?

It seems to me that my letters are a continual chorus of, please buy me this, please send me that, and so on. I am sure they must be most interesting to read! It must have been most exciting to suddenly feel there was something wrong in my direction, and to find me disappearing out of the window, but somehow I don't think I would have been harmed even if I had fallen. I suppose I would have landed on my feet or my head, either would have done.

1 Her bridesmaid's dress for her brother Jack's wedding earlier that year.

Dorothy must be quite a business woman now, with her dancing and music, and higher classes. Is she nearly ready to sprout the wings yet, not having her tempter–in–chief nearby?

Mr Hastings is a man of clear judgement and good sense, and I agree with him heartily, that a more promising set of rising militant suffragettes is not to be found anywhere than in our neighbourhood. Dorothy is the future Mrs Pank. (shes in the Geneva papers, that woman) and Chris and Mona are her aide–de–camps, and the other small fry will smash the windows and the other small jobs, leaving the bombs and Prime Minister to D. and her aide–d–c.; the only drawback to the little arrangement being that there will be some little disputes, now and again, at head quarters, and some bombs are likely to be wasted, but all will be well in the long run, and they will be put in Westminster Abbey afterwards. I have noticed D. practising to need forced feeding, already, sometimes.

Its just like Jeannie to want to send me some stuff for Halloween, but, as you say, I hope she will count the cost, which will not be light. Couldn't you warn her in time, although I would like to have the stuff, as I don't suppose they ever heard of Halloween here.

Jeannie's scones would be a revelation here amongst these sickly indigestible cakes, and indigestible bread.

When we get eatables sent to us, we have to give them to Mad and she doles them out to us all, after picking the choicest morsels for herself!! How absolutely horrid of you to order the honey after you had got me out of the road. You might at least have not mentioned it. I think you all seem to take pleasure in tantalising me. Phyllis writes telling me all the ice–cream, sweets, fruit and cakes that she has been eating lately, and you are just as bad.

What a ripping P.C. the kid sent me, thank her very much for it. I have not put it on the wall, as I happened to lay it on the top of a box, and it looked so pretty there that I stuck it onto the lid, and it looks most artistic. I am so pleased with my walls now, as they are so pretty and so interesting. I have my photos on one side above my little cot bed, and the P.Cs on another wall.

The Fates seem to take a pleasure in making me wait as long as possible before I read my letters. Sometimes I havent got a chance all day, and if I don't have my music lesson, then I have to practise. Oh, those music lessons, that man, he gives me a new piece every day and generally two or three, and then he is surprised I cant play. He lets out an ow! every time I play a wrong note, so he's kept busy.

We were at Lausanne again last Sunday and were shown the place this time. We went up a hill in a little kind of train, and who should we see in our carriage but a big nosed long faced tall English Minister. He just had the English air about him. Olive said at once, English! when she saw him, and then she started making him and us laugh by saying, "A rose between two thorns," and other silly things — there was one of the girls sitting between two gentlemen. We were also shown the University and went in to look at the pictures. It's University, museum and picture gallery all in one and a lovely place.

Mad has a nephew there, and he joined us, with a friend. It was my turn to walk with Mad, but when I saw the students looming up, I fled precipitously and contented myself with being last of the line. Everybody laughed when they saw the Pensionnat with two students at its head.

I am collecting things to bring home already, and have some quite decent things.

What a horror, heres my fourth sheet, and I cant stop yet. I am sure, my dear Daddy, that my letters must be a trial to you, you who likes letters which only take five or ten minutes to write. Unfortunately I cannot write my home letter in less than two hours and often am drawn to take four. I guess it takes about five or ten minutes to read them, sometimes!

Today I am just the opposite of last Sunday, as then, I could only fill two pages, and that with great difficulty, and today I have filled three quite easily.

Really it is awful. Mad has it in her head that I rise in the morning, very late, and, with much difficulty, and therefore she has deemed that I have to practise every morning at half past seven. Now, that's gross injustice as I get up at about half past six or seven, always, and, sometimes, six (I don't deny that its only with difficulty that these results are attained), but now I cant get on with my lessons, and have to get up earlier still (when I remember). Do you know I have been fined one penny for having a cold. It was this way. I was all stuffed up and miserable with cold, and couldn't get to sleep, in fact, I lay awake for four hours and a half, and only got to sleep a little before getting up time, and so was late to the school room, and so was fined one penny!!!

I shall have to write the kid's birthday letter today and post it later in the week, so I shall have to hurry up.

Has Thomas survived or succumbed, and how is the valuable blue grey Persian kitten keeping (what a title)? Bye the way, whats its baptismal name? (Tea! Bye bye, butter today as well as jam.)

Good luck today at tea, one of the girls, who was laying the table, is rather a decent sort, and she helped me most liberally to jam, and by my economical method I made four pieces of bread necessary to finish it. I havent tasted salt butter since Paris, and never missed it. I hope I wont shock you when I return by placing my bread on the table cloth, and tearing bits off and shoving them into my mouth, and by eating my jam with my teaspoon, and by eating about three slices of bread at dinner, as we do all those sorts of things here. But I am learning other good manners, as I always eat my vegetables with my fork, and never use my knife except when its absolutely necessary. Also I wash every night, to the waste (sic), in cold water (please watch for the commas in this sentence.)

Awful tragedy. Madonna's going off to Paris with family for winter, and intends not to show a too great anxiety to return.

I suppose the parties are beginning (ask Phyllis if you want to know). I shall take a marked interest in them all this year, so don't forget to tell me. You will have a very nice excuse this year for not giving a party. You can say, oh no, I havent the heart to give a party this year without my dear Flora to help and to enjoy it!!!

With tuns (sic) of love to you both,
your loving daughter
Flora Marion Ewing.

Its awful, I only got two letters this week, yours and a one sheet from my loving brother.

Délices Voltaire

Délices Voltaire
2 Nov. 1913

My dear Mother and Daddy,

I have got three and a half minutes stolen from learning punishment French Prose (for my memory, once more), and I intend making use of them. Boohoo, don't I repent of my foolishness now, when I think that at this moment the kid's enjoying the Cousins' Halloween Party, and that its through my own foolhardiness that I am not enjoying it.

Sunday. I got such a ripping surprise last night. It was a box of stuff from Jeannie. There was a tin of bulls eyes, such rippers, and a lot of nuts, some apples and scones and chocolate, and caramels. We ate the bulls eyes last night and they were most highly appreciated by the girls. Then the scones were heated up and served up at breakfast this morning, each got a half, and Olive, Marjorie and I got a whole and a half. Oh, there was a pot of bramble jelly too, and each girl got a little spoonful. Mad was very decent and said I could keep the jam, and about six scones to myself if I wanted to, and gave me the remains of the bulls eyes. It is just like Jeannie. She has remembered all the things I liked, and sent them now.

I wouldn't object to a little cold, and oh! for a roaring fire! We are hot again but I cant take off my winter things. Mad says they never had an autumn like this before. The trees are absolutely wonderful, the colours! I simply cant explain but I do wish you were here to see them too, as you would appreciate them so much more than I do. They are lovely golds and yellows and pinks, and reds and purples. To see a clump of trees from a distance is a sight.

It was indeed an effort on Dorothy's part to give away her rag doll, she must have been very much fascinated. It's a distinct improvement, as I have seen the day when she wouldn't part with even an old one.

Its such a relief to my troubled soul to know that you like the little medal. I think it is only Voltaire they make at Ferney, at least it was only Voltaire things I saw. You are horrid to underline 'World Wide Celebrities' like that as Mad had just been rubbing it into me that Voltaire was not at all popular, and that it was a very silly thing to send.

Our neighbourhood is, as you know, Délices – Voltaire. Well, Voltaire lived in Geneva, and Délices was his property, and he lived in a house opposite my bedroom window. Our garden and all the surrounding neighbourhood belonged to him. Then he started making himself disagreeable in his books, and otherwise, and, naturally, the people got ratty, and Monsieur Voltaire had to skedaddle double quick. Now he couldn't live in Switzerland, and France wasent having any of him either, so he deposited himself in Ferney – Voltaire, which is neither French nor Swiss, and which was evidently highly honoured at his presence as it has graced (or disgraced) all its fountains and market crosses with his image. It's a good thing they tell you who it is otherwise you would wonder what they were doing with a monkey there!

I am quite sure that the Oggs, Hastings and Robbies will be most mightily grateful for your honey, be it as messy, ten times over, and the messiness will not spoil the taste, I think.

Its true that Mad is not very high class, but I will have to take back what I said last Sunday, simply, that I don't detest her any more. She is an uncut and unpolished diamond, and a very rough one too, but she is a real genuine diamond for all that. She has a very kind heart and a very quick temper. You see, I know all about it now, as I have had some oppurtunities (sic) for judging, this week, specially on Friday. Goodness, I was nearly worried off my head by my accounts. I had received seventeen francs and found I had spent about eighteen, and had another in my purse. I think I had about half a dozen girls helping with the old thing, but their efforts were in vain. Now, I had once got a girl to change some of my English money, and with that I bought some chocolate, of the which fact Mad was in blissful ignorance. Well, I found that these two different monies were going to get beyond my feeble control (I had not got them mixed this time, but it was muddling me). So in desperation I chucked all aside, and said, I'm off to Mad to tell her I am done for, and so, with fear and trembling, I approached the terror, and made a clean breast of all my sins and troubles. For a wonder, she took things very calmly, and even managed to get my book nearly right (I have still spent forty centimes more than I had) for which I have very great respect for her. Then she demanded where I bought the chocolate, but it wasent my pleasure to say, so I refused, as we, a lot of us, had done it together, and I knew I'd get skinned if I told, but Mad guessed all the same, after which she gave me a long lecture, and was like a perfect angel.

What excitement there was just now in the garden. We were all walking so nice and peacefully together when, all at once, one of the girls screamed, "Oh, zurch! Zurch!" and, of course, we all rushed to the place of excitement, and, upon looking up to the place where she was pointing, I saw my first aeroplane (sic). It was the noise that first attracted our attention. I cant help thinking how the future generation will laugh when it hears the excitement a little areoplane caused for their grandmothers. It was just an ordinary two winged long tailed one, but it was very high up and you couldn't even see if there was anyone in it. It looked just as if it was sailing away by itself.

Unfortunately, we have had an epidemic of cold here, and Mad has said that all windows must be shut, so I am defeated and the kid has triumphed. As to her vanity, humph! she is typical Hungarian and is almost brown. They never even heard of Halloween in Geneva, even Mad, who was at an English school.

As you see, I was not allowed to go to any expense at all with Dorothy's present.

I absolutely <u>howled</u> when I heard that His Royal Highness, Sir Patrick MacMaster had made a speech. Oh how I beat my breast, tore what hair was left and gnashed my teeth because I couldn't hear it too. I would have helped bravely to swell the titters. Cathie wrote to me and told me about it too, and gave me an example of what he said, and how he said it, which caused more giggles.

Its so funny, you say the same things in your letter as me, sometimes, and when I send a short letter you send a short one, and when I send a long letter <u>you</u> send a long letter.

This week has been such a nice one for letters. First came yours which was a specially nice one, then at tea–time one from Cathie — 14 pages! And a type written epistle from Mr Turnbull which has something specially nice in it. Bye the way, your post–cards were specially nice this time, thanks muchly.

Did the eleven year old Miss Ewing have a nice birthday,

and how did she enjoy last night?

Heres this photo at last, and I wish you the joy of it. I am absolutely dried up now, and cant say another thing so I will do something else.

Got something. We have absolutely got to clear out of this old hole of a house by the first of April, and Mad is hunting high and low. She has seen a house which is in every way perfect, except the price which is enormous. The house is in the aristocratic neighbourhood at the edge of the lake, and is much larger and newer than this one, and has a beautiful garden. It is seven minutes in the train from Geneva, and it would be ripping to go into it, so I do hope we so.

I havent time to finish as I have had to write other letters in between, oh the worry of these Sundays.

With much love
from your loving
Flora.

I think I am getting on all right now, the lessons are not very difficult, and now that Mad and I have made it up things are going very smoothly. I shall be home in no time if the time goes on passing so quickly.

Forgot to tell you I have grown at least half an inch, and am already fatter, but my clothes fit still.

Délices Voltaire
7 Nov. 1913

My dear Mother and Daddy,

It's a girl's birthday today, and we went a walk into the country instead of lessons, so I have an hour to get on with my atrocious correspondence. I have at least six letters owing, and can only get two written each Sunday, so you can imagine my hair whitening rapidly.

Its really awful these birthdays, because if its <u>your</u> birthday you have to spend five or more shillings buying cakes for the girls!!!

<u>My</u> and <u>our</u> colds have departed once more. It really is awful, this heating apparatus. You are boiled in the hall and frozen in your bed–rooms.

Even I gasped when I heard that Miss McFarlane cleaned her silver with <u>bath bricks</u>. I never heard of that method before. I don't suppose you would like to leave your precious house, and still more precious contents, to Miss McF's tender mercy. I expect you would have visions all the time of her getting to work on your precious silver with bath bricks!!

I heard at the gym class that if you were always tired you should take deep breathing exercises, so I am going to try and get rid of my born tiredness that way.

Every girl here adores Marjorie, and they all like Olive very much, <u>but</u> (you see there is a <u>but</u> here), they all say she is a very nice girl but she does boast and blow her own trumpet a bit. And she thinks, "What a good girl am I," a bit, too.

My deah Mama, you should never say that your dress and

furs are swanky. You should say chic, that is the educated and aristocratic word.

Somehow I cant imagine that stony dentist giving way to the tender passions. Its quite like him to make a sensation though. It will be small loss to anyone if that superior maid does resign.

D's letter is very candid, very candid, its all you can say for it.

The mountains are covered with snow today and are so pretty. The snow makes them so nice and fresh.

Do you know that wedding was a blessing in more senses than one, as the girls here have the most frightfully grand dresses.

Sunday. I dreamt last night that I had come home again, but somehow home was in Switzerland. Also I was most frightfully disappointed because I could speak English straight off as easily as possible, and only three times put in a French word. I hope it wont be as I dreamt, as I found that I couldn't talk French any better, after a year, than now.

Do you know I absolutely will be home again before you know what I am about, as its nearly Christmas already.

The concerts have begun and the first four girls went in their splendour last night. I don't know when my turn comes. I have on one of those Viyella blouses today. It was not money spent in vain, as they are so comfy and warm and everybody admires them so.

Do you know the latest. Mad doesent like my fur hat with my costume, and we have to wear costumes to church, so she said, "Write home and ask them to send you a winter hat." Here winter hats and summer are two totally different things. If you don't want to send me a hat I can always get one here, but Mad's taste does not accord with mine, and I am mortally afraid that she will give me a little thing with a walking stick in front. She is desperately fond of those sort. If you do send one, just get a black felt thing with a pretty ribbon, a round one. Nearly every girl has had to send home, or buy, a hat.

We are having it hot again, and go in the garden without a jacket. Have you cold weather now?

I understand quite a lot of the sermon now, when I remember to listen, but I always forget.

Its so ripping, when we move into another house, we girls are to go for fifteen days to Montreux, at the end of the lake among the mountains. Wont it just be lovely, that's where Chillion (sic) is, you know.

You don't know how learned and accomplished I am becoming. For one thing I get piano music that is miles too difficult for me. Also I can do Richelieu embroidery and English embroidery. I can sing French songs and speak the French language!!!!

We played such a funny game last night. Marjorie got a Bible and tied a key so that the handle projected into it. Then she put her finger under one half of the round handle, and another girl put her finger under the other side. Then one of them asked a question, and if the answer was, 'yes', the Bible swung round, and if, 'no', it stands still. I asked it if I was sixteen and a half, and it said, 'yes', and neither of us had budged our fingers. Olive asked if she would receive a letter from a certain friend next week, and every time, it said, 'yes', at once. Ever so many true things it has said, but never once made a mistake.

What a joy, today its jam <u>and</u> butter, and tonight, before we go to bed, cakes, as it was a girl's birthday yesterday.

Wasn't that a fearful accident near Paris, with the two trains.

1913 is making a record for itself that wont be forgotten in a hurry. I hope there were no letters for me in that train, as I get few enough without that.

I shall have to be seeing about Christmas presents soon. Couldn't you send me some hints as to what anybody at home wants. Its so difficult when you cant just go and wander about town till you see what you want. Here, you have to say, straight off.

Is Dorothy slandering me just now, as my ears are burning like fire, and its somebody beginning with D, who's thinking of me.

I am afraid this letter is very short and uninteresting, but I really cant help having nothing to say.

With much love from your affect.
Flora.

Did you get my P.C. and letter at last? I hope you weren't anxious.

Délices Voltaire
15 Nov. 1913

My dear Mother and Daddy,

That was a ripping budget you sent me last Wednesday. You cant think how many letters I got on Wed., yours, Daddy's, Kate's, Mrs Thornton's and Mrs Smith's (Sunday School). Then I got two again today, so I havent done badly.

I was very angry with Mad, too, about that hat. This year, for you, will just be one long continual drain, as we are always having to pay for this that and the other thing. I tell you this that, when you receive your bill, you'll sit up with a vengeance. The hat you have bought me seems to be very pretty, and it doesent matter tuppence if it doesent suit me exactly to a tee, which it is more than likely to do, as its not once in a life time that you have bought a hat for me.

The photos were ripping. I was instantly besieged with crys (sic) of, give me one, give me one. I had to hide them and say I would <u>think it over</u> etc, and then give them to the really decent girls. There are some really decent girls, now, so decent, in fact, that two of us have just been separated at the dinner table because we giggled so. Its such fun, now, though, as Mad has put a perfectly typically German between us, and now we do our absolute best to make her laugh, but with little success. Mad warned her that she was to be firm and hold out against the wiles we would be sure to practise, to make her giggle, and so get our revenge.

We had some ripping fun the other night. Mad and some of the girls had departed for a concert, so, when the cat's away the kittens will play, and we were especially skittish that night. The girls in Olive's room, next to mine, asked me to come into their room, after bed time, which I did, basely deserting my small Hungarian, who, in revenge, burnt a lot of the candle, a thing which is strictly forbidden. Well, I sneaked in (by the door, as it was raining) and was offered the half of a square inch of bed, but managed to stick on, as they had shoved all their beds together. Then the fun began. Olive had constructed a Bible and a key too, so we commenced to pump it concerning various things. I, always blasé and sceptical, began by asking it if the next day was Friday, it said, yes! fortunately for itself. I also asked if Dorothy was coming here afterwards, and it said, yes!, so you will have to send her, so as not to spoil fate. I guess Miss D. Ewing would have a very good time here as she is just the kind of girl Mad likes, gay, sharp, actif (sic) and clever. Oh yes, Miss Ewing would get very much into Mad's good books indeed. We also asked it which girls Mad liked, and it said right, every time. Oh, bye the way, I asked it if I would write books when I grew up, and it said, yes! also it said they would be a great success!! So let us hope! It said I would marry 'B.N', whoever he might be. I have not the pleasure of his acquaintance yet, but it persisted that it was 'B.N.' every time I asked.

Sunday morning. (All the rubbish about the fortune was written this morning, too). Do you know, I have learnt one thing, and that is to get up early in the morning, which I can do without hardly a pang, and it feels so nice, afterwards, when you're up and dressed, specially when you see the shivers and hear the sighs and groans of the other girl when she is trying to make up her mind to get up about an hour after me. Another thing, too, which is very nice for my rising, is that, on week days, I wake up always at the right time.

(There's the gong for when we have to be in the school room, there'll be some fun in a minute – its begun, there are remarks like, Oh, I am not finished yet, and, Oh, my shoes etc.) and on Sundays I always sleep right on till eight o'clock. This morning I wanted to get up early so as to get on with my frightful correspondence, so I said in bed last night, I will get up at seven, I will wake up at seven, and I did. Its always like that, when I want to wake up at a certain time, I always do.

I have got such a lovely soap, this time, its almond and when you scent it, you think of the country at once. I thought of a bunch of wild flowers when I smelt it. Its absolutely ripping, I must bring some home.

Its so funny, somebody said, Wasent that an awful storm last night. I looked up in mild astonishment when I heard that, and said, Storm? The others laughed, they know me.

Bye the way, did you ever hear or see a storm (thunder) in the month of November? Well, I both heard and saw one the other night, but it dident destroy my sleep as much as a pair of wretched cats serenading each other the night before. Oh, those cats, they caterwauled, they growled, they spat and they squealed.

Goodness, how I longed to strangle them, but, alas, the joy was not to be mine. Then a pair of dogs got ratty at the row these prima donnas (would be) were making, and started barking in the most disgusted tone you ever heard. I agreed with the dogs but wished they would hold their tongues. Mad said she had never heard such a thing as a thunder storm in November, and especially to last all night too.

Do you know, I think I have come here just at the right time for everything. First, the boats never ran for so long before, they went right on until the end of October, an unheard of thing. Then, they never had an autumn like this before, so warm and so beautiful. Also, Mad is not fining us when we talk our native tongue. We are not supposed to talk any other than French, and she is very angry when she hears anyone talking German. She never hears us talking English, because we don't, because we are not daft. Sometimes Olive and I say the word in English because we don't know the French, but, only about three or four times held a conversation in English after the first fortnight, and that was confidential as we are very good friends now. I said we were not daft to talk English, as the Germans are always talking German, and they don't get on nearly as quick as us.

Been to church, such fun, walked with Olive. Geneva is simply crammed with English, and so is Victoria Hall, our church. The foreigners!!! All say that the English woman on the continent is not a spectacle to be proud of, in fact she is generally dowdy, her hair awful and a general air of un–chicness. Its sad, but it, alas, is too true. Well, today Olive and I were especially exasperated by the continual flow of English which we heard around us and, when we got outside, we began to let off steam upon the subject of our wrongs, because, you see, our great ambition here is not to speak French like a native but to be taken for English, so Olive who was feeling specially low said, Look here, lets speak English every time we pass anybody English. That was an idea which had not struck me, but we proceeded to put it into practise nevertheless. It was great but the greatest was when I discovered a girl I used to see often in Edinburgh. Phyllis and I used to make scathing remarks about her toilette which was very much à la mode. But here she is in Geneva and is living across the road from our Pensionnat!!

One of the girls paid me a very nice compliment the other day. She said that I spoke French very well, much better than at first, and that I knew a great many expressions, which is true, as when ever I hear a nice expression I repeat it over once or twice to myself, and then pawn it off on someone else, after a bit. Also, at last, I am beginning to get my verbs into order, and my sentences, as they have been rampant and confused for some time, but unfortunately I can only stammer and stutter and say, 'tu' instead of 'vous' to Mad which is a most frightful offence.

I am getting quite a connesseur!! (sic) on the subject of pictures as I have been to see about ten or more collections. We were at two different collections this week, will tell you about them after dinner. Bye, bye....Well, the first collection we saw was a 'sticklar', it was the paintings in the latest style of a friend of Mad's and the sister of my singing mistress; in the first place the colours were impossible. There was a picture of Adam and Eve, and the poor things look so ill. They are a bright yellow with red spots. There were others which consisted of squares and triangles and splatches of colour which gave a kind of picture puzzle look to the affair, but was worse as you couldn't tell what it was. Also they were atrociously badly drawn, some of them. In fact some of the worst looked as if they had been done by a little child, you know the style, triangles for skirts, curved feet, no features, and a splatch of paint for hair. It dosent seem the fashion now for picture people to have eyes or noses, or at least I dident see many there. We were all much more taken with the lovely eastern carpets which were decorating the place!

The second was better painted but less interesting, except one wall of Egyptian maids which had slits for eyes, plaster complection, carmine dots for mouths, and no nose, and who were in the most impossible positions. One interested me muchly, she was sprawling along the floor on her knees. She had the most substantial legs I ever saw. Then she had the body of a starved cow, all hills and dales, and skin and bone, and the top of her arm was no fatter, if as fat as her ankle!!! She was a beauty, you see.

We are lugged round all the museums and art galleries in the place, which, tho' it is very interesting, gives me a frantic headache and feet ache.

I am going, at any rate, to ask to learn how to embroider the initials on handkies and things, so your handkies will be a good excuse. You know it is a bit awful, tho' its quite modern, that I never had touched a piece of embroidery till I came here.

Bye the way, some of the girls here take lessons how to make designs on leather. You know that little pen–wiper, fawn leather with bright green flannel. Well, its that kind of work, and they do much prettier things than that. Well, I was examining one of the things one girl had done, and she said you don't need to have any talent at all for painting etc, to do it, and its very cheap, the lessons are about eight francs or ten, seven or nine shillings for a month. Do you think I could have a month's lessons? Do you think it would be worth it? The girl said, most unflatteringly for the other, that the other girl who took the lesson hadent any talent at all, but you should only see the most lovely writing case she has done, but that, of course, was most frightfully expensive. I would like very much to have a course of a month, but if you think I have enough special lessons already its all right. It would come all together for a month to not much more than £1, which is enough and to spare. If you think its not too much for my small whim, could you send me a P.C. so that I could begin at once, as the next lesson is before your letter arrives, and I want to get my four lessons finished before Christmas so as to make a present of what I make. If you think, no, then I shall know if you don't send the P.C.. Thanks awfully much, if you will let me.

Do you know its getting to be quite a proverb, 'If you are in doubt go to Rentons.' If you have searched all the town for a thing and are still without, 'Go to Rentons.'! I am quite sure the hat will be all right if it was bought at Rentons, and 15/– is ample, as you say, when you don't know whether it will gain me another beauty prize!! or not.

Thanks awfully, awfully much for buying the tartan things for me, you know, really, you are awfully decent, you at home, there. I just have to mention anything and you instantly do twice as much for me, and I would be an even worse character than I am if I dident try to make the best of the advantages you have given me. I really do work now, tho' not nearly hard enough, but I have learnt quite a lot already, not only in the scholastic line. You can make yourself content with this, that you have seen the last, for good, of the lazy, ill–tempered, discontented fat lump that used to make life a burden for itself and others, as I have had my eyes opened here, and shall take care not to get them shut again. Please tell me if D. goes right to the end of R.Crusoe, as I read the interesting bit, but basely deserted it at the end when he became a tea–merchant or something.

Your experience of the pictures seems to have been very much the same as mine, as your description of unnatural colours, and being heaved on, answers the pictures I saw very well. The 'Herald's halberd' is very nice indeed, and has got a special place on my wall.

There are groans of envy from various girls when they see my letter, as half of them seem to be suffering from nothing–to–say–ness, but I don't know what it is, today, that has made me so garrulous. Olive wants to write twelve pages home but was stuck at one and a half until I gave her some hints, but she seems to be getting along all right now.

I also wondered, when I read of the gay time the young bride seems to be having; it was just one long monotonous flow of, I am going here, I am going there, we're having such and such a person in, etc., it kind of took my breath away.

I am glad my chrysanthemums are doing well. Did D. nip the buds as I said, as that is very good.

It is a tragedy that Mr Stephen leaves, and just after he was doing so well, and you were getting settled down again after all the fuss. I suppose you will have to start all over again; hard luck.

I think my voice has improved a little, sometimes, but other times I don't, but I always have something in my throat just at the back, and that hinders me dreadfully. I have had it for years, and I can swallow or clear my throat as I will, but it always comes back again. Do you know what I can do to get rid of it, as it would improve my voice greatly if my throat was clear.

I hear Mrs Pankhurst has made what she calls an escape, but, which was an escape which nobody tried to hinder, and which therefore fell flat. Is that the last of the P.s, or is Sybil there still?

I am sorry the kid's cough is not away yet. Is it as bad as ever, or better?

I asked Mad about Calvin's grave but the old pig said, Don't know where it is, and that was all I could get out of her, but the Pupil Teacher says that perhaps some day we will go into the cemetery, and that I can hunt for it then. I am very, very sorry indeed, but the girls say that Mad never knows anything about things like that. However, I am going to find out, whether Mad knows or not.

How absolutely ripping that would be if you could only come in your cycle to see me. Couldn't you boat over the Channel and come for your summer holidays?

I wish you wouldn't fling that Corsock reputation of mine into my face like that, as I am ashamed and not proud of it, as it is not very much in my favour, if I can have two such utterly different reputations as my Corsock and home one.

I can absolutely understand all the sweet little 'Italian Art' man says, and am even beginning to venture a timid remark now and again. I have always had full marks when he has questioned me, except once when I had shut my book and said I was not to waste my time over that, and in consequence he pounced on me and demanded just the part I hadent learnt. I am beginning even to understand the literature,which is a strict advertisement, as it is very difficult to make out what he says, at all.

I cant and never will believe my affect. little sister misses me, except when she has to go a message, when she will suddenly be overwhelmed with violent longings for the 'Touch of a Vanished Hand.'

Gracious, this is my fifth sheet, what garrulousness. I never thought I was such a magpie, but I believe people who talk a lot don't do much in the letter writing line, hence the curtness of D's 'billets doux.'

It will be a great triumph for the kid when she can sail gracefully into the ball room and commence waltzing divinely to the tune of a ravishing waltz, and to see her big sister commence first by tripping over her own or her partner's feet, and then by retiring into a quiet and unseen corner and hide her diminished head.

"When I come home I'll have but'rand jam fo' tea. When I come home I'll have but're an' jam for tea," always, as its horrible with only jam, and rotten jam at that, and the same jam all the year round, except for summer, for a little.

Its something awful the plans and plans I make for what I will do when I come home, which are always either squashed or forgotten by the fact that I have nine months to wait before I can carry them out.

By the way, I never finished enumerating all the reasons why I had come just at the right time, here. Of course, it's a very distinct advantage not having to pay when you speak English, but at any rate I can speak French easier than English, much. In fact I cant speak an ordinary lengthed sentence in my native tongue, but discover that I have finished it in French. I couldn't speak English today to Olive. The last time I tried speaking English to Olive, she burst out laughing in my face. She apologised after, and said she couldn't help it as I spoke so funnily, which was true as I speak in the most stilted and pedantic manner.

I remarked once that Mad was a diamond and also that she was a rough one. Well, I have been finding her very rough indeed lately, but she still shines.

Seen that lovely blot on the other page? that is the result of my desk being the end one and the girls fill their pens on it and they make blots on my brown paper cover, and then I shall have to pay to get another one. This time the blot was on the wood and so I dident see it and consequently placed my paper on top of it!

Mad is going to have someone in every week to do something to the hair of those girls who are losing it, like me, so I hope I shall be able to preserve a little of it yet.

Tea time.

Could you really send me more of the photos, as I think they would do very nicely as Christmas cards. Thanks awfully much, they are very nice indeed.

That soap scents of sweetbriar now, it encourages me to wash oftener.

I will write a P.C. to Mrs Peebles and try to write to Miss Johnston, too, today. Miss Johnston wrote a very long letter, but somehow it dident leave anything behind it. Have you framed my photo yet, as she was asking about it, and her book, 'Kings and Queens of France'.

How awful, I shall have to be seeing about Christmas presents soon. The gay times are coming soon, now. In a fortnight is the first party, and then Christmas, which is a round of gaiety.

I must stop now as I cant put another page into the envelope as it would be too heavy, and the girls are kicking up a most infernal racket.

Lots of love to you both
from your affect.
Flora.

Are you writing to Miss MacFarlane some time? If so could you send mine with it, as 2 ½ c is too much for a little sheet like that.

Délices Voltaire
23.11.13

My dear Mother and Daddy,

The packet came all right on Friday night and I think the hat is perfectly ripping. It really is most awfully pretty, and suits me too. The little tartan things are absolutely, absolutely — they are frightfully lovely, but I am sure you have spent too much on them. The little note book and the hanky are absolutely the pick of the bunch. Bye the way, that little calendar is... I have used up all my language and havent any expression good enough for it now. The colour of the hat goes very well with my brown costume, and is ripping with my blue.

How funny you having cold and blustery weather. We are having it still mild and lots of sunshine, only it is very cold, sometimes, in the mornings because of the snow on the mountains, and very often misty, now.

I am going to try to get some decent photos of the different places and send them round, but I believe they are expensive.

I would willingly write less long letters, but I cant. I always have such a lot of things I must say, and, besides, it's the weekly treat which I look forward to all week!

It is a very good thing that the 25th is a Sunday this year, that we have all our festivities on the 24th. Saturday night we come into the D. room, and there ranged on tables are all our letters which have been kept from us all day, so remember to send your letters in time for the 24th. All the girls say that the Christmas week is a most lovely week.

You are lucky to hear Evans. I should like to have heard him very much too.

Is Dorothy invited to any parties this year? I guess Phyllis has commenced her season.

If Mr Hastings goes to school now, I suppose that means he is better. Is he quite better?

So D. is quit of St Georges. Why don't you send her to 'George Square'? You really should, tho', as I am sure she would have a ripping time and the teachers are so nice. I guess she would get a special interest taken in her as the sister of the notorious 'Flora Ewing'. I don't think there was a teacher in the school who hadent had to present me with an order entry, at some time or other.

You have rejoiced me very much by saying I can have the leather lessons. Thank you very, very much indeed.

I suppose you have got my P.C. of the mountains; well, I will commence to recount my adventures on the Salève.

We started off after dinner and were raced off to the tram, and in consequence of the first half going so quickly, the second half lost sight of them and went rambling gently on till it discovered it was in a region unknown. We then retraced our steps with the German pupil teacher storming and raging and saying we would have to go back home. Fortunately we caught sight of the other bit of us crossing the road, and made a dash for it. Then we met Mad and got into a tram which took us to the foot of the Salève, where we descended and got into a mountain train and were hauled up the mountain. We had a simply magnificent view on the way up. We could see the mountains and the plains for miles. The Swiss houses all seem to have red roofs and white washed walls. Then we got to the top and got out and made to the tea room which is kept by an English woman. After ordering tea we started to explore. Mountain air always makes me frisky and so I commenced frisking, as much as I dared, but was withheld by Mad's cold glares. I have stood on the very highest point of the Salève. On going to the Geneva end of the mountain we looked down upon the town. I had never been so high up in my life before. It was just as if I was looking down on a plan of the country. There were little hills and hollows, and little curling roads, and little cottages and trees, and fences, also little streams, but a big, big lake. We were so lucky that day, you could see the mist hanging over Geneva and the lake, but the Mt Blanc and the other peaks couldn't have been seen plainer. It was really and truly a magnificent sight. All the top of the range was covered with snow. The mountains rise abruptly out of the valley of the Rhône, with the river Rhône running at their base. It was so lovely to see the last sunbeam creeping slowly up the Mt Blanc, making it a most lovely gold beside the already grey neighbouring peaks.

We went to the theatre last Tuesday, but it wasent much. By far the nicest bit was when we came home and found Mad had left two biscuits and three quite big little packets of chocolate for every one of us. The first play was boring and sad, and it was an opera, so I couldn't understand it. There wasent a scrap of movement in it and they posed all the time. The second was funny and not all opera, and the dresses were very pretty. It was Greek and really awfully pretty. The theatre wasent as big as some of our Cinema Houses, even.

Miss McFarlane sent me a P.C. and the most sweet little Scotch sporran, like the one you sent me, only black and white. Its really lovely, and helped to stop me appropriating one of those you sent me, as they were a great temptation and I had given away three of mine.

I have got such a ripping book now. Its my third, as I made a great effort and finished my awful first one, and then found the second quite interesting, quite thrilling, in fact, and had to finish it in my room, but I often couldn't make out the words. This book, however, is just as if I was reading an English one. I can get straight along with it and simply forget it's a French book.

You really must send D. here afterwards, as perhaps Olive's sister comes and also the Madonna's, and they are all the same age and are all mischievous. (Poor Mad). Also I can comfort you with this, that you will not have so much expense with her, as I will know and be able to give her a lot of things I have had to buy here.

I have got on my green dress today for the first time. At first I thought I was going to have an accident with it, but fortunately remembered I could take off something underneath, which made it all right. It was most frightfully embarrassing with the admiring glances and remarks.

Olive has a necklace, exactly (almost) the same as mine, and also a green dress but quite another shade. There is nobody here with such a quiet artistic shade as mine. We have both got on our necklaces and dresses today.

Oh, by the way, if you want to have less work cleaning the front of D's dresses, make her a few aprons like mine, and make her wear them. When I come home I am going to wear them still. We wear them all day here, and its so sensible. You would be saved a lot of trouble.

Olive sends her love to you, and so do I.

Just imagine, I have written your letter and Miss McFarlane's and its only three o'clock. Its unheard of.

Oh, bye the way, it was such fun last night. Mad was at a concert so I sneaked into Olive's room and was offered a share of her bed, which I promptly took. Its so beastly boring in my room that I have to go next door when I want rousing up. It was ripping last night and I stayed for nearly an hour, when suddenly the peace was disturbed by my hearing a distinct rumble. It was only instinct which told me what it was, as it was only very faint. I jumped out of bed in the middle of Olive's speech, grabbed my dressing gown and slippers in my hand, opened the door and went flying bang into one of the girls who was already there. Mad was already on the stairs and it's a miracle she divent hear me. Fortunately my door was open, and I entered and was into bed in a moment. Do you know, I was so excited that I trembled till I couldn't hardly sit up, and you could almost have heard my heart as it bumped and thumped.

With lots of love to you both,
from your loving
Flora.

Mad said today at tea time that when she was little she was called an animal without bones, as she was fat and lazy, and hated going for walks, and liked nothing better than to go into the garden with a book, and then, all at once, she changed and became what she is now. That is a being without rest, that cant sit still for two minutes and has to go for walks. Is there any hope for ME!!!

Awful luck — have just been aching to recite and let off steam like that, and Marjorie has just asked if I will recite at the next party. I shall say 'Lochinvar', as you can put actions into it, and its easy to understand.

Coat of arms of Switzerland

Thonon-les-bains

Délices Voltaire

Mont Saléve

Marjorie

Ma chamber á coueher

Délices Voltaire
29 Nov. 1913

My dear Mother and Daddy,

Er — um — well, I had a lot to say once upon a time, but I seem to have forgotten it all now. In consequence I shall begin with the last and most important thing, which is, we had our first party last night — and this morning. Ow, it was scrumptious, absolutely, — at least the last part was. The nephiews (how do you spell it?) and nieces!? of Mad, with a brother-in-law or two thrown in, also a few friends (musical), well, these various items together with one piano, half a dozen or so violins, and one flute, and a violencello?! made up the orchestra. They really did rippingly, you know. In the middle we had cakes and a cup of tea, and they recommenced with renewed vigour. After the fixed programme was finished, some of our crew was called upon to perform. Olive sang; Marjorie[1] played violin; another the piano, another the mandoline. After we had got over these various duties, the real work of the evening began. We went into the dining room and played musical chairs, and, after that, a perfectly ripping game. You all sit round in a ring, and, behind every chair, there is a person. There is one chair that is empty, and the person behind that chair has to make eyes at somebody sitting. That person has to try to get to the empty chair, and the person behind that person's chair has to grab hold of that person, and stop them from getting across the room. It was most thrilling when some of the nephews ex-

1 Marjorie and Olive are Eliz's girls.

postulated at being forcibly withheld, and started off across the room dragging the chair, and the person who was holding on behind, after them. There was some good displays of feminine muscle at that game. After all was finished, we commenced dancing at one o'clock, but were packed off to bed speedily. It's a case of 'after the ball', now, with us all with great black lines under our eyes. I demanded, at once, when are our next gaieties. Its in a fortnight, joy, joy…

We are going to see 'Little Lord Fauntleroy' this week, in French. On Thursday we were at a museum, and, ugh, the things we saw: stewed cats, baby's heads with no brains, stewed pigs, sheep with two heads, goats with six legs, one pair sticking out of its back. Skeletons of all sizes and sorts. But the worst things were models of the human head. I. was showing the veins, one side of the face showed decomposition and the other all the veins. It was horrible. II. was a head also representing death, and with the skin shrunk to show the nerves. It was gastly (sic). III. was — I gave one look and nearly yelled; as it was, I clapped my hands to my eyes and fled. After a bit I ventured back and examined it. It was a head with nothing but the veins, black and red, like gastly (sic) branches, and, in the middle, a pair of wild staring eyes.

Upstairs we looked at the birds. There were birds from all over the world. Birds red, blue, green, black, purple, yellow, orange, some with about six of these colours. Birds big, birds little, some were only about an inch, the sweetest little things.

It was a girl's birthday that day so we had a lovely kind of merangue (sic), all icing, sugar, cream, and that lovely biscuit merangues are made of. Then we had tea in the school room and dined off the cakes the girl had received for her birthday.

Oh, bye the way, I must tell you an awful joke. When we went to the theatre we went in four cabs, all in a string. Well, this girl whose birthday it was wrote to her mother telling her about it, and said it was as if it was Mamoiselle (sic) Albertine's wedding, and we were the brides maids. All well and good, so far. But the next thing we heard was that Paula had got a letter from her mother, and in that letter there was a little billet–doux, doubtless full of friendly counsels etc, for Mad. Albertine, the mother having taken the matter up quite the wrong way. Fortunately the mother had mentioned what was in the note, which was torn up at once, amidst howls of laughter. I never saw a girl in such an absolutely blue funk as that girl. She was most abjectly terrified that M. Albertine would get to hear of it.

Have you heard that Bertie Ogg has been trying to commit suicide. Mary told me that he and Donald Mc. had been making toffee (wouldn't like to have had to eat it) and afterwards they went for a cycle spin with some of the toffee. Bertie, after a bit, felt hungry and put a bit in his mouth. The toffee began to fiz–fiz! And had a most gastly taste. Fortunately for his reputation it wasent toffee he had put in his mouth but a lump of acetyline for his lamp!!!

Every week the hairdressers come and friction those of our heads which are greasy or losing our hair. I got frightened the way my hair fell, fell, fell and spoke to Mad. I got most horribly snubbed and scolded for my pains. (The Madonna's mother is just here this minute, they leave on Tuesday.) We heard a series of bumps down below. We suppose it was Lada jumping, as she is franticly (sic) excited.

Would it be too much to ask Dorothy to copy out the 'Earl

king' for me and send it, as I am going to recite instead of playing the piano, and the Germans would be more interested in that than in anything else. I should be very much obliged indeed if she would. Its — I think, it will be — in any poetry book. I have locked away my own book, which is an awful nuisence (sic).

Thanks so much for the photos. The kittens are absolutely sweet. I have them up on my wall, in great state.

We havent had it really cold yet but we have a lot of rain and mist.

This is another photo of us, but it isent frightfully good. I have a quite decent one of me ordered, but, naturally, its very faint.

Its awful trying to buy Christmas presents here, as Mad, as nearly as possible, wont let me buy anything, and makes mock of me like mad, but I am gradually storing them in.

It never struck me until a little while ago that our party continued until Sunday, so we were trespassing into the Sabbath, so to speak... I wasent asleep until nearly three o'clock, but, even then, was first into the school room.

Some people have all the luck. There's the motor horn which signals the last of Madonna and family. They are going to stay in the hotel all night, and only come back to finish packing. Then they are off tomorrow night for Lyons, and then to Paris, where they will have a round of parties. However, I decided I dident envy them, as they wouldent be here for the next party.

We are going to have butter, jam — <u>and</u> cakes for tea today. Do you know its something awful walking with some of these girls here. There isent one who walks straight. The English can walk straight. Well, when you walk with a girl she starts off beside you, all right, but in a half minute or so she gets tired of that, and takes a little dance over to the other side of the pavement, and then comes back with a bang which almost sends you off your feet. Then she walks along with you for a bit sticking her elbow into you and trying her best to shove you away. I walk purposely as exactly in a line as I can, which is perhaps the reason why we bump.

All my dresses are beginning to get short again, and I have outgrown the measure mark I put on the wall.

Must stop, want to write to Jack.

Much love,
yours lovingest,
Flora.

This paper is so nice to write on, tell D.

Délices Voltaire

St Albands Road, Edinburgh

Délices Voltaire
6 Dec. 1913

My dear Daddy and Mother,

I am writing for the second time today. I was saved the last time, as I folded up the letter small and Mad just shoved it into her envelope. I suppose you will be recovering from the blow when you get this letter.

I have just finished my singing practise, and am a bit elated, as I have noticed an improvement. My high notes are getting quite decent, but they squeak off in all directions terribly. Madame Bailly says too that sometimes I get a note very nicely. (One note!!!). She says I must get the others like it. It can be taken for not at all complimentary, that.

The photo of the house was absolutely ripping, especially the little bit showing 'how it works' — Daddy's shadow. The thing which struck me very much was the general air of cleanliness and tidiness. The house looked so compact and nice after these ugly sprawling, beshuttered things. The road too looked well kept. It would put to shame our ill kept muddy things. On the pavements down town, even, on a rainy day, if you don't look out you go splashing into a sheet of water two or three yards long and six inches deep. I know, 'cause I have had experience!

They tell me in 'mournful numbers' that I have to design a programme for the approaching party. I cant and flatly wont. There'll be trouble but I hate making an exhibition of the talents I havent got.

The Christmas holidays have almost begun now, as we are

given very few lessons, and we do our embroidery during the lessons.

Do you know, its cruelty to animals the way we are treated here. We have to wash every night in ice cold water; we get one little bit of butter which, if you put none on your first piece of bread, you have enough for the second.

You should see my walls now. At first I tried to keep the views at one side and the photos at the other, but I have got a lot of those silly cards now, so in consequence you have St Nicholas Cathedral perched above the Sphynx, and side by side are two grinning maidens and the grim Sphynx. It's a most motley crew.

We went to see 'Little Lord Fauntleroy' last week, and it was magnificent, absolutely. Little Lord was a girl with golden curls. Mad said she would be between twenty–five and thirty, which rather flattened us. But, in any case, she did splendidly. She was so natural, she never once put on, and yet she was old fashioned, and exactly the picture painted in words, in the book. The Earl was splendid, he was tall, tall and a regular b'r–net, don't cher know, and what a temper — ow, but he *did* give those around him a hot time. Little Lord was simply killing: when he heard he was to become a Duke he plumped down in his chair with such an expression, and then he said, "But what <u>will</u> Mr Hogg say?"

There was a little extra morsel too which was absolutely, absolutely. It was a chemists shop. The door opens, and a little girl comes in, and <u>what</u> a toilette — she gracefully pulls up one of her wonderful stockings before beginning her speech. Then she turns round and opens her mouth to its fullest extent and says she wants to speak to the chemist. She says she doesent want to buy anything but just to ask a favour, but by the time she has got that length, the chemist's patience has stopped short, and she goes out of the shop double quick. Then the assistant comes in, one hour late, and gets the benefit of his master's temper. When all is quiet they find out they have given a poison to a baby instead of a medicine which is very similar. Then the fun begins, the chemist wrings his hands and moans and groans, then he asks his assistant to say it was *him*, but the assistant isent having any of that. The chemist says he has all his life behind him, but the assistant says he has all his future before him. Suddenly the advocate comes in, and the assistant flees and the chemist faints, nearly. It turns out Adv, has a sore head. He tells his symptoms, but the C. never listens and starts asking what happens if an assistant gives a poison instead of a medicine. Its killing the way they are both so interested in their own case, and don't pay any attention to the other. In the end the C. says it's a little rehumatism (sic) and gives him a little lotion which he says, afterwards, at least wont poison him. Then he sits down absolutely flattened out, and mops his mouth, and speaks with a voice thick with emotion. Just then the little girl comes in with her Sunday best gracefulness, and demands if he has recovered his temper, yet. He very soon shows he hasent, and she goes out of the door with a yell, only stopping to put her fingers to her nose, which unfortunately he misses. Then a magistrate comes in – fresh flutter – but he only wants medical advice, too. He departs with something which wont poison him, too, and the little girl comes in again. She goes out jolly quick, and the C. is nearly off his head by now. The little girl comes in again and demands for two tins of Vaseline, and then begins to talk. She begins a long rigmarole about her brother's sister's brothers–in–law, or something, but comes down to the point which is that their baby is ill, and bought some medicine there — remarkable!! The C. is interested, and afterwards the little girl says the medicine wasent wanted after all, and she has come to ask him to take it back. He takes it back and gives her three — for it. She explains she doesent want the Vaseline, as it was only to speak to him she had asked for it, but the delirious C. gives her that too, and opens the door for her, much to the astonishment of the Assistant who comes in at that moment. The A. starts being cheeky about the subject, but the C. who is lighting his pipe in peace serene, asks him what he is talking about. He says he doesent know anything about a bottle of poison, and then says it was all a trick to punish him for coming in late.

I meant only to give a little outline of the story, but, as usual, I couldn't cut it down. I hope you arent bored, as I havent time to leave out this page, as I would like to.

The concert last night was MAGNIFICENT. There was an orchestra of over a hundred, the violins in front and the trumpets and 'cellos behind. There were trumpets, flutes, violins, 'cellos, harps, drums, bells and a lot of other little things. The 'extras man' was most interesting to watch, he bobbed here and there and got crimson in the face sometimes. The first violin was very much first violin, indeed, and he knew it. He had a face absolutely shriekingly musical, and had his hair brushed straight back which heightened the effect. And his tail coat and figure!! Perfect. By the way I watched all the hands of the violinists, and they did hardly at all waggle them. There was a pianist too, and he was splendid. His hands just flew up and down the piano. One time he would dash up to the top, and then he was off, top speed, to the bottom.. His fingers hardly seemed to touch the notes but they just sang. I never heard anyone play like him, so dainty and delicate, he just drew the sound out of the piano. It was music, and real music, and all off by heart. Sometimes he played so quick that you saw ten fingers on each hand. The orchestra played magnificently too, and just made their instruments do anything they wanted. They played with their fingers and bows, and made tunes by just hitting their strings with their bows.. The last piece was something about water escaping and the agony of a man who is trying to stop it. It was comic and they played it comically too. You simply heard the water and then as it thumped against the side of a tin basin, and then the man yelling with fright. The men themselves laughed. It was so funny, once, one of the men wanted to sneeze in the middle of a piece. He gasped and gaped, whilst playing on heroically for about five minutes, but alas! Suddenly it came out. What a look he got from his neighbour, but really he couldn't help it. The audience giggled.

At half time we went out and promenaded in the grand salon among all the brunettes. Oh, the toilettes, and the powders — and the paints — and the heels!

We went to service in the Cathedral today (St Peters). Its an old grey dark place, and most frightfully difficult to speak in, as there is a frightful echo. Its all grey stone and arches.

In the History of Art lesson this week Monsieur Valaton asked what was the peculiar trait of the English nation. He said it was energy! I wish he hadent!! I met Mad afterwards and she jeered, where was that English energy, let us see it. That was the beginning but unfortunately it was <u>not</u> the end. However, I am going to tell her next time that it's the exception etc.

It's a most awful nuisance really, I always think my adjectifs (sic) in French, and have to translate them into English. In consequence, they are a little queer, sometimes.

For goodness sake tell somebody to write to me. For the last fortnight, minus yours, I have had one short letter from home. Its awful. Phyllis has written once!! Have you started looking for another organist yet? Hows the kinder spiel getting on. I expect the shops are looking ripping now with all their Xmas things. They are nothing special here.

You needent be alarmed about my appetite, as it is quite normal now, in fact, I feel inclined to strike, sometimes, when Mad says it would be a great pleasure to her if I just took another morsel of that (tough rotten) meat.

The reason why I thought Xmas was on a Sunday is because I have a calendar which marks all the Sundays in red and also it has the days in German, and the two combined helped my conclusion.

I am still wearing my blue on Sunday as it is quite warm enough. My brown coat I wear in 'bad weather.'

What happens to Mrs Gardner now? Is Mrs Angus ill? What was the name of the poison he took? Is the place closed now?

The old blue dress is lengthened and put away for the spring. I am going back with my blue costume skirt as it is too short 'again'.

Its not my luck to have the piano out of order when I am not there to get the benefit of it!

With much love to you both,
your loving daughter, Flora.

Rev. William Ewing (Flora's father)

Dorothy, Edinburgh, 1913

Délices Voltaire
13.12.13

Dear Mother and Daddy,

I am not going to write a long letter this time for the simple reason that I cant, as I have only about a dozen others, but that always takes time.

For, o'night is our party for Escalade. I will explain all. I do 'Lochinvar' and a tableau 'L'Age d'Innocence.'?!!! must stop. Hope all goes well.

Sunday. All did go very well.

Escalade is a national fête for the Genevois. Geneva, up till a little while ago, was a little republic of its own, and belonged only to itself. In consequence every country in Europe has had a shot at it, but they were always repelled. The country of Savoy, or something (Savoyards), made attempt after attempt, but never succeeded. Naturally the Genevois became a very hardy race, and always alert. The last time the Savoyards attempted was in 1602 or so. They blackened their helmets so that the sun would not shine on them; so as to come quietly, then marched along the banks of the river Arne. Everything went well and the Genevois heard nothing.

Early the next day, at about four o'clock, a good woman got up to make the soup. The soup–making was evidently a great event, or perhaps it was this special kind, it was rice. Well, the woman was getting on fine with her job, when she heard a noise nearby (her house was almost on the walls) and went to see what it was. She was just in time to see a black helmet pop up over the wall, and a hateful Savoyard face beneath it.

Quick as thought, she seized her cauldron and let it fly at the head. The head disappeared! The row alarmed the guards, and they came out. I believe the Savoyards even got into the town, but the plucky Genevois fought like mad, and eventually completely routed the Savoyards who were perhaps six times more numerous. The Genevois, who were religious, accounted their victory to having God on their side, otherwise they could never have withstood the attacks of big armies. They had thanksgiving services and that sort of thing. That was the last attempt the Savoyards made, and a while after, Geneva asked to be let into the confederation of the Swiss. Isen't it quite a little romance, the fight of a plucky little republic, which was only a little town, against great armies. Now every 13th Dec. the Genevois celebrate their Escalade with family reunions and dinners and parties. They seem to celebrate three days: 11, 12, 13. We went to the Cathedral to hear a patriotic service upon the subject; although we were there more than half an hour too soon, it was already very full. It was magnificent in the place with all the lights. It was most impressive. After the service we went down town (I always say 'down town'.) The shops were so pretty with their Christmas things. The children were all dressed up. There were 'pierrots et pierrettes', there were Red Indians, there were every kind of dress imaginable; you would have to scatter to right and left to make way for a band of charging Red Indians, or a group of children in their national dress.

The next day (12th) Mad said she would make us a present of our Grammar lesson and said we could take it over again for the next time. Then we descended for dinner – and what a sight!! In the middle of the table was a big cauldron all made of almond toffee and a coloured sugar monogram of the arms of Geneva. All round were red and yellow crackers, piles and piles. Also at every place at the table was a small chocolate cauldron filled with chocolates. I have not begun mine yet. After the meal we pulled our crackers, ate the contents and then opened the big cauldron, and found it full of marzipan potatoes, big, big, and different to those at home. We were then all served with a little wine. I took it as I wanted to taste what it was like, but I shall not be so curious again as it had a rotten taste and gave me a still rottener headache even tho' I had only taken a desert (sic) spoonful. The next day (13th), and the great day, we were to have a great gathering. We had to get up a programme for the benefit of Mad and her guests. There were fifteen, and all relations, and only about a sixteenth part! We went to work manfully to prepare something worthy, and I don't mind saying that we did rippingly.

First a girl played, then a tableau: Faith, Hope and Charity. It was magnificent. The three were dressed in long flowing white robes. Faith and Hope had their hair down, and Faith had a golden cross, and Hope a silver anchor, all made by Marjorie. Charity was kneeling in the middle with roses in her hair and hands, and on the ground before her. The lights were put out in the salon, and in the dining room we had two little lamps with red shades that shed a sort of red glow on the scene. Then we slid open the sliding door between the two rooms, and we sang a song about the tableau. You have no idea how lovely it was, and those girls never moved a muscle! Next was a Hungarian dance by our native of Hungary land. She did splendidly (in costume, of course). Next came a tableau, 'The Two Sisters', Olive and a German. One is sitting, and the other, O., is standing with her hand on the other's shoulder, both are gazing lovingly into the other's eyes. It was ripping, especially their coiffures which were strictly classique. They had a blue light. They never smiled once, even tho' they were staring at each other. Then came 'I' and my eternal and infernal 'Lochinvar'. I don't mind saying that I did quite decently, and Mad said this morning that she was going to give me no peace now, but was going to worry my life out till I pronounced my French as distinctly as my English, and that I was going to recite in French before I left, if she could help it. She even said something about, 'When you have such talent,' etc.; she said that, even she could not understand very well, as a recitation is very difficult, but she said that even those who could not at all understand were interested and amused by the mimic. Then came an absolutely killing thing but which I missed seeing. It was the Bohemians or strolling minstrels. Marjorie with a handky on her head and a ragged red shawl, and a ragged purple skirt and her violin; another with a pair of huge checked trousers, a flowered waistcoat and jacket and little hat, and a mandoline; another with a ragged red jacket and a pair of gym knickers and blue stockings. There was a pair of Mexican trousers for her, but they most unfortunately split!. She had a guitar. Another was just a little girl, with those hollow bones that you clap together. She had black hair and a yellow handker, a blue blouse and red tie and dark skirt and red bracelets. These various items sang and played. Then came your illustrious daughter disguised as 'The Age of Innocence'!! I had a pink ribbon in my hair, a night gown of Marjorie, and pink stockings. It was gracefully posed so as to show my little pink toes, my hands clasped tightly upon my bosom and my gaze fixed into space (not to mention a gorgeous pink sash). They had to guess what it was, as Mad thought it was very well known, but they dident know, but, after they were told and saw the picture, they said that, of course, it couldn't be anything else. I heard a patronizing voice (masculine) saying, "Its good enough, that, you know." Then came Olive with her song. She sang better than I have heard her for a long time, notwithstanding the fact that she cracked atrociously, twice. You know, she has an absolutely magnificent voice, that girl. Mad says it is already placed, which is remarkable at sixteen. Then came tableau 'Gleaners', you know it. There were girls with the appropriate costumes and positions, and we had a lot of straw scattered about. It must have been awfully tiring standing there in stooping positions while we sang four verses and four choruses. Then four girls, piano, mandoline, violin and guitar all played tunes — great success. The End.

We had tea after that and cakes — fortunately I only ate four small ones. Then we started the games. We had that one with the chairs and the people behind them; it was most exciting, this time. One young man asked me what part of Scotland I came from, and if all Scotch girls were as tricky as me. I think I tried every way imaginable to get off that chair, but in vain. At last, I seized the chair next to me and, by brute force, managed to get onto it, and held onto the bottom of it, while I was tugged in two directions. The two opponents declared pax afterwards, and I was saved. Then we played a most exciting and amusing game. We all took partners and started marching two by two from the dining room to the salon, where we divided and marched off to meet in the dining room again. Then we went out at one door and in at the other (somebody was playing all the time — rotten for her). Then we made a single line and marched upstairs into the schoolroom, made the tour and descended to the lower regions, then went down into the cellar and made a tour of that, singing to frighten away the creatures who live in the dark – it was absolutely pitch black. Then we came up again and ascended up and up, and – made a tour of the bedrooms… It was one of Mad's nephews who was leading, and he seemed to be quite at home, all about the house. It is a game that they play year after year. Then we went into the schoolroom again and (I know now its 'Follow my leader', I never thought of that) we had to climb over the desks in the dark, always hanging desperately onto each other. (You should see those desks with the big boots of the students, they are scratched and frayed and in a most lovely condition. Mad doesent mind, she is very decent like that. She would sacrifice a lot so long as you enjoy yourself.) By the way, I saw a chair in the dining room which is more white than brown, and its not alone. If you were on the chair and wanted to get off it you, very often, were driven to knocking the chair over, in the hopes that the person behind it would fall over it! Again, Mad is quite apathetic.

It was so funny, one game we had all to go out and come in, one by one, and do some mysterious obstacle game. Well, I waited till the end, and by that time I had a good enough idea of what was going on. Naturally, I got a bit excited, and when I was asked to come in I felt a bit funny. By the time my eyes were bandaged I was all giddy, and things hummed. I stuck on, however, and went through my performance, but with the same feeling all the time. I wondered if I had fainted and was just dreaming. I dident feel ill but just funny. I told Olive after, and she took me out and gave me a drink. Mad came and asked me what was up. I told her — she said — you've eaten too many cakes. Fortunately I had only eaten four and was able to reply in the negative. The feeling passed off after. I think it was all the excitement. I was in the most awful blue funk when I had to recite. I think that had helped, but wasent it funny? We ate the toffee cauldron, sang songs and afterwards, when the guests went off to dress, we danced, despite the fact that Mad had put the light out. We went to bed at half past one, much too soon! And I was so little tired that I made a promenade on the roof. It was an absolutely magnificent night, frosty, clear and so light.

We went to Mad's church, instead, today, as we were up so late. There were only four of us who went, as it wasent obligatory. You see, Daddy, that your influence in that direction still works, even tho' I am not directly in the road of it.

It was so funny about you sending that article of how our church was built, as, just that Sunday when you sent it, Mad asked me what our church was built for. I couldn't tell her.

Xmas, don't mention it, I never was in such a mortal funk in my life. Instead of rejoicing that its near, I get more worried every day. I have payed for every present I have bought, as yet, with my own money, and don't think I shall have to use any of your money. All the things can be easy enough sent without expense. I am going to send Aunty Harriet's to you, first, as I don't know her address.

I hope you get a nice man in place of Mr Stephen. It is an awful pity he parts, or rather, has parted.

You made me green with envy when you mentioned the book you are giving D.. D. can take this, that at least her big sister will very much appreciate it when she comes to the fore again.

I am going to tell you something very dreadful, its this: if you sent for me to come home now, I should be most wild. I will not be troubled with longings for home, up till March now, when the gaieties cease!

Much love from
your loving
Flora.

This is a short letter. What is a long one like!!? I have discovered that your Xmas is on Thurs. while we celebrate it on the Wed. Can write next Sunday.

Délices Voltaire
20 Dec. 1913

Dear Mother and Daddy,

I have, at this moment, a very difficult task before me, namely: to write a long letter and not put much in it, as I must write again, for Xmas Day.

The book, I know, has arrived, as the maid told me; the other things, I suppose. (I shant thank you yet till I get them properly into my clutches). Mad is keeping all our letters, already. I dident know and was very pleasantly surprised when Mad said that she had been keeping the English letters, already, for a long time, and for me too. She hinted that there was a lot. I hope so!

Olive is absolutely <u>cracked</u>!! this last week, ever since she heard there was a packet here for her.

I have seen the Xmas tree arriving, its big, big, and all frosted. We don't put any presents on it,'cause Mad says when she did, her bothers–in–law and nephews made for the chocolate etc. and the tree suffered..

Yesterday we started packing our presents; what a business! We cut and tied and rummaged and — squabbled — all the afternoon, and then we found we had no boxes and no paper for the grand finale. This morning we started again, with the necessary articles, and spent all the morning; Mad did them for us, fortunately.

We are on holiday now till the 5th of Jan., good luck. We can read, write and embroider all day long — so Mad says — Marjorie says differently!!

How absolutely spiffing of Miss McFarlane to give you a fur coat!! you will feel swell in your motor, now.

I hope you will get that man you want for your organ. He sounds all right. Cathie said Mr Stephen comes back in a year, does he come back to his post?

M. Valeton, our History of Art master, has just been showing us pictures of how the paintings progressed. They first were flat and without a scrap of movement. One Madonna was absolutely awful. First, she had jaundice awful, so had the angels who were in lines behind her, so many with their heads on one side, and so many with their heads poked to the other. Then he showed us a Madonna of Giotto, and there you saw the first picture with movement. It wasent so much, but a distinct improvement. The picture was carried in triumph around the town.

We are just getting a resumé of the life of Leonardo da Vinci, and its most awfully interesting. When I come home I am going to get hold of a book with fuller details. We have just been shown his 'Last Supper' and told the story of it. He was asked by some monks to decorate the refectory with a picture. He chose the last supper. He worked at it for years, and at last the monks got impatient, and one came up and spoke crossly to him, one day, when he was deep in thought, and grumbled about their money he had taken, and a lot of rot like that. Leonardo let him finish, and then said, "I have been searching for a head of Judas, but, thanks to you, I have got it now!!". The paint he had mixed with some preparation of his own, which looked much better than oil, but in a few years the paint began to peel off, and, also, the monks knocked a hole in the picture to have a nearer passage to the kitchen, then it was damaged at the French Revolution time, and now there are only a few traces of the great picture left.

Vinci seems to have been a most awfully remarkable man, he was born or had the ideas of two centuries later. By the way, I suppose you are rejoicing over the return of your beloved 'Mona Lisa'. She had the honour of being the one and only woman Vinci ever took any took any notice of, and she died before he knew her, hardly. He had nothing but checks and drawbacks all his life, that man. His pictures decomposed, his ideas and inventions he daren't make known, his statues were destroyed, and his inventions met with accidents, but, through it all, he just dident care, he was quite apathetic. I am just wild to hear more of him.

Do you mean me to have the boudoir as a bedroom? I would prefer to have my room — minus Dorothy — but I can come down, all right, it would make a very pretty bedroom. I would find it very funny after living for eight years right on top.

How ripping of you to send M. and O. Xmas presents. M. will be very pleased to have the book, and Olive will be <u>most</u> gratified with the scent sachet. I am going to give Olive that little tartan book for the addresses, but she can do what she likes with it. It is well — very well — that we did not meet until we were a bit older, as we should have had some awful rows!! Every now and then, there is some little thing which has to be carefully treated!! I like her well enough but she grates on me every half hour or so, and fishes for compliments, awful.

You have made out the items all right on the bill, the extras, some of them, are very expensive, laundry especially.

Its most awfully cold here now, but it does not snow yet. Are you getting many presents this year — cakes, etc.? we shall live on stale cakes till the end of January now, as all the Germans, Austrians, Bohemians etc. all get boxes cram full of eatables. I think it must be rotten to get nothing but eatables for birthdays etc. I couldn't stand it.

We are going up to Mad's sister's house at four o'clock today to see the Sunday School Christmas tree, so I shall have to busy up with my correspondence.

We are all a little tired, I think, this week, as we are all a little snappy. I could slaughter someone, sometimes, and cant bear anybody to touch anything of mine, or even look at me — too many gaieties.

I really must stop now. What am I going to say again, tomorrow?!!!!.

With much love
and best wishes for (tomorrow)
Flora.

Délices Voltaire
21.12.13

My dear Daddy and Mother,

A very merry Xmas and a happy New Year. May it be the best Xmas you ever had and the worst Xmas you will ever have!

22nd. When you get this it will be Xmas morning with you. I hope you will have a very nice and happy day. I will think of you at night eating your Xmas dinner. We don't get mince pies and plum pudding, anyway.

We go to church on Thursday morning and then spend the rest of the day in the drawing room, reading, I suppose. On Wednesday Mad says that perhaps we will go up the Salève again to see the 'Sea of Mist' down below. It will be magnificent, and will give us something to do till five o'clock — that's why Mad is doing it!!!

We were at the Christmas tree yesterday, and it was so nice. The tree was only decorated, and lacked colour a bit, but looked ripping when all the candles were lit. All the candles were attached to an inflammable string, and they lit one part, and then little flames went dashing and leaping all over the tree, lighting the candles. The children sang Xmas carols and recited pieces telling the events at the birth of Christ. Then two gentlemen told the children a story, and then all the children got a book and an orange — we got oranges too — it was all so pretty and happy that I was very sorry when it was finished.

Today we slept till half past eight, when we have breakfast. I came down fastening myself on the way, and found in the middle of breakfast that I had forgotten my collar! After breakfast we went for our promenade, it was so nice outside, so cold fresh and nice. Once, as we were going along a lane, we saw a squirrel up in the trees, and when he saw us he began racing along the branches. It was simply wonderful to see him, he would spring from one tree to a branch on another, and light right on the end, and hardly even bend it. He ran for a long time in front of us springing and running, just like a playful little kitten.

It was so funny yesterday, I had to walk with an awful peculiar kind of girl. She is only just sixteen but she bosses all the show, Marjorie included, and corrects everyone. Well, she is frank, very frank, she said so herself, and I got the benefit of it this time. She commenced, "Really, you know, when you first came I detested you and hated walking with you, in fact, it was a punishment. Now I don't mind at all, and, really, I like you quite well (compliment). When you came you were not safe, you were wild and you had a figure like a sack, now you are much better, and your figure is much improved!!!" I giggled inwardly but looked reverent. I could have returned the compliment about detesting walking with her, but thought better of it. But, really, I do wonder, sometimes what will become of me if, at nearly seventeen, I am still capable of getting under the table to tickle a girl's legs?

Did you take the tea–serviettes for handkies? I asked for cheap handkies, but Mad refused to get them, and at any rate I had begun the serviettes. You must remember when you are examining them that they are the first piece of fancy work I ever did.

I am afraid that the pictures wont be much use to you, Daddy, but it was absolutely the best I could do — minus handkerchiefs!! I thought I would spare you, this time.

They are going to begin decorating the Christmas tree, today, so we will have to keep out of the road.

How many cakes have you received this year, I should like to know — not as many as us, at any rate. If I die of indigestion you will know the reason why.

There is some mild excitement among some of the girls as they are getting corsets and things like that in their packets, some of them, and the nephews will be there when we open our packets!!

I cant realise one little bit that Christmas is in a day or two. I don't know why but perhaps its because we have been having such mild weather up till a week ago. I hope you have been reminding people that they must write to me for Wednesday and not Thursday, as I expect I will get most of my letters the week after Xmas.

I hope my P.C. came in time to warn you about the big packet.

Oh! Its cold, its not the first time that I have been driven to crouching before the mouth of the heating apparatus in a vain attempt to get warmer.

I have got my first song from my singing mistress, and, of course, my accent spoils everything, but I heard two girls reading English, and that made me think that perhaps I talk funnily too, and then I watched the children singing last night, and I went home and did likewise. The result was a surprise for Mme Bailly. She turned to me and said in mild astonishment, "That goes better than I ever thought it would". I have awful bother with my pronunciation, I cannot say, 'plus' right, I always say, ‘ploo’ (English). I get my ‘ploo’ chucked at me everywhere.

Well, I hope you enjoy yourselves today and have a happy Xmas.

With much love and best wishes,
from your loving
Flora.

Coat of Arms of Geneva

Délices Voltaire
26 Dec. 1913

My dear Daddy,

Thanks awfully, awfully much for the simply ripping book, you couldn't have thought of a better one. I started reading 'Leonardo da Vinci' at once. The other book I was very pleased to have as it had a lot of photos I knew. I have started reading it already. It was most exciting opening the packets, especially when the string would neither untie or slip off. We shrieked and we gasped and we oh'ed and we ah'ed. Thank you all very much for your letters. I liked my letters very much, as now that I am away everybody starts saying nice things about me. You know it does comfort a bit to know you are a little bit missed.

After we had examined our things a bit, we went to supper. Oh, that supper! — it lasted an hour and a half, and only a little bit was occupied with eating. I did not take any wine this time!! I am more impressed than ever of the toughness of a boy's stomach. The four youngest nephews were at a little table by themselves, just behind us. They kept us busy!! They emptied, amongst them, at least one and a half carafes of water, and at least one whole basket of bread. That wasent including the wine and various items like turkey, soup, fruit!! They ate fruit during all the intervals. We enquired if they were well, next day. We were told, oh, yes, very well!! We did nothing special afterwards and went to bed at half past one. The next morning we went to church to see another Xmas tree. The little room looked beautiful. It was decorated with long garlands of ivy and evergreens, and there was a big Xmas tree in the middle of the room. At the moment given, they set light to the gunpowder string, and the flames went running all over the tree lighting the candles. I thought of the squirrel I saw, as I watched it.

The great question now is what to buy with my money. Naturally, I want books, but now I want decent ones. I shall buy the 'Talisman', and perhaps 'Jane Eyre', and then I am stuck!

We have just been for a little run on the lake, and I saw my second aeroplane, but quite near this time. It turned and swerved and flew about in circles, and then descended onto the water, and sailed into its harbour.

Do you know I am beginning to think its an awful pity that I am so infernally lazy, but I absolutely cant help it, as I havent, not even a half ounce, of energy in my body. If only I had energy, I perhaps could do something, or at least work, but its an effort to do anything, and I am sure to miss my oppertunities (sic)!

The Geneva air, I find, is very good for the eye sight, perhaps in two senses, I don't see any difference to my physical eyes but the others — rather too much, for my peace.

You really must send the kid here afterwards. I shall be able to help her French enough to smooth away some of the difficulties I had.

With much love,
and thank you,
your loving
Flora.

Délices Voltaire
26.12.13

My dear Dorothy,

Thanks awfully much for the ripping box of peppermints, you sent me. They were <u>very</u> welcome, I can tell you. Also, your card was a miracle of high art and talent. I will keep it for you, if you like. You said you would like a cauldron, I have not touched my chocolate one yet, not even the sweets inside, so I could keep it for your museum, but it might be rather dangerous. Perhaps I can pick up one more durable! In any case I shall keep mine.

How goes the work–bag? Was it pleasing to your Gracious Majesty? They are all the go here, so at least you are in the fashion. What else did you get?

You seem to be gay enough, anyway, with all your parties an' a' that. When is the Sunday School party? Do you play the violin at it, you should.

How many bars of chocolate did you get? You will have it all your own way in that direction, this year, at any rate.

Did you take out the Xmas tree this time?

I havent got anything to say so shall not say it. If you see Cathie, thank her very much for the things she sent me and say I will write as soon as possible. Tell Phyllis she is an angel, she will know why.

I'll chuck it now, so au revoir.

Love, Flora.

Délices Voltaire
26 Dec. 1913

My dear Mother,

Thank you very much for the lovely scent bottle. Its simply magnificent. I shall hide it, if possible, as I am afraid to look at it for fear it breaks. I never possessed such a lovely thing, before. I am content — I have five books, one from Daddy; one from Phyllis; a lovely soft leather covered Indian papered thing from Aunty Harry; one from Mad!!!! And another from Daddy. A handky from Miss Smith, another from Miss Waugh, and one from Uncle Sandy. Ten shillings from Mrs or Miss Steele, which I don't know, what am I to do? Five shillings from Uncle Fred, and three from Corsock. A tie from Cathie and a calendar. Dorothy's sweets, and a little dish for the pins etc. from Mad. And a most beautifully embroidered collar from the girl who was in my room before, and all because I gave her that little tartan broach (sic) — I havent done badly?!!

It was so exciting waiting upstairs in the schoolroom till Mad had finished and dressed. We were all ready at half past five and had to wait till nearly seven. The guests arrived, meantime, and had to wait with us. We played games — and tricks — to while away the time. At last they rang the gong below, and they stopped everything and fled — some of us — I locked the door on some of them — we entered the dining room and arranged ourselves before the folding door between the salon and the dining room. Melle Albertine had to hold the door and hide the chinks. Suddenly, there came a loud knock. A sudden and intense silence fell upon us. We waited with bated breath while Mad unfastened the door. Then! — she flung it open wide and we saw inside. There, in a far corner, was the tree, lighted by myriads of candles lighting up all the room, and (much more important) on tables on each side of the room were boxes, letters and packets, all in confusion. We all stood in front of the tree and sang a Christmas carol. Mad's brother–in–law then read the Xmas chapter, then we sang again, and then made for our tables. I looked at mine and then gasped — all that for me!!

We spent all yesterday in the salon, after church, and ate and read and sat on the sofa. It was mostly for eating the packets of almonds etc.

I had a cracking headache this morning, even tho' I hadent eaten half what some of the others had. Its off now, however.

This note is brief but I must write two others for home yet.

With much love
and thanks again,
your loving
Flora.

Flora's mother

Délices Voltaire
27.12.13

My dear Mother and Daddy,

What a day!! I have written letters all day, when I could, and must write at least six or eight more. I shall have no time tomorrow as we are having some poor children in for a Christmas tree and presents. We had to make kind of overalls for them, the dressmaker cut them out so we only had to baste them and then give them to be machined.

I was at a Christmas Tree meeting last night in a big hall where we were shown lantern slides of the birth of Jesus, and some scenes in his life, also there were some speeches. It was very nice.

I gave your little tartan things, and the girls were delighted with them.

You asked my opinion upon the nephews, now that I know them. Well, here goes: Maurice, the eldest, he is clever – very, think – sensible and very lively – helps to make things go, a good face, though not awfully handsome. Mad is cracked on him – bought him about six Xmas presents. Everyone likes <u>him</u>. Olivier, the second, is just as different from his brother as the day is from the night, in two senses – he's dark, the other fair. He is absolutely mortally shy, which, of course, makes some excuse, but he's a bit of an idiot, at any rate. He giggles all the time, says things he thinks are wise but <u>arent</u>!! His very expression is earthly and sordid. That's for him!! Margaret, the niece, is very shy too but very pretty and so nice and <u>so</u> clever (by the way, the one redeeming feature for Olivier is he talks

English magnificently!). The other children are all little but very gay and very nice looking. They nearly all have that clear cut profile, the pointed nose and chin and look so 'class' and pretty with their hair in two plaits drawn straight back — the straighter the better. There are other two nephews who have been here, and others who havent, but all and every are very gay.

They say that Mad invites all the young men she can for our evenings so as to accustom us a bit and learn us to talk and not be a lot of idiotic stookies — I am still an 'idiotic stooky', but surprise myself sometimes, talking quite the thing, but those times are so rare they couldn't hardly be counted on the fingers.

Mad has a collection of fancy clothes up in the box room, and, every time we need more, we buy and make and add to the collection.

Please don't bother about my recitation book or the Earl King as I shant have need of it, as Mad wants me to learn to recite in French!! For goodness sake don't open my box!! For, once its opened, all the things will come out!!

You said you could find nothing to do but eat! It strikes me that's not a British but a German!! thing to do!

Its so funny that you should be having the same things at your lectures as I am at my lesson, only mine is more particular and yours general.

The mints arrived quite safely, not even the boxing damaged. They were very much appreciated.

I do sing better when I am excited or in the evening, but never well when I have my lesson — my high notes are scrapes and my low ones are — !!! I have got a song but I don't think

I shall ever sing it before Mad. I couldn't, you know, it would only be mockery when there is Olive! And also I am afraid of Olive as she is not altogether above sneering, you know. I could never recite properly when there was someone there who could do much better than I, but I think I could amuse the Elders, all right.

You made me giggle audibly when you remarked on the friendliness of Mr Stephen and Miss Stewart!! And about its apparently falling flat. It was my fortunate privilidge (sic) to hear a little more than most people!!

I have not overdone the eating. I was quite abstemius (sic) compared with the Germans etc.!! But nevertheless I had awful indigestion, as nearly everything had nuts in them, and nuts and I don't agree very well!

Do you think I should buy a camera with the Steels' 10/–? I could get quite a decent one for that, and my soul always longed for a camera to take lasting prints of the glorious scenes around me! (ahem). I shall wait till I hear your opinion – so hurry up and send it!!!

They call these the holidays – I havent seen the holiday bit of it yet. I am working all day long, writing letters, going down town, doing messages, etc.! When we flit in March, we girls are to be sent off to Montreux with Melle Albertine for a fortnight. That amusement wont seem much to you perhaps, but you are only to see Montreux once to know what it means: mountains and the lake and excursions all the time.

It has been threatening to rain for two days and now it has come, just when Mad is having the children in. They will be wet and make a mess of the house, and perhaps wont be able to come. – Poor us – her temper does not sweeten under her trials, not it!!

Just imagine, I have been here nearly four months!! The time does fly.

You seem to have got hold of the idea that I am doing well with my French, etc., well it isent true, as, really, I don't know half what I should have known in the time. I am a little bit of the opinion that I have been wasting my time again.

I must stop as the kids come at three o'clock, and there will be lots of things to do. I have to have charge of one child all the evening, and look after its daily wants, etc.!!!

With much love from
your loving
Flora.

Pensionnat Mange
Délices Voltaire
Geneva
Dec. 30th

Dear Mrs Ewing,

Thank you very much indeed for the book you sent me. I like it awfully. It was good of you to remember us.

Flora will have told you what a busy Christmas we have had, with so many trees and parties. All the girls seemed to enjoy themselves thoroughly.

Yesterday we had snow for the first time, but it did not last. It is beautifully frosty and fine now.

I have just finished with a cold and sore throat, which made me miss several outings, but which began, happily, shortly after Christmas.

Olive and Flora soon picked up enough French to jabber away with the others. They have both made heaps of progress in the four months we have been here. I can hardly believe I have only two months now to wait for coming home time.

I expect Flora has already described the girls. I like most of them very well, and put up with the others.

Tomorrow is a great fête here, and everyone is getting quite excited. At 7.30 a.m. they are going to let off 100 cannons, then there is a grand procession which has to pass through the whole town. In the evening we are having a family gathering here and I expect we will play games and enjoy ourselves.

One of the girls has asked me to go and stay with her at Prague before going home as we are both leaving at the same time. It would be awfully nice if I could.

I shall have to leave off now, and I hope you all have a very happy New Year.

Yours sincerely,
Marjory.

Pensionnat Mange
Délices Voltaire
Geneva.
Dec 30th

Dear Mr. Ewing
thank you very much indeed for the book you sent me. I like it awfully. It was good of you to remember us.
Flora will have told

Original letter (fragment)

Délices Voltaire
30 Dec. 1913

My dear Daddy and Mother,

A very, very Happy New Year to you all. For me at any rate 1914 is likely to be anything <u>but</u> uneventful.

New Years Day will be very quiet, we will go to church in the morning and then read in the drawing room for the rest of the day.

Tomorrow we are going to be gay. In the morning we are going to see the procession which is composed of all the soldiers, students and people of all the social status!!! of the town. They make a circuit of the town. Then we will go to the cathedral, probably to hear a patriotic service. Bye the way, all this is because this is the hundredth anniversary of the deliverance of Geneva from the French Power. There will be dinners and a' that, I suppose; tomorrow morning, at eight or nine, the cannons will be fired — 101. Then the cortège will start. We will be in town all tomorrow, most likely. Then we will come in and dress for the evening, as they help out the old year with a good dinner and games, till eleven o'clock or so, when we will start watching for the New Year. It'll be the first time for me.

Tonight we go to see the students put the crown on a historical monument!! The intelligent children here in the room don't seem to have the ghost of a notion which.

Last Sunday we had some poor children in, for whom we made some overalls, and, also, every Sunday we give a half penny for every Sunday there has been in that month — that goes into the poor–box. Also every time we leave things about or are very naughty! we must give a penny for the box and learn ten lines of prose — they got ten pence out if me that way, and then I chucked it and was careful only to be just as naughty as I could be without overdrawing the limit. Well, with all these items, the poor–box is not left empty. The money then goes to buying toys and stuffs for the party. Each of us was given a kiddie to look after. I got a little brat with hands like coal and a squint, but he turned out to be an angel — in disguise — as he behaved like a little saint and, afterwards, asked for an orange for his little brother.

We prepared a big tea for them, three huge plates the size of which you never saw. They held at least thirty or forty buns and rolls, also the table cloth was all covered with white papers. The kiddies finished every bun on the plates, and some from another.

After tea we went into the drawing room, and they all sat on stools in front of the tree, and then they recited us little bits of poetry and little songs, after which we,(some of us) played the piano, violin and guitar. Then they got their presents, and each little girl called her doll after the girl who had had charge of her. Mad even gave some games and dolls, which she had over, to those who has little sisters or brothers at home.

Mind you say if I can buy a camera. I asked you because Agnes Maitland said her father said photography was too expensive for her just now.

It has been trying to snow for the last two days, but it has never done anything serious, as it just melts away. Mad, however, is furious with the weather, as she says, Geneva has only to think of having a procession or anything like that for it to rain or snow at once.

Are you having good, bad or middling weather? I hope you get your little packet in time. You see, Cavillers chocolate is like no other chocolate I ever tasted, so I thought I would just send you a little to taste it..

I am so glad your new organist is going to please you. It would be rotten without an organist during the festive season!

Perhaps we are going to go to the mountains a little sooner this year, as there is snow at last. They havent been able to have any decent sledging this year yet.

Tell Dorothy that I will send her my badge for the 31st Dec, when I have finished with it — for her use.

I hope you will have a very happy New Year.

With love and best wishes,
yours lovingly,
Flora.

Délices Voltaire
4th Jan. 1914

My dear Daddy and Mother,

Thanks so much for the nice letter, also thank Dorothy. I couldn't help thinking that it wasent altogether the raw meat which made her kitten bite!! Thank Mrs Thompson for the pretty card – ought I to write?

All your things came long before time – in fact I only got a stray handky or two after Xmas. I don't understand, however, how your things dident get you till Friday night, as they went off on Saturday afternoon, and Mad said that was ample time. The Reavells' got there on the 25th at night. Everybody, but Olive and Marjorie, got heaps of sweets. At least I got yours so we were all stuffed with one another's bounties! It seems to me that this year, just when there is one very hungry mouth less to eat them, D. has been getting more sweets than ever. Was that of Mrs Bogie as big as ever? Bye the way, don't worry about not having sent me more sweets – it wasent at all necessary!!! The – d'oyleys!! – were really meant to be tea–serviettes but perhaps you can hide them better if you put cakes on top of them. I thought that it would be quite a good idea to put them in D.'s museum!! Allow me to inform you that whatever you use them for, you must 'take them up tenderly, fashioned so slenderly'!!

I was thinking of you and your late dinner on Xmas Eve.

Olive is horribly clever all round! – and knows it. Don't you worry – we are quite friendly. Unfortunately there isent one chance in ten of another English girl turning up! I don't see any difference in what you are pleased to call my figure!! Also I havent the slightest remembrance of being wild, at the beginning. My own opinion is that I am a very quiet and humble person here. The Flora at home and the Flora here are two very different persons it seems to me.

The Salève is only a local hill — and three times Blackford Hill, for all that.

You are not the first who said it was funny — these boys — also, in a girls' Pensionnat too, but Mad doesent think it funny, and the nephews only need to be asked — to come, rejoicing. They wont go away, when they do come. Mad has to nearly shove them out at nearly two in the morning — but that's on the party nights.

By the way, I thought when an author got an article into a mag., he or she was generally sent a copy — I havent heard anything about mine yet. I have written to Chrissie McCallums to send me one however — I dident even know if it was accepted or not.

Now I'll begin with the news.

First on the 30th it began to snow, and in the evening it began properly, and soon all was covered. That night we went to the town walls to see the students put a wreath upon the Commemoration Tablet — this tablet was placed in memory of the day when the Austrians, coming to attack the French, passed through Switzerland and, incidentally, released it from the French power. That was 30th and 31st December 1813.

Well, we all set off, and, of course, had our beloved galoshes on!!! You cant put even you nose out of door but you must put on your galoshes!! Well, I found out there and then that it was possible to slide with galoshes on. Its an unwritten law of the sliding season, with the juvenile section, that anyone with galoshes must keep ten miles off the slides. Well, we went off and slid gaily all the way, till we reached the walls. These were covered with flags and borders and garlands of ivy. It was, of course, all red and yellow – everything, the Genevan colours. The tablet was wreathed with garlands of ivy, and had a Genevan flag on one side and a Federal one on the other. All along the top were Chinese lanterns, ten red and ten yellow, alternately. Then the students came bearing the wreath, and also came the firemen bearing big escapes, which they placed against the wall, and then two presidents of some two clubs or other climbed up leaving an enormous holly wreath tied with red and yellow ribbon. They themselves had national sashes on. After the placing of the wreath, the students sang a song or two – oh, bye the way, during the ceremony and behind us, there were 'fires of Bengal', some red and some green; these lit up all the decorations and made the place as light as day. The only thing which rather dampened our enthusiasm was that the smell of sulphur nearly choked us.

Then we all sang God Save the King in goodness knows how many tongues, and then we went home by town to see the decorations. I'd have given a lot to have seen all the lights etc, from a long way off.

The next day 101 guns were sounded. Then, after breakfast, we went down town to see the procession. At nine o'clock punkt (we all say punkt here) the procession started. There were brightly hued soldiers of all kinds with and without bands, a few pinched, bedraggled and shivering students, some with pretty caps and some with ordinary black velvet. (The students here wear caps according to their station or society. There are black velvet with red and yellow braid, white, blue (sky), green velvet which sags at one side.) Each of these bands had a leader or two who had gorgeous!! sashes and beautiful banners. (All the companys (sic) in the procession had flags, and some most beautiful.) There were also some worthy citizens, all in furs and fat! Also some sailors, also gendarmes, all with beautiful banners. Humph! They don't learn how to march here in Geneva, even the soldiers just shambled along, anyhow. (Oh, there were boy scouts too, but they looked miserably cold and not smart like ours.) After that we went to catch another glimpse of the procession as it streamed past the National Monument,(two women, probably Switzerland and Geneva.) As they passed, they all took off their hats, and the scouts did their salute. Then we went up the walls again to hear some old Jonny make a speech. He was so fat he hadent room for a decent voice, and so he just squeaked. Naturally, we heard only the squeaking, but no words. The procession ranged itself in front of him. We saw nothing but the banners. After that they sang their patriotic song, every company playing its band. It was magnificent really, the sound of all those men's voices, and the bands.

Then we (literally) dashed for the cathedral, and just managed to get standing room near the door. We were just like sardines in a tin. The silly leaders, or whatever they call themselves, hadent the sense to shut the doors, so we were getting packed tighter and tighter by those trying to get in. At last some women lost their heads and started scolding and trying to get out. Oh, my, how they carried on. They shook their fists and they fought. They were got out, and the doors were shut, at last, and the service began. We were much too far away to hear the words, but we heard the magnificent song, all right.

Now, we knew that Melle Marie had said that she wasent going to bother herself getting up early, and was going to go straight to the Cathedral and get a decent place. Well, we knew that she would start crowing over us because she had had a better place than us, so when we met her afterwards we started, before her, to say how nice it had been all, and that it was much nicer to be near the door than to be away in the middle, etc. etc., and we refused absolutely to be convinced that M. Marie had had a nicer time than us, which was absolutely right because we had had a taste of everything, and all the excitement of the crowds, etc. to bargain..

Then, that afternoon we went down town and had tea in a confectioners to celebrate everything. I have had a chance — like my usual luck. I have seen and done things that wont be seen and done for another hundred years, so it isent probable I shall do the same things again. The next item on the programme however is the hundredth anniversary of the joining of Geneva to Switzerland. That's in June, so there will be very gay doings then.

After, we went on a sort of carnival affair, and went on the merry–go–rounds. I went on twice and was finished for the evening. Luckily I felt better after supper. It was then, on the way home, that my hat went gallivanting, and was recovered with difficulty. That settled it: Mad called me a HAT–PIN!!

After supper — the nephews came!! — and we played games till eleven, when M. Raymond read some stuff about the Restauration (sic) — wasted an hour with that — by the light of the candles on the tree, till it was time to dress to go out into the garden. We started singing till Mad suddenly yelled 'A Happy New Year to you' and we dashed into the garden to hear the bells. We stayed in the garden for more than ten minutes, racing round the house in the clear frosty morning, and then went in to be scolded by Mad!! Then we all got a glass of hot wine — more water than wine — and sweet. We drank and sang toasts till half past one — I had three glasses and had to do all I could to prevent having a fourth. Then we went to bed but not before Olive and I had celebrated our English New Year — one hour later than here.

Bye the way, I have bought a pretty little alarm clock, in nickle (sic), for eight shillings or so. Its not more than two inches square, but I have still ten shillings burning a hole in my pocket.

Hows the kid's cough after a dose of nursery life?

We went to the cinema — for the first time in four months. It was quite decent. Melle Marie said!!!, "Oh yes, it was nice — very good — but it is a pity that such a wonderful machine should be wasted like that. What imence (sic) good might be done with it. They should show instructive things, of factories, etc., also! Did <u>that</u> interest or amuse you?!!" Our opinion was that we dident go to the cinema to be instructed!!

Golly — you could scrape the powder off M. Marie's face this afternoon!!

I think I'll dry up now, having said enough rubbish for the present.

With much love,
yours lovingly,
Flora.

L'homme de heige

St Georges

St Georges

Olive Reavell

Délices Voltaire
10th January 14

My dear Mother and Daddy!

Its been an' gone an' snowed and been and gone again. It started snowing on Tuesday night and in the morning everything was covered nearly six inches deep. The trees had piles three or more inches high on them. Naturally we went out after dinner, and we made snowmen.

The snow lasted till yesterday when it rained, but the snow still held on. Then it rained again today, but its still there. All about the streets are huge, huge snow heaps.

Tomorrow is Mad's birthday — we have a holiday today!! Humph! But we had to pay 10/– each for it, all the same! We went to the theatre yesterday to celebrate it, and what do you think I saw — Charlie's Aunt! Its always English things when we go. It was really awfully funny, and the man who was the Aunt was really — patent — he was the only character in the piece I liked, or rather, he was the only actor I liked. I don't like the French actors at all, the men arent manly. I ache to see the English version with English actors. The theatre is most aesthetic, all grey and gold and lofty, and a magnificent grey curtain with aesthetic figures and birds and colours and a beautiful fringe.

Bye the way, thanks awfully for the 'Fragments'. It was so funny, I got one from you and one from C. McCallum by the same post, but it was all right as Olive wanted to copy my letter to send to her mother, so I made her a present of one. I don't like it much now, my letter, as of course it had huge chunks chopped out and the language has been very much modified, which spoiled the effect, rather!!! Also, I am like Mrs McPherson in 'Wee Johnnie Paterson': "I cant tell one story without branching off into a hundred parenthetical observations."

There's to be a family dinner tomorrow — and its my turn to lay the table!!! Two girls are chosen every week to set the table, and the next week these two clear away. At breakfast we have to wash the cups, saucers and spoons!

I don't think I ever gave you a sort of outline of what we do all day, so, as I havent much news tonight, I'll tell you.

Monday 6.30, a big dinner gong is rung just outside my door — or at least it used to be!!!! That's for us to get up or something — we don't!! till seven or half past, except when we have to practise at half past seven. At eight Melle Albertine rings for breakfast. After breakfast we make our beds and tidy our rooms. Then we do prep till ten when we have a little lunch. Then we have a Dictation — first sight, always! At first, I made thirty and forty mistakes, and even then wasent the worst. Now I have come down to twenty, so let us hope… one or two memorable times I have had less than Olive!!! After that we have history: all about the French Revolution, and, now, Napoleon. Then we have dinner: soup, meat and fruit, always! Then the promenade and the Hairdresser for we who lose our hair; then singing! Then tea — bread and rotten dyed jam. Then, sometimes, the promenade. Then prep. Then supper — meat and pudding. Then we embroider till nine or half past, when we go to bed. Our room and the one off it are the coldest in the house!

Tuesday: 9. Painting or leather working; 11. Correction of the dictation!! Afternoon we go an excurtion (sic)

Wednesday: 10. Reading lesson; 11. Literature. Afternoon, fancy work lesson.

Thursday: 10. Grammar!! etc. till 12!! Evening, gym, also on Monday.

Friday: Recitation and History of Art. 2. Mending.

Saturday: 10. Grammar etc. 2. Singing class. Evening: Dancing. We are leaning the — Tango — now!! The girls wanted it.

Sunday: Up half an hour later. Church. Dinner, letter–writing till six. Go to drawing room. 9. Tea, bed.

The dinner is over — but the after thoughts are only beginning. We drank eight bottles of wine and champagne, at least not the English girls. I refused but Mad passed a glass of champagne down the table to me and said I must drink her health with it, so I had to. Champagne isent awfully bad, but I much prefer lemonade! But really, I think it is a bit disgusting when a girl drinks six glasses of wine, and all alcoholic, as some of them did.

I hope all your colds are quite away now.

I cant say that the news of the friend of your infant days coming to Switzerland, and the probability of his visiting me, rejoiced me fearfully!! I am going to wash my lace collar, and tighten my skirt a bit, and try a little bit harder to get my hair tidy.

I have written all my duty letters now, thank goodness. I shant buy a camera, and will just keep the 10/– and buy anything I may want by the way.

Did you only find out recently that I am frightfully 'slangy,' when I am beginning to forget it all now, and will be quite presentable when I come home.

I got a P.C. from J and K this morning. It was a photo of their party taken while on a motor spin, but for the life of me I couldent tell which was K. and which Ella!

All the Xmas cakes and chocolates are finished now. All the chocolates had liquer (sic) in them. I emptied one out of the window, the other day!! Have you got the little packet of chocolate I sent you for New Year?

I do hope you are all better now.

With much love,
yours lovingly,
Flora.

L'Hiver dans les bois

Olive. The countryside, Gimels

Sur la glace

Délices Voltaire
14.1.14

My dear Mother,

Many, Many Happy Returns of the day – er, I hope you will be happy and prosperous and have a very nice year.

I cant send you a present for the simple reason that, as usual, I havent finished it. I am really awfully sorry, but its me you have to deal with! I can only hope the letter will arrive in time. Bye the way, I got a long letter from Mrs Cousin today. It was awfully decent of her to write to me.

Please, from who are the handkies you sent in my letter. They are so pretty, and so dainty, and just what I need.

It has snowed again, and has been at 10 degrees below zero, once! It is resting at 7 and 5, so you can imagine we are cold!! We took a walk along the lake side one day, and it had been very windy the last two days, and the wind has lashed the spray onto the rocks, and it had all frozen.. It was beautiful. There were stalyagtites (sic) and all sorts of things: the grass was frozen, the rocks were fluted, the trees were ice–bound, and the rushes and all; all, all ice, just like a fairy garden.

We are going to the mountains on Tuesday, probably. We will sledge all day long, and go sleidge (sic) runs on a big sleidge, sometimes, so we are all very excited.

We are going to see some plays the students are doing tonight. They say it is better than the real theatre, their acting.

Did you ever hear of going out in the dry crisp snow in galoshes!! Four of us got a bad mark for going to our gym with no galoshes on, and it was dry, dry, and the streets were cleared of nearly all the snow. Well Mad found out, and!!!!!!! Its her war cry: caoutchous for ever!! If it rained last week, you put your gs on this week.

I am teaching my small Hongroise to speak English now. (Mad doesent know and wouldent need to!!!) Its so funny, she has such a pretty soft accent — and oh! those 'ths', what a time we had with them. She gives promise of learning very quickly and of being a very good pupil.

Bye the way I made up my mind at the New Year that I would really work a bit this term, and, really, I have been trying. Well in my last first sight Dictation I made only eight mistakes — and four less than Olive!! Well you can imagine the gasps that went round the class — school girl frankness. Mad turned round and said, "Oh yes! But Flora is on the good road, you know."

I have puzzled it out that there are, Marjory on top, then an Austrian, then a German, then a line. Then a German and a line and another Austrian and another German; these are all about equal, then me and the tail!! Well I make less mistakes in my Dictées than the second Austrian, and see lots of mistakes in her speech, so I think I could vanquish her; then the German — perhaps; Olive, no, so I can perhaps get fifth on the list, and we can see about afterwards!! I am going to work now, as ambition is at last beginning to awake!! I am a bit conceited but I don't care.

What ho! The gibberish of M., the Litterature Master, is beginning to become a little more intelligible, and I am being initiated into the works of Molière and Corneille. We get bits read to us, and then we learn the plots of the masterpieces, so, at last, I am becoming instructed.

I am writing this at ten miles an hour, as I have about five minutes till supper, and this must go tomorrow.

Supper!

The students were – magnifique! last night. It was a thousand times better than the theatre. They gave it in an old theatre and, so, had scenes, seats and all. It was magnificently acted, and so much *fresher*, and not so obviously *put on* as so many actors and actresses.

With much love
and best wishes,
yours lovingly,
Flora.

The garden with the hoar frost upon the trees. Délices Voltaire

Délices Voltaire
17.1.14

My dear Daddy and Mother,

Its all settled now, and we are off on Tuesday to St Georges (funny how the Georges haunt our family!) up in the mountain. We will have the most magnificent view imaginable, lots of snow, also a place to skate, good food, good bed, good heating – AND good eating.

We go with Melle Albertine, the young one! so will have a spiffing time. We are hiring six pairs of skis as we all want to learn. I shall buy a pair of skates with some of Mrs Steel's 10/–.

I am going to a concert tonight to hear a woman singing – Italian and German! But there will be the orchestra.

We went last week to hear a man giving a sort of demonstration on Elocution, at least he recited a lot of pieces of different natures. He recited beautifully and the pieces were very pretty – except one!! Someone who had never heard of Militant Suffragettes had written it, very evidently. This person explained why he dident like girls. He said they daren't climb trees, play games decently, without shrieking!, talked and talked, even in bed at night; they lifted their little fingers and behaved generally like idiots; and gushed – a thing was superb, exquisite, ravishing, etc.; and, oh horrors!! also they laced their corsets much too tight. There were some of our number who must have found that remark rather personal.

Bye the way, I sent you some chocolate at New Year. Well, yesterday a battered looking parcel came in – returned by the post – no explanation!! We ate the chocolate ourselves, and felt rather obliged to the post!! I shall bring some home instead.

Please, from whom are the handkies?

My voice is settling down! I have tried opening up my lungs and making a dash for it, but can only give a miserable squeak at G high, but can touch C below; low Doh squeaks too. Olive can sing up to highest Doh, and still farther!!

Its snowing again today. Have you snow or ice much?

So the kid goes to Craig Mount?

The students' play was ripping. They did, 'The Barber of Seville'. the barber did better than any actor I have seen for a long time — so fresh and lively and — perfect! The young girl was absolutely beautiful and a perfect actress for her part. Her expressions changed every moment — and what fibs she could invent on the spur of the moment, unblushingly, and then say, "Oh why, why havent I got the face of a woman of the world, who never gets confused, etc.!!!"

It was a great success, even tho' they did make us pay tenpence for the programmes, which dirtied all our gloves.

The Swiss have four languages: French, German, Italian and a dialect which is a mixture of all three.

Mad has just been giving us a long lecture upon the Tango subject and also about the 'Apaches'. What an absolutely atrocious thing that club is, and in what calls itself a civilised society. It seems, to get to be a member you must commit a murder!.

I cant say that Phyllis keeps me very current in the church or any other matters, so I don't know why they havent been at church, but I know that they used to go to Liberton when they were late for our church. I have asked Cathie if anything is wrong, however. Cathie, by the way, is a real brick, she writes regularly every month, and drops me an occasional P.C. now and then. She keeps me in touch with all that goes on:

Salt, Beechams pills, Sunlight soap, a penny stamp, a penny packet of turnip or some other vegetable seeds, or a potatoe, Amoniated Quinine!! Scots Imulsion, a cake of soap, a tooth brush, Antifon!!, a mirror, a piece of cheese, a penny tawse!! I think the soap is good enough, although none are very brilliant.

Do you know Mads latest. Olive said something about gaiters for golf on wet days, and about bringing them here. Mad turned round in horrified scandalisation, "Whaaat! Do you not wear *galoshes* when you play golf!!!" Poor Mad, how she loves her galoshes!

Do you know that your dearly beloved daughter has the honour of being absolutely the worst player in the Pensionnat? Consequently I always play first on our *exhibition*!! nights. Mad and the girls all talk while I play — as softly as possible. Then Mad says, "Yes, er — I think that goes better, Flora!! But wasent it a little faulty!" (it was!). By the way, in my garden, right at the back, there are some white bluebell affairs. Well, ask Dorothy to pick off the flowers as they come, as they arent at all healthy, and will come up much better next year!

Out of my year, there are only seven months left.

I am beginning to find my feet again, evidently, or rather taking up old habits, as the other day Mad gave my back an awful *dunch*! to make me sit up straight, and then snatched up my book and stumped off with it. She gave it back at night, and told me that some girls dident read enough, but, I read too much!! I don't read so much as the little Hungarian — her average is one book in half a week — but then I (ahem) have more sense!! and do my lessons before reading; she — reads before doing her lessons!! Also, she doesent do much letter writing!! She is the youngest here, just turned fifteen and — awfully, awfully babyish. We make a nice pair, together in a room!

Can you please tell me what I must do to look my age, or at least not look a baby, as when I told one of the girls I was nearly seventeen, she nearly toppled over, and then said, "What! Seventeen, why — I thought always, at the most you were sixteen, the very, very most." I then unburdened my bruised soul to another girl, hoping for sympathy, but alas! "What! You nearly seventeen! No, you, that's not true, etc." They say I look so babyish and have childlike ways. I have been studying all the knowing expressions I can think of in my looking glass but don't find the results satisfactory, so have decided that I'll be old soon enough, and I wont grumble if my youth lasts longer than most people's!!!

Remember to say where the sweet little handkies came from.

Oh! So cold! What an awful winter this seems to have been, or is! Mad tells us harrowing tales about the cold and storms in Italy and elsewhere.

Bye the way, could you give me some information about this earthquake or eruption in Japan, I heard Mad speaking about it — the Daily Sketch will be in its glory!! I wonder if the end of the world or something is coming, sometimes, when I think of the way thousands upon thousands of people are being exterminated every month.

I have just written a Post–Card to Mrs Thompson, so my mind is a bit green!! Who else now? What awfully nice note paper you have got.

I aint got nuffin' more to say now, except that my English

pupil makes an alarming progress; she knows all the room (names), and all the furniture in the bedroom, also two verbs, and makes sentences already, in four short lessons.

I have decided that I wont be *finished* when I come back, but only *begun,* and want to work at home, still. I would like to learn German, as it seems easy enough, and the Germans go into extasées over my accent which they say is not a bit English!

With much love
yours lovingly
Flora.

Pension du Signal
Gimel
24 Jan. 1914

My dear Mother and Daddy,

I have got a free afternoon, as Mad said we all looked tired. It was as well! I got a letter from Phyllis this morning, and couldent read it till now!! — It wasent long before the other girl in the room was looking for water, which she poured down my neck, but alas! I commenced laughing worse than ever in a minute, so she fled for help, and then emptied a whole glass of water down my neck! I was soaked but couldent calm down. 'Oh! for the touch of a vanished hand!' Phyllis wouldent forget the touch of mine very soon, if I could get hold of her.

I have been skiing all morning, as my back and neck will tell tomorrow. Really I took very quickly to the ski. I can do fairly long runs without tumbling, now. Ski is awful sometimes. You forget your feet are about two yards long, and you go tipping over them or treading on them behind, every minute!! Other times you are climbing slowly and carefully up again after a run down when, suddenly, your feet begin to run away from you. Naturally you go with your feet; you generally end on your back or nose. Other times, you are coming down finely, when suddenly one foot starts off sideways. You watch it in agony but cannot stop it, then the *other* starts, and then — c–r–a–sh!! Bump! And when you start collecting your feet again, you generally have to roll about in the snow for a bit before you can get disentangled. You would roar if you saw some of us. I saw one girl crawling up a slippery slope on her hands and knees, waving her feet in the air. The skating is going off all right too, now. I can go with my hands in my pockets!! But we have only a little pond of ten yards or so to skate on, so it isent great sport!

For the sledging, however, we have magnificent places, although a bit exciting! A snow drift here, an ice pool there, a stony bank there and a ditch there, but in between these items the road is very good. On the other side of the hill there is a perfect run, but — alas for me — there is a little bank at the end. I tried this side once and, at first, all went well, I went whum, whizzing through the air, when suddenly — space! Burrrrrrr bump! — bang — crackkkkk!!! on the top of my head, and then the sledge and I went rolling down together. When I had collected my seven senses and my various pieces, I found I had a funny feeling in my head, also a feeling which was not at all funny in my right leg. Just then Mad yelled down, "Are you hurt?" I promptly yelled back, "No," and started walking back, slowly and carefully, backwards!! as that dident hurt so much! I got a good scolding, and then tried again. I tumbled again but dident hurt myself, and was ordered off the pitch.

We dine most sumptiously (sic) here. Honey–sirrup (sic) and bread and butter with coffee or chocolate for breakfast; three of the biggest pieces available for me! Dinner: two helpings of some scrumptious savoury, two of meat and potatoes, two pieces of bread, and dessert. Tea: three or four good slices with honey–syrup, and rotten tea. Supper: two helps savoury, two helps meat, two helps pudding, when available. Guess what we got one night: meringues with real beautiful cream!!!

We can have hot water bottles, and sleep till half past eight.

Of course, everybody admires Marjorie very much and also likes her — Nobody admires Olive, I don't think, but she is very popular with her long tongue and tricks.

Olive is very concientious (sic) in her work, that's why she always knows it, but I learn much easier and quicker than her — and forget it!!

My writing is changed because I hold my pen a different way. I found out that, by holding in that way, the writing looked quite different, and much, much easier to get neat. I have tried sloping it to the right, and you have seen the results! I have tried sloping it upright — and you know again the result, so now I try to the left and have had at last a little success. I am writing this holding my pen in the old way, do you like it? This is sloped to the right, do you like it? I cant get it to slope that way at all, now. I think I will stick to the way I have; if I become great, people will excuse me — and say I am original!!

I am snow burned, like a lobster but will cool down rapidly after — next MONDAY!!! when we return.

That lace collar was most awfully welcome!! as my other one is not respectable, as I need it for everything.

I have heard nothing from your cousin yet.

We have been working all along in spite of our funs — you bet!

The only part of you that gets cold here is your feet, and how!!

I must stop now as I have another letter to finish for a young lady who says that if she doesent get a letter this very week, she will never write to me again — most Madonna like!!

With much love
yours lovingly,
Flora.

Délices Voltaire
1.2.14

My dear Daddy and Mother,

We are being frizzen alive in this hole today. There is a mist hanging about and it freezes all the time. The trees are all covered with hoar frost, thick and sticking out in little pointed spikes.

The hoar frost at Gimel was absolutely magnificent. It was inches thick and lasted all the time. All the woods were white with it. It is a thousand times prettier than snow, even.

Do you know I was never cold for a moment up there, and only felt it for the first time when we arrived at Genève again. We even pitched away our woolen jackets, sometimes, and even then just roasted, literally!!

(It strikes me just now, on comparing the two, that my writing is not like Aunty Flora's but a little like yours! turned the other way! — I hope you arent altogether insulted!)

Even when we were still, we dident feel cold, except the feet. I always get cold feet, I have them all day here. My skates are beauties — 5/–!! But I longed for Blackford Pond to try my skill upon, as you couldent get up a decent run on the little patch of ice we had.

We had only little, one– and two–seated sledges; Mad refused even a three–seater as being much too dangerous.

We went to hear the Requiem of the great composer Verdi last Wednesday. It was magnificent, all in Latin. The choir sang beautifully, and there was a huge orchestra conducted by M. Stavenhagen — ever heard of him? He is a great lord about here!! Conductor in the big concerts.

There were also four solos, two women and two men. The first lady was a soprano, a trilly voice, very pretty, sky scraping, a little past its first youth. She was a disagreeable, conceited little thing; her expression absolutely ruined her voice.

The second was a mezzo, tall, thin with her hair done Greek wise with the bands. Her voice was very nice and very dramatic, an improvement on the other. Her expression was modest and nice, and she looked so young when she got her colour up. She made me think of Olive, somehow, perhaps her coiffure, as that style goes awfully well with Olive.

Do you know, if Daddy was one day hard up for a job, he could turn court dressmaker with the greatest of ease. All you have to do is to — lop off a piece of material, cobble it up a bit in draperies, preferably as little bodice as possible, run a thread through the waist, the position of which imports little — up at the neck or down at the knees — then take a band of braid, lace, or ribbon, and pitch it on, and sew it as it comes. Then, if you like, you sew a bunch of flowers, anywhere, it doesent matter. Sometimes you put a piece of chiffon over the bodice, like a shawl, and there is your masterpiece — £1000! and cheap at that!

You know, I don't know if I will find it so monotonous as you think, at home. I never found it monotonous, and the idea of just being able to be alone! absolutely alone and quiet, now and then, appeals to me very much.

What do you mean by, "my taking op a career"? What is it you have that you want me to do or be? What I want to do when I come home is to study — First–aide (sic), History, Literature and cookery, but not!!! at Athol Crescent.

You certainly don't seem to have been much impressed with

the Sunday School party, but I await Cathie's version of it.

I sent Mona a Christmas card with writing on it, and she replied. I shall have another shot at it when I have time — which is not today, as I must write to Jack who has sent me 25 francs for Christmas e.g. £1, wasent it decent of him?

I also have intentions of writing to Isobel some day!

I'll see about the H. article for D.'s mag. But I am beginning to be bombarded with these beastly contributions! Cathie and Phyllis are in the editing line just now too.

I have no doubt that Carlyle knew what he was talking about when he said that about the beginning of knowledge, but it seems to me that I have had my eyes opened to my ignorance for a very long time, but there I am stuck!!

How exciting and romantic — three engagements!! Mr Forsyth!!! What a cooing and a fluttering there will be in that little dove–cote! What an event in their quiet little life! Mr David Steele — his grin will be less come–offable than ever, and Miss McDairmid!!! Cant I picture it, Mrs McDairmid blessing the culprits, and saying to Jessie, "My child, I shall now die in peace! my duty being done."

I don't think much of Mad's taste in the book line. They are all and every the same. They all commence with two children who get parted, and meet after years, and fall in love, each thinking the other doesent love it, and go about with face one yard long, heaving huge sighs, etc.. Then one falls ill and refuses to get better, but hangs on. Then someone tells the other one that the invalid is dying for love of it, or something., and the other goes and falls on the invalid's neck, or something. Book after book carries on the same way, and I am getting most awfully bored. The present one, they are both most atrociously miserable, and he is in love with her, but daren't confess it. She has a secret sorrow. They will make it up, sure, perhaps he will fall ill!! Oh, for a book with some go in it. These are so empty!

Does D. need silver paper, by any chance, as I can get heaps for her?

Marjorie goes home, or rather, leaves in about four or five weeks. Doesent the time pass quickly!!

My accent is becoming more moderate now, it seems, by reason of going to sleep over the last half of the words, and making contortions with my mouth.

They have chosen our new house now. It has a garden three times as big as the present, which is almost as big as the field over the way, counting the house. There will be ever so many more rooms. We will be one, two and, at most, three in a room. Altogether it is an improvement. I believe it is an old château.

On Sunday at Gimels, Mlle Albertine asked what time was church. The landlady said, nine or half past; the maid said, no! no! its at ten, sure. Then Mad asked in the village; there she was told, half past nine. That was too soon, as we breakfast at nine, so we went skating. It was really at ten after all!!!

The morning and the afternoon, we walked to a village some miles higher up. There was a long descent for the ski there, with some little hills. I did it twice without tumbling, and can lift one foot up in the air while at full speed, so feel accomplished, but, alas, if ever I have another chance, I will have to begin all over again! But it is ripping and much nicer than sledging, as there, if you try to guide, you get a lot of stinging snow in your face and eyes. Sledging bores me now!! I do hope Blackford will freeze next year.

Must stop. Much love, yours lovingly. Flora.

Pension du Signal
Gimel
7. 2. 14.

My dear Mother and Daddy,

Here we are once again at Gimel! I certainly did choose he very best year possible to have excitements and events which don't come every year.

We returned home from Gimel the 26th January. Well, straight away that night Mads mother became ill. Well, on Thursday night she took a very bad turn. Bronchitis!! She has been an invalid in bed for <u>seventeen!</u> years, rhumatism (sic) and a lot of other things. She has always coughed, since I have been here. Well she coughed most frightfully and was worse on Friday. Bye Friday afternoon her throat was so swollen that they had to give her oxagen (sic), to make her breathe. They found, too, that she had something in her throat which should have been cut out long ago and which stopped her getting enough air. She suffered frightfully for want of air. Later they injected something into her arm to help her, but at night her breathing was more and more difficult. She had awful spasms of coughing and then couldent get her breath back. At night the doctor came and stayed till ten at night. I think some of the relations were there too, as we heard people talking, talking, talking all the time.

She died at half past five this morning. They gave her something near the end to ease her, or to put her to sleep. She died in her sleep, perfectly calmly.

Naturally, yesterday we all went about on tiptoes, and whis-

St Georges

pered dismally. You know I think I knew from the beginning that she wouldent live, as, ever so many times, I caught myself thinking of what we would have to do if Madam died, and at night I felt it more strongly. I sort of knew she would be gone by morning, although we weren't at all sure the night before.

We were left to sleep this morning till half past seven, when the gong was rung, and those who heard it said at once they knew what had happened, as it was rung twice as loud as other times. One of the girls wakened me afterwards with the words, "Flora, get up, its twenty–five to eight. Madam is dead." I just looked at her, it left me the same as if she had said, Good morning. I wasent one little bit surprised, but so as not to shock her altogether I said, "Ohhhh!" You know, there is something missing in me. I think it is the power of realising. I don't know Madam is dead; it left me cold when they said she was dangerously ill, and suffering horribly.

In bed I felt she was dying, but slept well all the same.

This morning after breakfast Mad said that we were to go to Gimel for three days, just till the funeral is over.

Mad's brother in London was not warned, as she died much sooner than expected, so now he was sent a telegram saying she was dead. He will get here just in time to see the last of her, and for the funeral.

Melle Albertine is in a most awful way, as it has been her life's work looking after her mother. She had sort of consacrated (sic) herself to her. Now her work is finished, and she is left. She refused, time after time, many offers in marriage, so now she is absolutely thrown upon herself. All the others are married, and Melle Marie has her school, so all have some means of forgetting their trouble a little. Melle Albertine hasent slept a wink or been off her feet for four days, and only has been able to rest, a little, the other part of the fortnight since our return, so she has broken down completely. She shut herself up in a room at the top of the house and refused to see anybody; they could hear her sobbing and sobbing awfully, all alone.

Melle Marie was much more composed, as she had to arrange everything, but the poor thing, it makes you want to cry to see her with red eyes and huge lines under her eyes, as she hasent slept either and hadent even the comfort of being able to nurse her mother, as her mother would have no one but Albertine near her.

Good gracious! What ever have I been doing, here have I been filling up four and a half pages with things which, at the most, can only harrow your feelings and make you uncomfortable. Well, just another word and we'll change the subject: its this, that the half of us have never seen Madam, except through her window in summer, so the only difference to us will be her cough gone. But for the rest, otherwise: all the house turned round that bedside. Maman had to suggest this and criticise that, and her opinion was always being needed, so she will be missed.

It is good for all that we are leaving this house in April, except that they had chosen a beautiful room with a lovely veranda, and everything, for Madam.

The new house has twenty rooms and an immense garden and electricity, etc.

There is still a lot of snow at Gimel, but we must only go for walks all day long, as we have no sledges, etc!!!

I have started my daft tricks already. The last day we were here I spilt a bottle of ink onto the table cloth! It however disappeared by dint of hard rubbing with lemon, soap and water — and thanks to the amount of water that must have been in it. Well, today I thought I would like to take a little Eau de Cologne, as they say its good for heat spots, in which I am rejoicing just now. Well, I put a little in a bottle and packed it; upon unpacking, the odour of E. de C. made me stagger. Upon exploring, I found an empty bottle — <u>and a full collar</u>!!! Various articles were sprinkled with the odour, also with the blue from an exercise book. The collar I put into the water; the bow I dried upon radiator which both dried and puryfied (sic) it. Luckily the Eau de C wasent very valuable as I got a 1/3 bottle which was ¾ of a foot, if not quite, in hight (sic)!!! Again, that funny instinct I have told me the scent would spill, and also that my collar should have been elsewhere, but — !! We make another attempt to go to church tomorrow, ten o'clock this time!

MOTHER! Are you aware that in your last six or seven letters, its been Pat McMaster this and P.M. that, till I am ready to go on strike, any moment. Whats he done to you, or what have I done, to get his praises dinned into me like this. Allow me to tell you that our select circle have our own opinions upon the subject of that young man, and that they <u>don't</u> flatter him!!

The other half of my letter is with Chrissie, as I sent a contribution much too long, and so they cut it in two.

We are in the middle of the Juras, and have a most magnificent view of the Alps from here. We left Geneva in the mist and dullness, and came up here through the mist into the sunshine.

It was the sledging which blackened me; the ski I took quickly enough to. Oh its spiffing when once you get into it.

I am attempting to write this sitting on the floor, and writing on a chair. It doesent help the inspiration, so I will defer the account of the Salève and its misty seas till I can get a table and a chair. Meanwhile, I will read!!!

Sunday. 8th. Well here I am in peace and quiet, except for the clacking of hens, crowing of cockerels, and the distant murmur of voices. I am in my room with the window wide open. If only Melle Marie could see me!!! But its absolutely spring like this morning, and outside smells so good! The sky is as blue as blue, and the sun is shining hard, the birds are singing, the snow is melting, and the faint breeze wafts in the smell of dinner, and poultry. Even so, many times I have just shut my eyes and thought I was in Corsock, the scent of the country and the noises and all, except the dirt; if you want dirt, pure sheer dirt and stinks, look for it in a Swiss village. Its atrocious!

We went to the village church today. It was so funny! The seats were made of unvarnished wood and all scratched and worn. The floor was of stone, so we had a wooden board under each seat to stand on. The windows were plain except at the top, where they had some marvellously coloured glass. In form it must be very like what Corsock church is now, but half as big; its vestry door was in the same place, the pulpit and the arched space behind the pulpit, with some more empty seats. The interior seemed at first sight to be built of huge blocks of fine grey stone but, alas, for the impression; upon turning my roving eye around, I saw a place where the wall had got knocked, and there underneath the surface of the stone was something which looked suspiciously like plaster. Further investigations found that this was the case. However, there was a very decent organ with pipes and a' that, and two galleries. Two ministers, one who had a robe and bands, first I'd seen since home. The place was heated by a wood stove, which the ministers stoked, from time to time putting on more wood.

The preaching minister was a little timid, but did all right; the bibles, etc. looked a bit dusty and old, like the rest of the building. The girls sat on one side and the boys on the other, and the adults in the middle.

We are here in charge of a sister–in–law of Mad's brother–in–law, if you can comprehend! She is horribly fussy, and worries this that and the next way. She gives me nerves, horribly, and I have to sit next to her at table!

Rennes.

Bye the way, this masterpiece which I enclose, is your belated birthday present. Its — supposed — to be a card case! and is the first thing I did. I have two other things finished now, but shall keep them till I return, I think.

I was going to tell you about our adventures on the Salève, so here goes.

We left Genève all dull and horrid in a stuffy old tram which made me fearfully sick! As we continued, the mist got thicker and thicker until we were right in it. Then, after a bit, we began to see the sky, and then the pale glimmer of the sun, and then we came up right above the mist into the blazing sunshine. (we havent had sun in Geneva since Xmas, I think, always that abominable mist.)

At the foot of the Big Salève, the most of us got out and started to walk up. There was only a little foot path which was covered with frozen snow!!!! However we struggled bravely on. The fat girl and the little Hungarian were the worst off. The fat girl was fat and frightened, the Hungarian was frail and fearsome. The fat girl managed to get up — just, the Hungarian had to be hauled and pushed by poor Marjorie and another girl. I had to give a friendly shove now and then to the girl in front of me, when she started a backward course, or got stuck altogether; it was most exciting. But the view at the top was worth twice the pain.

The Alps were covered with snow and, lying at their feet or rather, literally at their middle, was a great sea of mist all around us. Wherever we looked was this sea and, here and there, were little islands sticking through. Just below us was a house built upon the hillside, but which seemed to be built on a ledge of rock in the sea. At the other side you saw the Juras, just a little.

After tea we came out again to see, and this time all was changed as it was sunset. The Alps were a most lovely pale rose, deepening here and there. The Little Salève was a lovely gold. The mountain feet were a beautiful dark purple, and the sea was all wrinkled and rose, while at another part it was greenish grey. The Juras were purple blue, and the sky, blue, yellow and golden rose. It was magnificent, and the sky melted off into different colours, so beautifully, making the dark Juras stand out more clearly than ever. The mist was thick, thick and beautifully white, and all little heaps and hollows, like the foam on a windy day. No, its no good trying to describe it, as its indescribable, altogether.

Here too we see the Alps very well, but just now there is a faint haze hovering before them, which gives them a sort of unreal look, just as if they were painted upon the sky.

Do you know, the Hungarian and I are a most lovely pair to put alone in a room together. I think that, if possible, she is a little worse than me in sensible matters, but then she has a year and a half less than I, which explains and equalises all.

We are always late, our drawers, cupboards, and desks are a treat. We break all possible rules, talk till eleven, read at every spare moment, are equally erratic and inconsequent – and frank, but you should hear the things we talk about!!!

The other night we started: I told her she wanted too much, that she wanted the moon. That brought up the question of the size of the moon, then about the stars, then about the population and civil conditions of Mars. Then we discussed the affairs in the Balkans and the probabilities of its becoming – (Oh, those hens! – the indignant and outraged Hungary has been dancing with impotent rage at the row they are kicking up, and has been slaughtering me into the bargen (sic).)

Well, to continue: the probabilities of the wars becoming international, and as to who would side with who, etc., and we let off a little steam on the subject of Russia and its aims.

We then discussed the writing of poetry, books, and the bringing up of children, and human nature and the judging of it, and various other subjects.

All the smudges on this page are due to the hens and the indignant Hungary, who threatened to kill me if I dident stop them, so I had to shut the window as far as it would go, and stuff the curtains in the bits that wouldent shut. Then just as Hungary was settling down, it let out a wail of despair and started banging the bed and yelling: the hero in her book had a long fair moustache! She wailed and wailed and refused to read further, saying, "Oh, oh! He'll have a long moustache, blonde, to the end of the book, now. Oh, oh!" Then the hens started again and then Hungary came to me with a ferocious look, and shaking her fist at me, said, "If you write a book with a long moustache in it, I'll kill you!" Then she flounced off to tell her woes to the others, and leaving me a moments peace. She's most awfully excitable sometimes, but awful fun and so intelligent.

The Madonna is a native of Bohemia, and has returned to her native land where she has a Mademoiselle and high jinks. She wont return if she had her way of it!! Olive calmed down after the first flood of tears.

Olive and her father are going to make a tour in Italy before returning – Milan or Florence, etc.

Do you know I have put on two pounds since November, in spite of all my sports, etc., and I have grown ¾ of an inch!!! But my face is getting disgustingly fat; it wobbles like jelly when anyone shakes me, but one of the girls has put on nearly eight pounds since November! And another, six! Which rather puts me in the shade, but I have more to show for it, for all that.

I shall find the meals funny, at first, at home, as here we have two heavier dinners and two light meals, but I shall find it so good to eat a decent tea with butter and jam, and decent bread! We get magnificent vegetables here, but our puddings and meats are miles better.

Cathie wasent much impressed with the Sunday School Party, either.

We have great 'loyalty' fights here sometimes, which sometimes become a little dangerous, as the various partisans wax hotter and hotter, also we discuss politics, and I am getting quite proficient in the various little bitternesses between the different nations.

I really must stop now, so, with much love,

your loving d. Flora.

Gimels

Marjorie Ravell

Délices Voltaire
15.2.14

My dear Daddy and Mother,

We are having spring at last, the sun shines and its quite warm; we are sitting with the windows open.

'When the cat's away the kittens will play.' Our kittens are playing hard enough, at any rate. Mad, M. Albertine, and the brother are all gone out to dinner, so leaving the kittens free. At dinner we kicked up an awful row, and ate!! Now they're taking photos. The girls have got on their night gowns and their hair down, and are being taken like that. The open window is a sure sign of Mad's disappearance.

I think it is a very good idea, that of buying a book for me, but not the sending of it. You could buy me a nice book and then keep it for me, as I am not allowed to read English, and I will subtract 10/– from the sum I have here. I would prefer a book upon artists, or something; is 10/– too little, as I have visions of a very pretty work box for my table, and it will probably cost 15/–. We are getting Raphael just now, and after, Michel Ange.

Bye the way, if you could find something in the line of Greek or Roman History, like Dorothy's book, or something, I should like that.

I have fallen upon my feet this time at any rate, in the book line. But not through any fault of Mad's!! It fell about thus wise: Hungary and I had both finished our books at Gimels, and Hungary's stray remarks and interjections, while reading had roused my curiosity concerning the book. Well, we changed books – which was against the rules, you know. Well, as

I said, I fell distinctly upon my feet that time, as the book, at last, is interesting, in fact, thrilling. It is titled, 'The Necklace of Pearls' and is translated from the English (one reason). It is in the time of Elizabeth and Catherine de Medici and Charles IX of France. The massacre of St Bartholamew comes in and Sir Philip Sidney, etc.. The plot is ripping and you absolutely don't know one little bit how it will end! Something quite refreshing after the transparent articles I have been having for the last six months.

What excitement: in the intervals of writing this last page I have been three times up on the top of the house watching for the aeroplanes which are to be here today. We have a little roof affair right up on top of all the others, and from there we can see the Juras, the lake and the Salève, and, once upon a time, the Mont Blanc before they built these wretched sky scraping flats in front.

We have seen the new house now. It looked very dull and out of repair, but it is all to be done up. The garden is huge, and has huge trees and walks and a nice tennis court.

Do you know, I actually saw a copy of Punch whilst in the Juras. The English lady, we met there, lent it to Olive and us, I swallowed it whole. She dident speak English, however, except twice, but complimented our guardien upon us, as she said she thought it splendid the way we all spoke French, all the time, even when no one was there. That was *almost* true — *almost* — but there are a group of Germans who talk German very often, and had just been having a little bout that day.

I find that the Germans don't count truthfulness amongst their cardinal vertues (sic), nor have they the code and law against telling tales! If you dident do a thing then your duty is to find out who did, and give them away, if possible. Fair play, they never heard of!

I enclose some photos of Gimels. Please don't throw them away, as I have only got the originals. I am also enclosing a beautiful portrait of self with the galoshes. The sun was so strong that I had to shut my eyes, in spite of all protestations!

1. Snowman in the garden at Genève, I wasent in it.

2. Some of us on the ice – what ho! How goes my pose? Marjorie is in the corner. Behind are the Juras.

3. Marjorie.

4. Another skating place, with Mad Albertine disappearing in the distance, is Hungary. I was over at the left learning painfully to ski, at the moment. That figure near the trees might be me, or that dot.

Please excuse the French on the back, but that was written before I thought of sending them to you.

Two more of us go tomorrow, which leaves us ten – out of sixteen. However, we are to have cakes etc., in their honour!

Have been up on the roof for nearly an hour and have seen the aeroplane at last.

We were all there and were searching hard, some were tired and had gone down, but we faithful were at last rewarded, as, all at once, it came out from behind a house.

It flew here and there, high, high up and then quite low. It nearly stood still, sometimes. Once it just started doing the loop, when it went behind a rotten house! (swears, etc.). It did nothing extraordinaire, however, except flying right up over our heads, until tea–time. Then, we had to go down. I dident want to and kept lagging behind and then, when the others were gone, I went back – reward of disobedience: the thing began to get lively, and <u>then</u>, just at a nice hight (sic), it started looping: swoop, twirl, twist, there it went, and then it flew a long way upside down, and then turned with a most beautiful swoop and swerve. It was magnificent, and so graceful, then it disappeared, and then reappeared below the level of the houses and turned again – then I saw Mad entering, and <u>fled</u>!! pell mell!! Just wet my hands and flopped into my chair, and started eating, but I was so excited that I could hardly eat, but <u>wasent</u> it luck, and hard luck for the others; just when they weren't there all the excitement came. Its just wonderful to see the thing dropping head foremost, and then to come up all of a sudden and swoop off in another direction. I couldent help thinking how funny our enthousiasme (sic) will seem to the people of fifty years hence, and what a wonder the object of it to the people of fifty years ago!

My letter is a little empty this time, but we havent done much this week.

I went to a conference upon Madame de Sévigné and her letters, and heard a lecture upon the different styles of letters, and how the letter <u>always</u> showed the character or nature of he writer, and he gave us examples.

With much love
your lovingly
Flora.

Saw it again, and it looped and looped four or five times in succession.

Délices Voltaire
22nd Feb. 1914

My dear Daddy and Mother,

We are now quite settled down again, and, really, to us the house is very little different, as we never saw Madam at any time.

No! it was Melle Marie who started the school. She has her twenty–five years jubilee next year!

You know, I always feel more at home when it rains here, its more homely! How lovely the lawns must be with all the crocus and snowdrops. Here, there is not one single flower in the garden.

Our Hungarian is a native of Budapest — she doesent have any difficulty in speaking, at any rate!!! Perhaps she exhibits the national oratorship — once start her, and you'll be clever if you can put in a word edgeways! She astounds me more and more with her intelligence, every day. Last night we discussed the probable state of the world in the year 20 or 50. I persisted that we would have nothing more to do in a few thousand years, as all would be done by machinery. She said that we would have to work, as we would have to work the machines, and to get the materials for making them. I said they would have machines for making the machines and for getting the stuff. We decided, however, that, as man was made to work, there would be something else for him to do that isent invented yet. Also, she says that, as the successor to the German throne was likely to bring about wars, he would become unpopular. The successor to the Hungarian throne was unpopular, and also that of the Austrian. Perhaps there would be some huge revolutions, and then these countries would become big republics, after which the other powers would follow their example. She said that in some thousands of years the earth would be one big republic, that being the ideal state of affairs.

She has explained to me all her national genealogy, where the Hungo came from, etc., also the relations between Austria and Hungary, etc. so I am learning History easily and modernly.

I don't know if you would altogether approve of our 'Loyalty fights,' if you heard them. I think, upon the whole, we try to avoid them, that is, those who have a little sense, as the feeling runs high sometimes. Its generally Olive who starts them, with some silly brag. You know, Olive isent <u>proud</u> of her nationality but <u>conceited</u> of it, and its people like her who will be the cause of a war between Germany and us, as the Germans get absolutely furious. When she starts bragging, she absolutely hasent one idea of when to stop, and when she has gone far enough. We had one awful row once, in which yours truly took a rather too lively part! And after that, we stop when we start. England, needless to say, won the battle, but Germany sulked, and only answered now and again, so we cant judge rightly.

But, really, I find the English, as a nation, are liked well enough upon the continent, except by those who are jealous, but even the Germans like us well enough. We got a lecture the other day in class upon the reasons why the British are always successful as colonists, and why the Germans, Spanish, etc. were not and are not. It is because Britain always manages to boss the people without hurting their feelings, and letting them feel that they are conquered, as the Germans seem to do.

I really couldent take cookery here, as I should have to take it instead of my other lessons, in the morning, which Mad would never permit.

We are going to the play of another student club. We are invited to buy the tickets because Mad's eldest nephew belongs to it. Mad will not go, but the little old wife who took us to Gimels will take us. Its sure to be ripping.

I saw an English picture journal of the strike in Johannesburgh, also a copy of Punch, with the ten leaders all in Napoleonic attitudes upon the Bellerophone, going to St Helena, otherwise England. What are they going to do with them now?

Olive knows already the date of her departure, and her father is to send her a map with her voyage marked upon it. She talks incessantly of what she will do at home, and of her journey. Mad scolds her for being silly, but she gets worse. She is to go to Italy with her father and visit Florence, Rome, etc. and return by the Mediterranean.

The photos that I have enclosed this time are mostly old, taken last autumn, except those of the snow. Six of the girls in the big photo have since left, which leaves us nine. In March two others go, which leaves seven, and at present we know of only one prospective new girl!

Its just awful today. I havent got one blessed thing to say. Before tea, I had to stop and take up my book.

In the evenings after supper, we all sit round and embroider while someone reads aloud. Well, as fate would have it, it was my turn to read, and the book is a most awfully funny one. Well, I started off all right but soon came to a funny bit. I promptly started to giggle, and I giggled and I giggled and

I could not stop. However, Mad told me to take courage, and at last I got off. Then again came a rotten bit, and, this time, I saw the funny bit and started to laugh before I had read it aloud, so the others dident know what was up with me. This time I just gasped out a word or two and then collapsed and refused to read. Mad got cross with me in the end, but all I could do was take a rush at a sentence before I was overcome. I am going to get hold of the book, if I can, as it is very interesting. It is a girl and her aunt who hate each other cordially and who have awful fights, the aunt being in the fault. The girl tells the story and gives observations which just collapse you altogether.

I think I shall stop now, being absolutely dried up.

With much love,
yours lovingly,
Flora.

Délices Voltaire
28th.2.14

My dear Mother and Daddy,

Here am I in my glad rags once more, it being my turn once again for the concert. Its a singer! The 'Zophinger's' play was rotten, and Mad's nephew said we were to expect something extra special! The students played quite well, but the piece was rotten and not appropriate.

I am in train of sniffing just now, having cotched a cold. Fortunately, Mad has not observed anything, as yet, otherwise it would be foutu with my night outing.

Oh! Bye the way, Mad has proposed making a little journey for the Easter Week, and she said we were to ask at home if you would object to us going to the Italian lakes. The cost will be at least five pounds. We would visit all the neighbourhood, of course, the lake Major, etc. Mad said we were to ask if you would object to the expense. I think that it wont go very much more than six pounds, at the most, for all, but Mad is making enquiries. I should absolutely love to go to Italy, although we wont see any of the big places. Perhaps, we might get as far as Milan.

If you object, we can go to some place nearer hand, in Switzerland.

How absolutely ripping that 'Stories from Rome' must be — just exactly what I wanted. Thanks awfully much! I should love to see it, but as I woudent be allowed to read it, its not worth while risking getting it damaged by the post — but I never said you mustent send me books for my birthday.

I should like awfully to have a book–case in my room, but you know that I find it very embarrassing to be asked what I want, as I don't know of anything special!

I will have to spend 4/6 upon cakes!! Isent it awful, its 1st March tomorrow; the time flies. To think its nearly the year ago since Marjorie was staying with us.

We went to see the new house, yesterday, and two of us went in and all over it. It has a huge staircase and big corridors with passages and rooms leading off, two drawing rooms and veranda, etc. The grounds are like a park, and we see the Alps, the Juras and the Salève, and are a stones throw from the lake. We have a little brook, and a wall which overlooks the railway upon which we can sit and wave to the girls in the train, going home. Its an ideal Pensionnat now, we say — we wont have any more fortnightly candles, at any rate, as its all to be electricity.

What ho! I took notes in the Art class last Friday and made a résumé of them, and have just handed it to Mad. I am not feeling very comfortable in my mind, just now, as it certainly wasent a masterpiece, as concerned French, etc. But at any rate, I will not forget Michel Angelo, again, I think.

1.3.14 I dreamt last night that Mad said that my résumé was very, very bad indeed, and that she scolded me thoroughly for it. They do say dreams go by opposites, let us hope!!!!

In the meantime I have broken my specs, one eye, and I shall have to wait a week before Mad takes it into her head to take them to be mended! They have succumbed, at last, but I think someone must have walked upon them.

Awful nuisance, I just wanted to write to Aunty Harry

today, she having asked me to, at Xmas, but I have just discovered that its much too near 19th March[1] to think of any such thing, so she will have to wait a little longer.

We are doing nothing special these times, which makes it difficult to write. I am writing this letter and another, and am going to begin another, all at the same time, and go from one to the other, accordingly as I find something to say!

Yesterday the concert was ripping, also the baritone had a magnificent voice. There was also a novelty, in some music written by a Jew, and conducted by the author. It was weird, and sometimes flatly discordant. Every instrument in the orchestra played in it, bells, drums, cymbals, scales and all. I amused myself in nick naming the men, and finding out which were friends, etc.

There is a book by Victor Hugo, I think, called 'The man who laughed', that's Danton or someone. Well, I have got a man for it. He has a funny little face, but knowing enough too, which laughs all over.

Robespierre is the first violinist. He's supercilious, spick and span and beautifully got up. Marat is one of the cellos, little, fat, dark and ugly. Our dancing master plays the violin there, too.

Bye the way, the latest in coiffure is the tower upon the top of the head. (There is nothing new in this world.) does that mean that those huge towering coiffures are going to come in again. Also the crinoline seems to be threatening, as the only thing needed now is the crinoline, the dresses are all getting bulgy.

Also, everyone affects dark chestnut hair just now, all

---

1 Flora's birthday.

sprawled over the head, so that you cant see where it begins and where it ends!

I am afraid that, if you are counting upon my coming back home reformed and wakened up, you are doomed to eternal disappointment, as I seem to be worse than ever. Last night Mad gave out the clean sheets, etc. and all the girls came and took their lot, except me. I was labouring under the impression that they were back from the wash, although never before were they placed upon the table from the wash. Well, I watched the girls taking their things but still I never dreamt of taking mine. Afterwards I wandered off leaving mine behind me, when Mad demanded if I had taken my things. I explained to her that she always kept my things, etc., etc. and it was only after a lot of trouble that she got me to understand <u>or</u> to remember that it was the day for clean sheets. Then I gave a girl two spoons, on setting the table, also I mixed up the Mads' serviettes — the storm broke — Mad lectured me for nearly half an hour on the subject of thoughtlessness, etc.

We are having sunshine now, but not awfully warm.

You couldent complain of my being thin, in the enclosed photo, at any rate. Mad told me that I would become a little round dumpling if I divent worry myself a little more, but I would have liked to tell her that I preferred to be fat and unwrinkled than thin <u>and</u> wrinkled.

In the other, observe the polite gesture of the maiden standing next to me; it, however, hasent come out very well (the gesture).

With much love to you both, yours lovingly, Flora.

Is Helen still there? Hows she keeping? Give her my love.

P.S. Please don't forget the halfpenny stamp, the next time!

Délices Voltaire
6.3.14

My dear Daddy and Mother,

We also are having spring now, only it snowed two nights running again. There are lots of primroses growing in the grass in the garden.

How on earth did D. find out about Mad's cousin? I told Mad, but she said she dident know her, and that she had cousins galore, that she had never heard of or seen.

Two new girls are coming some time soon, but, when, we don't know.

You remarked in your last letter that Dorothy was eating much better now!!! – what does that mean?! you did say once that she was nearly eating you out of the house.

Marjorie goes – a week next Sunday. She goes with another girl, and will voyage a bit with her, staying with some of her old school friends.

This week has been altogether a red letter one, for me, at any rate. One of the girls gave me a lecture in which she impressed it upon me that I was in the wrong always to be with my nose in my book, and that I should talk to the others, etc., etc. quite a sermon, in fact. Well I said I would see what could be done to remedy the matter, a bit.

(There's a wretched Italian in the house opposite, and he's banging upon a tin kettle piano all, the wretched dance tunes imaginable.)

Well, that very night, another girl and I made up our minds to do something daft. Well, I went upstairs and emptied a lot of cheap eau–de–cologne into a bottle, and afterwards took it and emptied it onto the very girl who had lectured me's pillows!! What a veritable viper she was harbouring in her bosom! But then she is an awful silly beggar, always lecturing, etc. Well, she got all the eau–de–C. upon her pillow, at any rate.

The same night, I put a brick in Hungary's bed. It had a good result: she yelled. Then she put one in mine, but I felt it, before entering.

Next night, I felt for my handky and found my pillow nearly sopping. No, it wasent that; I was looking for my flannel, which had gone astray. After a long search, I found it in my pillow!!

Next night, made Hungary's bed, and folded over the sheets so that she had only one over her; also stuffed her pillow with boxes, keys, brushes etc.. Next night, Hungary stuffed another girl's bed with little stones under the sheet, and the maid put in a big stair brush. Unfortunately, in placing the stones, she had disarranged the bed, and the girl found out.

Next night, on starting to get into my bed, I felt something hard. Without saying anything, I took it out. It was a brush... Upon feeling further, I discovered another, and another, and another, and another, and another. One of these obstacles I kicked to the bottom of the bed, the rest I removed. Bye and bye, Hungary began to sigh most heart renderingly (sic), and then she said, "Flora, you have got a good skin." I demanded why, most innocently. After a while the remark came again, but she refused to say why. Then I asked, most mildly, "Have you put something in my bed?" After she said she had, I then said, "That's funny, as I don't feel anything at all!" This obviously puzzled her, as she began to make observations aloud.

I shrieked inwardly but still appeared to be ignorant. Then Hungary said, "Look thoroughly in your bed and see if there's nothing." I made a great show of exploring my bed, and then brought up the brush at the foot. "Theres only one, here," I said. "Really," she replied, "I put six in!!" Then she even got out of her bed to come and examine mine. Naturally, she found nothing. She then made the conclusion that the maid must have taken them. She went to sleep puzzling out the reason of their disappearance.

Next morning, I being up first, I arranged all the brushes beautifully on her night table, and fled…

She came downstairs that morning whole five minutes sooner!! She must have been curious, to have made such an effort. I explained all to her carefully, and she did look disgusted!! She put big stones in my bed that night, but I never felt them as they weren't well placed!!

Mad has a cousin staying with her just now. She is rather peculiar e.g. she nearly made me jump once by suddenly putting her knife into her mouth!

Mad is making up my bill just now, and it doesent appear to be a small one. Also, I had £4 left out of the five you sent me last year, and she made me pay for my sporting outfit, and all those sort of things out of it, so its all gone, so please could you send me some more when you pay the bill.

Please, when has Aunty Harry her birthday?

I have just been in the garden, and I have picked such a dainty little bunch of primroses. The leaves are such a lovely fresh green. I am sure the spring is here now, all the windows are open, and we havent any need of our jackets in the garden.

You cant imagine what a treat it is to have butter and jam

together. Its better than cakes, I think.

Do you remember how, the last Sunday at home, I ate 8 eggs, that day. I wonder if I was trying, without thinking, to lay in a stock till I returned, as I have never since eaten a boiled egg. Mad has one at breakfast and my mouth waters awful, sometimes.

Do you know Mad came into the school room the other day with a book in her hand, and said, "Just come and see this." it was tenpence, the book, and in it were five of Racine's plays, written on nice thin paper, beautiful print, large, clear. The cover was nice red cloth, with the printing in gold; all that for the paltry sum of tenpence. I would like to have Racine, at any rate, as we are having him for the Literature class. Do you advise me to buy the four volumes which contain all his works? I would like Molière too, as we have just had him. I have still £1 from Xmas left, even subtracting the ten shillings which you were to spend for me on books. Was there enough left to get another smaller book?

I have been here more than the half of my year, now.

We are having the parting cakes of Marjorie tonight. Really they have been nice cakes here at Genève.

Whosoever comes to fetch me must be prepared to take me to the confectioners and there stand me a tea, and what a tea that will be, as the tastes of cake here have whetted my appetite.

Is Daddy still going to Palestine this year, because, if so, I suppose he would fetch me back.

With much love to you both,
yours lovingly,
Flora.

Délices Voltaire
10.3.14

Dear Daddy and Mother,

Mad has just finished making up the bill and has offered to let me write a word.

You will find a string of extras, these are the extras from the last bill, which you hadent understood about. I have paid for the extras for this term, but hadent enough for last time's. She has written the extras upon another sheet so that you wont muddle them.

I said that it was because they were written in French and in such small writing that you had made the mistake, so she got me to see that she translated them all right.

She said that, as I wasent getting German, she would cross out the price of house linen, which is the same, which makes things right.

We have no German pupil teacher yet, so cant have lessons, but, all the same, I have picked up some few scraps.

I know two words in Hungarian, a few in Latin, some in German, French, English, Scotch, Gaelic, one in Check (sic) and one or two in Italian, so I am accomplished (nicht war?). All the train notices are printed in three languages so we learn them by heart.

We were at the North Pole yesterday, at the cinema, a programme specially arranged for the Pens of both sexes. Needless to say, the female Pens overran the place. We saw seal hunts, bear hunts, different species of Esquimaux, their houses, food and customs. We saw frozen seas, and thousands and thousands of seals and walrus playing in the water.

We saw the workings of the great gold mines at Kimberley, or something. We saw the post and mails etc. and, you'll never guess, such a funny coincidence: the post master of a little northern desert village was called – Ewing – his name was placarded upon high for all the world to see. The Pens giggled – audibly!!

Really, I mustent waste any more time, as I have my literature to learn yet, and I must practise!

With much love
(and sincerest sympathies!)
yours lovingly,
Flora.

P.S. We are putting on summer hats, doing without fires and leaving the windows open. It is so homely today, as it has poured from morning till night!

Everyone likes my orange hat here, and even I get a sort of relief when I put it on after the big winter one.

Now I really must stop.

Fa–la.

Have just been stricken with a brainy idea. Did you have a little left over from the ten shillings I substracted (sic) from my private accounts for books? If so, couldent you spend it on penny and half penny stamps? If not, I will substract (sic) another three shillings. These stamps you could send me, and then, when I wanted to write to Aunty Harry or someone like that, who doesent live in Edinburgh, I just put on a 1d stamp, put the letter in with yours, you drop the enclosed letter into the letter box, and there, I have saved 1 1/2d. What do you think of the idea?

The Madonna has promised me a big photo of herself upon my birfday (sic). It is to come later, not being finished!

Poor Lada; her early depart has not helped her French; it seems she makes dreadful mistakes when she writes, but I never notice them in the letters she writes to me. If you want to find mistakes, you have but to look for them. I was simply wild at breakfast today. You see, Lada had sent Olive a letter with some sheets enclosed for the others. Well, perhaps it was that Olive was cross after having boasted that her letter had ten pages, and then to find that she hadent but four for her, but, at any rate, she started and mocked the letter, saying what awful mistakes there were in it, and how frivolous and worldly etc. Lada was getting. I wanted to say that she hadent made any mistakes in mine, that I could see, but I thought that I would just get snubbed for my pains — my judgement is not held very highly here, so I said nothing aloud but a lot inside.

Really, I think that is disgusting of Olive to critisize (sic) the way she does, as, although she may think it, she is by no means perfect in the various branches of the language, as yet! Probably, I think she is very jealous of the good time Lada is having at balls and theatre, and all her little love affairs etc., as Olive regards the trousered sex with by no means an evil eye — quite the contrary.

Deary me, how violent we're getting, to be sure. I think you must have a most atrocious idea of Olive by now. Poor thing;

she has her good points too, like the rest of us. In fact, summing up all, she is very human! I like Olive best at night, in her dressing gown, or in bed. There, she seems to throw off her affectation at the same time as her clothes. Then, I like her really and truly. It really is an awful pity — and nuisance — that she is so unnatural, as she would be so nice without it. She is so gay and full of fun.

My specs are mended now, and, I was so accustomed to doing without them, that, at first, I couldent bear them, and had to take them off.

Really, this is the end, this time.

Love,
Flora.

Délices Voltaire
14.3.14

My dear Mother and Daddy,

We are having spring, real and true at last. I roasted when out walking. Its lovely and sunshiny – outside, at least!!!

By the way, Mad has found out a mistake on her bill; she has put £10 instead of £9 for the extras.

You always talk about having wet, dreary, blowy, slushy, etc. weather. We – leave all the windows open, have hot sunshine, and thin blouses.

I think that, perhaps, the next bill will be a little smaller, as the Gym and Dancing lessons stop at Easter, but that all depends as to whether it comes before our big mountain trip or not.

I have got a piece of good news for you. Its this: we arent going to go to Italy, as Mad found out that it was going to be more expensive than she had thought, so now we are going to go to a little village near Montreux, from which we can visit Berne, Basel and some pretty places. Really, I am glad its not the other, as I was having melancholy visions of me sauntering about in the Italian sunshine, and you at home sitting round an empty table, etc., etc.!! Since your last letter, I have been bitten by the saving flea. I have a book, and there I mark down all the little things I have saved money upon. The book, I dident start now but long ago, but, up till now, the sum I have saved off different things doesent amount to more than 4/–.

Two new girls are coming, one this month, Monday week, I think, also two new pupil teachers, soon.

How uninspiring cookery sounds. I want to learn housekeeping, at any rate, but isent there anything I could do in which I could employ my – gift of the gab. If only I knew enough, I should like well enough to teach something, History, Literature, but, even that, I don't want much, so I suppose that, as I know nothing I want, I shall just have to take what comes. Is it difficult to critic books or to write articles for people? That is my only vision at present.

It is so difficult to know what one could do when one sings *a little,* recites *a little,* (there's for the stage – my last hope!!!); one is *good enough* in History and Literature, and has a little taste for composition in general.!

Olive has just been looking at an English paper, and there she has found an awfully clever guess.

If you saw an egg upon a music stool, what great poem would it remind you of?

The Lay of the Last Minstrel!!!

This has been a busy day for the post today, as four of us have received something — I, two books! Mad was on the point of giving them to me when she suddenly remembered that I had my birthday soon, so she took herself off double quick. There was a lovely fat red one, and one with a pale green cover. I dident get the chance to see the writing but I suppose it is from you. I am aching already to get at them. The big red one excites my curiosity muchly.

Then M. and O. received £5 each this morning. Then a German received a huge box with a skirt and blouse, but stuffed with sweets and cakes. We will have enough for nearly a fortnight of her bounties. Then, just as she was unwrapping it, another packet came, for an Austrian: two big tins of biscuits, etc. It never rains but it pours, and nobody's birthday, neither!

On Wednesday, instead of the North Pole, we went visiting the Alps, this time. We saw some beautiful pictures of snow and ice, mountain tops and valleys, glaciers, lakes, also the mountain cottages and inhabitants. It was very interesting.

I had on my summer things today.

Marjorie goes next Sunday. Poor us!

It seems to me that my very existence is being forgotten at home, as, barring yours, I havent had another letter for nearly two months, but I suppose the holidays are nearer here now, are they not, so perhaps someone will find a minute to spare!

We have been quite mild and uninteresting this week, the only thing I have done in the stirring line being an alarm clock under a girl's bed, being set for between ten and eleven. Here, we think ten o'clock very late, as at nine, often, Mad starts telling us to go to bed, and at ten we mustent talk any more. I imagine, at nine, here, and at eight, with you, we go to bed.

Here I will mention a fact which will probably rejoice you. It is: I have been writing to Mona for two Sundays now, but will have to wait till next to finish it.

One of the girls has two friends in for the day, so we had a big dinner, and will have cakes for tea and for after supper, when we have our weekly cup of tea in the dining room — great event!

Mad was really sporting today, she provided for tea today a huge big cake with pink icing and preserved fruits and marzipan. There was enough for seventeen people all to have two big slices, and to have two pieces left!!

Bye the way, when you send me Kate's letters, do you wish me to send them back again?

Please, do you find my letters very uninteresting these last times, as I really havent a scrap of news, hardly, and have to beat my brains horribly to get anything that could possibly interest you at all. We have been so very quiet these times, only going out once a week to have tea in town or in the country.

We had one very nice walk the other day, along the lake side, and had tea in a little village hotel, and — strawberry jam, if you please, first time for seven or eight months. After tea, another girl and I hurried out to see what was what. We discovered a see–saw, much to our delight, and soon set to work. Afterwards, the others came out, and, on seeing us thus amused, they came too. We se–sawed six and eight at a time, in fine style.

Really, the kids here are, for the most part, a spiritless lot, and afraid of everything, but this German and I have taken a solemn vow and covenant to try and stir things up a bit. She too had found the others spiritless, so we have joined forces, hence the apple pie beds, midnight excurtions (sic), etc. Even Olive proves herself very unsatisfactory, where real fun is concerned.

Now please don't start and worry and think I shall get expelled or not do my lessons, as we are like angels during the working periods — sometimes!!

With much love,
your loving
Flora

Délices Voltaire
22.3.14

My dear Mother,

Thank you very very much indeed for the P.O. I shall certainly get Racine with it, but, really and truly, I never thought what an awful skint I was giving you when I asked if I could buy the set.

I never dreamt that I would get so many things. In fact, I was hoping against hope that I would, at least, get a letter upon my plate, and, instead of that, when I came in, *there* was my plate surrounded with parcels and letters. D.'s book – spiffing; Daddie's book – absolutely – !; two books from Phyllis!! Letters: yours, Phil's and two old girls, and a card from the niece. Later I got 5/– from Aunty Harry and 4/– from Corsock. Also I got the usual three books from the girls, in the 1/– Nelson binding – cream and gold, awfully pretty. I got one awfully clever and funny story which we have just been reading at night, which I asked for, thinking of your possible entertainment afterwards. Also, '5th March', a historical book of the time of Henry 4, or something, of France; and then, what I have sighed for for many a long day – Napoleon Intimately, (the translation of the tital (sic) sounds rather queer!!),so I dident do badly, did I?

At night we played games in my honour – 'Simon says thumbs up'!! and 'Proverbs'!

They mercifully, put off the musical evening which was to have been that night, but it came in full force the next. Oh! those evenings, how I hate them! Everybody has to play or sing. I don't sing but I do play, and its agony, for me *and* for those who hear me! I can 'stew' a piece all my practising hour but when I come to play it before Mad — !! I make mistakes I never dreamt of making before, and generally disgrace myself. The last time but one, Mad said, when I had finished — "Humph! — sniff! Not much of a big thing, that! and much too short." I told her that it, to me, was quite long enough.

I, being the very worst player, always head the list, and make a glorious beginning. I often feel that, if I dident have to begin, I might feel less nervous.

Sometimes we have trios. Marjorie plays the violin, Olive sings and another girl plays; or M. plays the violin, another the piano, and another the mandoline. Its very nice.

The last time there came a sad accident. M. was playing with just the piano. Well, we all settled ourselves down to listen, and the artistes tuned up and prepared, at a given signal they both crashed out their opening cords (sic), and — !!! Oh!! Oh!! Oh!! Oh!!!! There came the most awful row imaginable — the piano had struck a cord one tone too low. We all shrieked!!

Marjorie and the mandoline player go today, at half past nine.

I do not envy you your spring cleaning, and I thank my stars to be out of it.

How ripping my room will be now downstairs, and the book case is a very good idea indeed. Thanks awfully much indeed. You don't need to bother about the writing stand, as I wont use the wash stand, so I can employ that as my 'secretaire.

Is it true that Ulster has revolted at last? Olive said she thought it was something like that, but wasent sure.

I really can make much more noise now than when I began

my lessons. At least, this last fortnight it has been quite different – my voice.

With much love
and thanks again.
yours lovingly.
Flora.

Corsier

Mimi
Pupil teacher
M. Marie
Alma
Linda
Louse
Marjorie
Hedi
M. Albertine
Paula
Lily
Flora
Lada
Olive
Olga

Délices Voltaire
22.3.14

My dear Daddy,

Thank you very much indeed for the lovely little, or rather, big photo album. You couldent have guessed better, if you had tried for a week, what I wanted, as for months I have been wanting one, and been wanting to buy one. The photos inside are ripping, but what a dreadful lot of time you must have wasted in putting them in. The photos were much admired, and so was the album, by everyone.

On my birthday morning I got up at half past six and started practising at seven, so as to have finished before breakfast. At breakfast I had to wait till everyone was in, and then, as I came in, everyone started to sing a birthday song. Then I had to go all round the table and kiss everyone — that was the rottenest bit. Then we had breakfast — I spent most of my time peeping into my packets.

Theres another thing ended — Marjorie and the other are gone, we have just accompanied them to the gate and seen the last of them disappearing round the corner. The other girl was in the room adjoining ours, and was just beginning to get very nice. She came after me, and was much older and cleverer than the rest of us. I cant realise that they've gone and shall probably never be seen again.

Everyone has disappeared now, but presently there will be a string of red nosed and bleary eyed demoiselles going down to church. I don't cry and wont. I often wonder what sort of inside I've got, as I never feel anything like that. Even

M. Albertine had tears in her eyes when the cab went off.

Marjorie will be home about Easter. She will visit Prague where she will stay a week with her compagnon, then she will stay another week or so with another old girl, then she stays a Saturday and a Sunday with another, at Berlin, etc., etc. till she reaches Hambourgh where she will get a boat right to Newcastle.

At dinner, for my birthday, Mad provided a lovely huge sort of meringue, all cream and biscuit, with my name upon it. We all get this upon out birthdays.

I hope Mr Smeaton is better now and that his gloomy forebodings are not to be realised.

We here are not in a very charitable frame of mind, as a new girl is coming tomorrow, and another the next day, and we have been together so long that we feel that the new girls will spoil everything. Mad has, however, lectured us long and loudly upon the subject of being nice to new girls, so we will have to be. One is twenty, and is only coming for three months — to repose! a little. This one, we object to — strongly!

We were on the lake in a big boat last Tuesday — already! It was ripping and just like summer with the sun and blue sky. Yesterday, the first day of spring, it snowed!!

Bye the way, on the way home, you *will* spend a day in Paris and London, wont you, please, just to visit the big things a little, as I have been reading tuns (sic) about Paris, and am aching to see it. Also the Tower and Westminster, I have longed for years to see.

It is quite settled that we are to go to 'Chebre', and there we will visit all the country side.

I don't envy myself all the letters I'll have to write today — nor the stamps, but perhaps you wont object if I enclose as many as possible.

With much love
and heaps of thanks,
yours lovingly,
Flora.

Délices Voltaire
29.3.14

My dear Daddy and Mother,

Its altogether spring today, sunshine, primroses and violets. We have just come in from playing in the garden – Diabolo and 'Charlie cross the river' sort of affairs!

Please don't think that I am moaning about the numbers of books that I have received, <u>not in the least</u>!! You made my mouth water dreadfully with your accounts of books and book cases, which await me. I much prefer linoleum to carpet on my floor!

Things are very behind here too. The first time for ten years that the blossoms havent been out at this time. It snows and freezes, and shines and rains, and blows, all by turns.

I have been worrying too, a lot, as to how I am to return with all my things. Lots of the girls get boxes sent to them from home. Couldent you do that too, when the time comes?

Please do forward me a few stamps, as we have a thing here for weighing the letters, and so know when they are too heavy. Also, for two heavy letters in separate envelopes you pay 5 centimes, and the two in one envelope 4c.

We have just been having the situation of Ireland explained to us in our History lesson, and I am very interested all about it. What is going to happen?

I gave all the class the creeps with telling them your servant girl story. How could she carry such smelly things as dead bodies about with her for six years, and what kind of bodies were they, and have they found out a little about her.

Weve been having revolutions here too. Mad has been favouring the new girl, so we objected.

On Monday, one new girl came; she isent anything special, except that she had a different dress or blouse on every day since she came. Mad doesent like her, as she isent pretty or very clever.

On Thursday, came the new girl, with her sister, from Prague. She — aristocratic isent the word for it; absolute nuts — both: powder, elbows on the table, curling pins — or rather, the effects of them, absolutely latest in dresses, etc. — no petticoat, and slit at the bottom, and broad sash at waist — twenty–two, and she is here because of a *love* affair…

Well, Mad neatly flattened herself upon the floor before them, and cringed, and he–he'ed, and haw–haw'ed, and a' that, until we turned sick

She came with a box twice as big as mine — for two months!

The first two days she went out a lot with her sister, all the time, and we never saw her, (but we imagined a lot, and said a lot too.) Well, we told Mad that this girl was going to spoil all, etc., and got badly lectured in consequence. However, the new girl made a good beginning by sending her sister home two days sooner, and by buying us a big box of chocolates. At night she gave us oranges, and a rapid résumé of her romantic life — ahem! It goes something like this — engaged to be married in a month, to a gentleman; suddenly becomes desparately (sic) in love with another, and breaks off the engagement; new man goes off for a year to the mines in Asia, so she comes here to while away the time till he comes back.

She is very pretty, in a dollish way, with her pretty hair and artificial curls. She is also very, very gay, and the biggest baby of us all, for games, etc. Her special charm is her imperfect French, she speaks so like a little baby learning to talk.

She isent a bit musical, and says it frankly. Last night, in the middle of the most thrilling bar of the orchestra, she turned to her neighbour and said, "Oh, how funny, what a lot of gentlemen have bald heads, here!" The other girl was most horribly disgusted.

We were at the last orchestral concert, last night, and, as it was held in another hall, we all went. There was a choir too, as they performed the musical affair that had been composed for the centenaire of Jean Jacques Rousseau, in 1912, but which had had to be put off as it had rained, as it always does when Genève has a fête of any kind. The toilettes and the coiffures were, to say the least of it, extraordinary. The latest colour is a brilliant cerise red, which goes hideously well with all other colours, and makes you shriek when you see it beside a sea–green, or yellow, etc.!

Bye the bye, I have a large and enormous crow to pick with Mad. It came about thus wise: Maurice – the eldest nephew, came to supper with his shy brother, Olivier. Well, Mad adores M. above all other earthly idols, so he had to sit beside her and listen to her words of wisdom (this part is an aside, my bit comes later). Well, soon Mad got confidential, and, to our horror, commenced thus wise: "You know, Maurice, its terrible with these girls, as I have to go running round the rooms at night to see that all the shutters are closed. If I don't, I discover a window with the shutters wide open, and with the light on, and the girls undressing, and carrying on, to the probable edification of the neighbours." Then she asked if it wasent he who had been looking into the rooms (not ours) by the means of opera glasses. The opera glasses he denied but confessed to have succumbed to the temptation, sometimes, of an unshuttered window.

This conversation, she enlarged and beautified, till we rocked, and the two poor nephews got like boiled lobsters. The shy one nearly fell under the table with embarrassment. The other giggled and tilted back his chair to hide his blushes, till we expected the crash to come any minute.

After supper, we heard a discordant series of screeches (Mad laughing), and then Mad came downstairs giggling, and saying, "Oh! oh! I kissed Olivier in my room, and then found that the shutters were open, and one can see everything that goes on, when the light is on." She is in for it, now, as, if she has been seen, her reputation is made, as she says. After this, we refused to give a concert for the edification of Maurice, so Mad got waxy and grumped, and told me that I was to do a whole huge lump of my embroidery before I went to bed. Most unfortunately, I found I had no sizsers (sic), and whilst looking round to see who *had*, a voice of thunder bellowed, "Flora, put away you things and go – to – bed!!! – I went – on to my bed but not into it.

We are now hoping that Maurice wont come again for a long time, as the excitement isent good for Mad's nerves, as she has been in an atrocious temper ever since, and that night, after he had left, she gave those left downstairs the most awful row, but wherefore, etc., we do not know.

You don't seem to have understood very well as to those extras. Its like this. In December there were a lot of things that I hadent payed for, and these were put in the bill. Well, you don't seem to have understood the small writing and the French, and it stood unpayed, so she put them in this bill.

Two pupil teachers and one new girl are coming in the beginning of April, and then, about the 14th, we start for near Berne.

We have been having the history of Venice in the last Art lesson; he does make us ache to see what he tells us.

The Easter holidays will soon be there, will they not. How quickly the time does pass.

With much love to you all,
yours lovingly,
Flora.

Délices Voltaire
5. 4. 14

My dear Mother and Daddy,

We have got the real spring weather, at last, and so hot sometimes.

How did the bazaar get off? Who stood in my – glorious – shoes!!

Thank you very much for the mags. I hope this letter shocked you less.

How is Mr Smeaton getting on? Better, I hope.

Had the servant girl her atrocious and spicey luggage when she was at the Rainys, was it there that she left it? What kind of bodies were they, and who?

Its just my luck; now, another new girl has come, and don't they just go and put Lily (Hungary) into another room, and jam the new girl into – my bed!! and I had to take Lily's. I always get the new girls, and shes German, and I had to – ahem – speak German to her! You can imagine the result, without my aide!! However she is really very nice, but quiet, great change after what I have been accustomed to, in the same room with Lily.

Do you know this house is absolutely overrun with mice! You hear them in the wainscotings, you see them in the garden, and now they come upstairs. On Monday, in the middle of the History class, a mouse ran down the shutter cord and into a hole. Soon, it came out and ran up again, but stuck at the top. After that it ran up and down for a long time, looking for an escape. Then it jumped onto the curtain and ran down the window ledge, till it tumbled, flop, onto the floor. There it scuttled about for a time, and finally, plucking up all its courage, it made a dash round the room, and disappeared for ever. Naturally, the words of wisdom of M., doubtless very worthy, were absolutely lost.

One of the girls, Mariele a German, was mortally terrified that it would run up her legs. The same day, the maids had a rare old hunt after a little mouse in the hall, which they finally caught. The same day, the – reposing – new girl went out with Mad and came in with two little mice with waggly tails. These we proposed to put in Mariele's bed. One, we placed in her bed, and the other, we attached to a long string and put it under her bed, another girl having the end of the string in her bed. The mouse in the bed was a – shrieking – success. Mad, who was in the plot, came running in to have her share of the laugh too. The mouse and the string dident succeed, as the mouse stuck and wouldent come, and the thread broke. The conspired against, rendered sharp by bitter experience, saw the efforts of the other girl to pull something, and knew at once what it was, and jeered heartlessly.

Then, last night, on opening out my nightgown, out tumbled a mouse, but, happily, a chocolate one! Some girls were frightened, one specially, when, upon pulling back the bed clothes to make sure there that were no brushes, etc. in it, the mouse tumbled, right plump, into her hand. She yelled!!

On Sunday we went for a lovely excurtion (sic). We started with the boat, till we reached a little village where we got off and started walking back. It was hot, but hot, you havent an idea how hot. I had a flannel blouse on, and I roasted. The sun shone in torrents, and the lake was like a glass with a faint heat haze hanging over it.

We walked along a country road by the lake side. Soon, we came to a field, quite open, and there we found violets growing in great clumps, all over the field. Naturally, we soon had our hands full of them, purple, heliotrope and white. I don't need to tell you that I trailed behind and had to run to make up.

Then we came into a wood, and here, on one side of a mud–puddle of a path, was a perfect carpet of lovely white starry flowers, and on the other, but behind a barbed wire fence, a carpet of daffodils. It was so pretty, and then we found primroses and violets and white flowers, all in profusion, at another place.

We stopped at a little country inn near the lake, and had tea outside, surrounded by dogs, cats, hens, cocks and ducks, all asking for something to eat — so romantic, wasent it?

After tea, we went down to the lake side for a bit, and then continued our voyage. Never in my life did I see so many violets and primroses, you could scarcely walk for them in the fields, and it was so hot!

On Wednesday first of April, I got up early, and prepared a little surprise for someone. I got an envelope, and posted an Austrian stamp upon it, and then forged the post marks, most admirably, with some charcoal. Then I took a sheet of paper and dessined (sic) some objects which were intended to be fishes (here, you are an April *fish*). Then, out of the mouth of the biggest fish, I made these words come, "Are you caught or are you not, Mimi." Then Mariele wrote something polite on the back, and, in the middle, we emptied nearly all the ink out of our pens, in making blots. This witty article I addressed to Mimi, the fat girl, who had boasted so loudly, the day before, that she wouldent let herself be caught, and put it in the letter–box. Mad gave the letter out at tea time, but, like a big spoil sport that she was, she said, "Mimi, heres a 1st April for you." Mimi said that she would never have known that it wasent a real letter, if Mad hadent said. So Mad was sporting enough to say that she was very sorry that she had said anything at all, but that she had thought that everyone could see that it wasent a real letter.

Then, at six o'clock, the two Mads being afar, I went downstairs to practise, and, after a little, crept out and took the gong stick, and banged and banged the gong, and then fled, coming back afterwards to ask who had rung and why, etc..

The gong had a good effect; only Olive, rendered misanthrope by the date, said it was only a farce, she having seen I and my accomplice giggling, a little while before. However, Lily got an awful fright, starting up and crying, "What is it, whats the matter, etc.?" The others were more or less startled.

But it was at night that we had the crowning adventure. The two Mads were out for the evening, and wouldent be in till late, so we were all alone, even without a pupil teacher.

Then, suddenly, someone suggested, lets dress up a figure and put it in Mad's bed; the suggestion was hailed with all the enthousiasme (sic) which it deserved. We dashed upstairs and raided Mad's room to see what we could do. We thought that a long handled brush would be a very good thing to dress up, but we thought, after that, perhaps Mad wouldent be very delighted to find a dirty old brush in her bed, however much dressed it was, so we retired to discuss the matter together.

Upon retiring, I caught sight of Mad's bed post, and then, in a flash, an idea came to me. I wanted to dress the bed post, as I had read in a story, but the others said it was best to do nothing in her bed or with it, so I got a nearly clean broom, and tied two sticks to it for arms; Mariele put her big coat upon it, and then I stuck my umbrella down its back, and another put her hat upon it, but it wanted a face, dreadfully. Then I had another brilliant idea. I got a white garden hat, and stuck it in front, under the hat, Olive wrapping her big fur round its neck to hide the rims. Then I drew some beautiful features upon the hat, which, fortunately, turned out to be my own, afterwards. The hat having a very large crown, it made a beautiful face. Then we gloved the hands, and arranged it nicely, and placed it at Mad's door. There the thing stood, arms outstretched and gastly (sic) face, till we became really frightened, ourselves. Then Mariele put her skirt under the coat, and pinned it and draped it, till it looked just like a leg. Then another girl arranged the face–hat in a way which made it much less startling, in the dim light. Then we began to wonder whether Mad mightened get a nasty shock or not. Some wanted to undoe all our work, but we hesitated, and then some scolded and went off. Then we arranged that each one was to come up the stairs, quite alone, and we were to try and judge Mad's feelings, but instead, we asked the cook to come up and give her judgement. She said, at once, that we needent have the slightest fear that Mad would be frightened, and that the lamp would be left lighted, all the time.

The cook is rather a decent sort, and she stayed to talk with us, instead of going down. She told us of the doings of the other bands, and of the tricks that she and the other house maids had played upon them. Once, they took some of the theatrical clothes, and cook dressed up as a man, and went into the room where Marjorie and some others were, and they thought it was a real man, and shrieked and yelled, till the others in the other rooms came running out to see what was wrong. This was two years ago.

Well, next morning Mad Albertine said that she really did get a start, at first, but was very amused later. She told Mad Marie that she would find something at her door, so M. was prepared. She said that, when she saw it standing there, with its arms outstretched towards her, she took it up into her arms, and took it into the schoolroom, and bundled it onto the desk of Mariele, knowing that it was pretty certain to have been the tender thought of Mariele, to give her a 1st of April.

We are getting our holidays on Thurs. next, but will only get a few days, as we will be going to Chexbres later, about the 21st.

Did you find your letter, all right, last Wednesday?

All the blossoms are coming out now, just opposite my window there is a cherry tree, and its looking so pretty, all round, with buds and flowers and pale green leaves.

We have been having high times, these last days, what with Mad going out at night. I have gone just to the other extreme, now, and have had my book for nearly two months, and have now read nearly fifty pages. Its true that its not frightfully entertaining!!

With much love,
yours lovingly.
Flora.

We are all suddenly very interested in palmistry. Could you possibly send me that little red book that is on the nursery book shelf. If it's a bother, don't, as it doesent matter. As Mad mightent let me have it, could you send it in an envelope. Another girl is writing home for hers, too. Thanks awfully, if you do.

Marielle

Délices Voltaire
10.4.14

My dear Mother and Daddy,

I was dreadfully sorry to hear of poor Mr Smeaton's death. Poor Daddy, it must have been an awful blow for him, he will miss him at every turn. What will Mrs Smeaton do now, all alone in that big house.

We are doing Sunday today, in our good clothes, and writing letters. We went for a long walk this morning, and got roasted through and through.

Quite an interesting little event happened upon the way. One of the girls has a male cousin here, and who should we meet but this object. He promptly followed us all the way. The girl was in an awful state, not knowing what to do, whether to speak or ignore him. Upon returning, he stood still in the middle of the road, so we told her that she'd have to speak, now, so she went — to the horror of those behind, who dident know that it was a cousin. Well, the pupil teacher and the 'reposing' girl were furious, also Hungary — why, we don't daigne (sic) to enquire. It was the fifteen year old Hungary who let off a lot of steam upon the disgracefulness of Mariele's conduct, and it was she who told the pupil teacher that M. was to stop talking to her cousin, at once. When Mariele came back, the camp was absolutely divided into two parts. We said that Mariele was perfectly right to go and speak, the others said that it was disgraceful, etc! etc!... Well, we knew by the pupil teacher's black looks that she would tell a fine tale to Mad, so we urged and urged Mariele to say, the minute she saw Mad, that she had met and spoken with her cousin. This she did, so well, that Mad had hardly finished welcoming us, before she burst it out. Mad grinned, and looked sceptical about the cousin bit, at first, but said nothing. Mariele wasent a bit too quick, however, as the pupil teacher came running up, and was opening her mouth to speak and looked awfully waxy, when Mariele spoke first. After that, upon the way home, our company was separated by a huge gap from the other. Now, things are a little drawn, the over vertuous (sic) ones holding a bit aloof.

Marjorie is in Bohemia, just now, and writes us P.C.s, often.

I am wearing the beautiful collar that an old girl sent me. Today, Mad said, "Is that the collar that Hedi sent you, no?" I said, yes. Then she said, "Did she do it expressly for that dress?" I replied that she had never even seen the dress. Mad said, "Really, how extraordinary, if you had tried for a week you couldent have found anything to go better," the border is a green exactly the same shade as my dress. The design is big flowers bordered in yellow, purple, gold, blue and red, and silver, a lovely thing, broidered upon heavy grey–brown canvas.

We had some ripping fun on Tuesday night. There was to be a play by amateurs in a hall down town, and we were all going. As it was very dirty and muddy that night, we had to go in cabs — three. Our cab was the last of the line, and the cabby, coming up at the last moment, obviously hadent been told where we were going.

All went well till we were right in the heart of the town. Then the cabby stopt (sic) and came and asked us if we divent know where we were to go, as he dident, and had missed the other cabs. We replied that we hadent the faintest idea as to where we aught (sic) to go. This seemed to disquiet the man, a little, however, he suggested some different halls, and we selected one, as likely, and set off…

On and on we went, hugely delighted, I can tell you. Well, we went right away into the other end of the town, until, at last, we became sure that this couldent be the right way, and I put my head out and yelled at the man to stop. He stopped and came down, and we confabed together, each of the <u>five</u> of us yelling another direction. However, we thought it might be the old theatre, so we turned back, and retraced our – wheel marks – and then went off in another direction… Once again, we were baffled, and then we began to be a bit worried about Mad, who would be in the dark as to our fate – otherwise, we shrieked with joy. Then the cabby enquired in a book stall as to where this play was to be, but the people dident know. Upon remounting his box, a man asked him if he was looking for some place. Upon being told our sad history, he suggested a likely place, and off we set, once more, amidst general grins, inside and out.

Once again, we were on a false trail, and, this time, we thought we would telephone home, and ask where the place was. We were on the point of dismounting, when the man suggested yet another place. After much – er – <u>squabbling</u>, we decided to put off the telephoning until we had tried this place, and set off <u>again</u>. Upon the way back, we met a cab, and the cabby, recognising us, asked, "Is it the Casino of St Pierre, that you are looking for?" and you should have heard the yell I gave: I just screamed, "Yes! yes! That's it," I, having heard the place mentioned by Mad, but had not payed much attention, at the time. The place that we were on the way to was as nearly right as the others had been. Off we set again, this time, right. Our only trouble was that Mad might have returned home, but we found her standing at the door, with such a patient, long suffering look upon her face. She greeted us with, "Well, you've come, at last, have you?!!" She scolded neither us nor the cabby, but told us that she'd never let us go anywhere again, without telling us the exact destination! We arrived nearly three quarters of an hour late, but only missed a chorus or two — that is to say that we did not miss them, if they resembled those that we did have the misfortune to hear!! The play was quite well played, except that the heroine was the ugliest, affectedest, silliest little idiot as I ever had the misfortune to see upon the stage. She spoiled the play for me, at any rate, and others said the same thing. In the book, she is tall, charming and fascinating, but that — !!!

11.4.14

We went for a ripping walk, last night, after supper. We went away out into the country, and along by the side of the Rhône. The mountains stood out black against the clear midnight sky — ahem!! We also went along the road by the cemetery wall! Just as we passed the cemetery, the girl I was with, who was telling me the story of one of Schiller's plays, came to the bit where the villain poisened (sic) himself, etc., etc.. I did think, then, that there are more agreeable places to pass in the dark!

By the way, I saw a real live pea cock, for the first time, last week. When we saw it, it had its back turned, and, although we called and called, it refused to turn. At last, someone clapped her hands. This seemed to annoy the bird, so we all started clapping, and were rewarded by the bird's wheeling gracefully round, and displaying its full glory to our admiring eyes. It really is wonderful how such a fragile little body can support such a huge tail.

When we had sufficiently admired his tail, we wanted to see him shut it, and told him so, but all he did was to make it shiver and quiver with a noise like the wind in the trees. Then M Albertine said, "Shut up your tail, old boy," and, at once, he let it curve gracefully down, and then swept it together and marched off — so did we, then.

12.4.14

These Easter festivities are impairing my memory, it seems. I have just been hunting high and low in my desk for my specs, making awful havoc amongst my books. In despair, I get up, and, don't I, find that I've been sitting upon them!!

We had a ripping walk yesterday. We stayed in the tram till we were right out in the country, and then we walked. We went through funny little villages along by the Rhône side, we being up on a cliff. We scramb led along a little path in a back wood, then we waded through mud and pools along a cart track, then we went through corn fields until we gained the road again. The woods were full of violets and primroses.

By this time we were getting a little tired, so Mad's brother–in–law, who was with us, promised us that we would only have a good half hour's walk before us, now. Thus encouraged, we marched on, jackets and — umbrellas!! fastened round our waists, and still roasting, till we reached a little village. Here we were told, half an hour later, that we had another half hour's journey before us, yet. We made some polite remarks, but staggered bravely onwards. Later on, we were told that we had either five minute's walk or half an hour's, by the brother–in–law. It turned out to be the latter... At last, we arrived, absolutely squashed, but ate a very good tea, all the same. Maurice, the eldest of M.'s nephews, cycled up and joined us, on the way. I discovered, there and then, that, added to his other beauties — or blemishes, he has delightfully bandy legs!!

Today, on coming into the dining room, each girl found a little packet sitting in a boat–shaped serviette. These proved to be sweet (big) little chocolate rabbits with nice blue bows round their necks. In the middle of the table were two plates of toffee and cream Easter eggs. These were from the Mads. This afternoon, the nine nephews and nieces come, and we are to have an Easter egg hunt, in the garden. There is a huge barrel in the dining room cupboard which contains the Easter eggs — chic, isent it?

I had better give you our address for Chexbres; we will be there for a week, from 21st to 28th or 9th, Hôtel Cécil, Chexbres, Suisse.

I have returned to my books again, and am now reading, at every available moment. I even got one of the girls to waken me up at six this morning, and then I went out into the garden to read.

Its awful, there are tons and tons of new girls coming later, and they are horrible animals, to begin with!

With much love,
yours lovingly,
Flora.

Marielle

Marielle with mother and brother

Délices Voltaire
19.4.14

My dear Daddy and Mother,

Here, we are in full muddle and confusion. We have almost finished our packing, only a few little things that we have need of, again. All the carpets are up, and the passages crammed with boxes and litter. The drawers and cupboards and walls are mournfully barren. This is our last day at dear old Délices. We leave just when the trees are white with blossom, and all the trees are coming into leaf, and everything is so pretty. Really, we have become very attached to this house.

We start tomorrow for 'Hôtel Cécil, Chexbres'. I shall probably drop you a P.C. when I am at Berne.

One of the girls got a huge box of great big chocolates, all liquour (sic), for her birthday. It was passed at three different times, and each time fourteen people got three, more than an inch big; the last time we got four even. Doesent your mouth water?

Oh, I must tell you about my — er — packing up!!!... I began all right, putting all my books at the bottom, then my shoes and various boxes, then I put in my best dress, then I thought that it would be better to put that as near the top as possible, so I took it out — (here Mother heaves a gasp of relief) — and put in some dresses. Then I discovered that I had forgotten about my brown costume. I considered a lot as to whether I should unpack altogether again, and put it at the bottom, or just put it on top. Vertue (sic) triumphed, however, and out came the dresses; I took the end of the layer, and rolled them, and placed the bundle on the floor. Olive, mercifully, folded the jacket for me, and then I put the bundle of dresses into the box, and unrolled it, and flattened it into order. Then, I discovered my tennis racket… This, I rumpled all my dresses for, in lifting them up, to put it beneath. This manoeuvre created a bit of a havoc, but I managed to smooth things down a bit again. Then, to my horror, I found that I had forgotten all about my cloak and oilskins!! Bye this time, however, I had had more than sufficient, and I wrapped my oilskins up in tissue paper, and put them on top of everything, another kind soul taking my cloak into her too big box. Then, I continued, happily, with my blouses, and put my woolen jacket on top of everything. All the little holes and spaces left by the boxes, etc., I filled up with tennis balls, gloves, bottles, sport articles and slippers. Then I rammed a few boxes and little things, forgotten, down the sides of the box, and then turned my attention to the second storey. Here, I put a few blouses and then, my best dress, then my fur, which I stuffed inside my best hat to make room, then my hats, and one or two little papers or boxes, which I had forgotten. The dress, I had left inside the bag, and simply folded in two. Then, I shut the box, and went off and read.

Bye and bye, Mad came along and said, "Flora, let me see how you have packed." Cheerfully, I opened the box, and *then*, the storm broke forth, in all its glory. 1st: "Is that your best dress, there, with all those hats and boxes upon it?" – point and scene number one!!! 2nd: (roar!), "Lift up that partition, and let me see beneath." I thought of the oilskins, and shuddered!! She poked about, and found a blouse which wasent quite dirty yet, and which I had rolled up into a bundle, and stuffed into a corner!!!! – Then!! she!! found!! the!! oilskins!! – I'd rather dra' a curt'in over the sceen whit followed!!! I unpacked again, and put the things at the foot, folded the blouse, and took my dress out of the bag, and folded it, with Olive's help, and then covered it over with the bag — but I did forget to put the paper underneath it.

My box is full, and I havent yet told you all the things that weren't in it. 1st: One big drawer crammed with *all* my underclothing, one bed jacket, one shawl, two dresses, *and* a big bath towel, one golf cloak, and one big coat, dressing gown, and baggage for Chexbres, and the things at the wash, also, all my hats!! Its my books and boxes which take up so much space.

We have discovered a new species of spiritualisme (sic), only the spirit cant always speak French, sometimes he is Russian, sometimes Italian, sometimes Roumanian, Hungarian, etc.. You have a piece of paper with all the letters of the alphabet, in a ring round it. Then you make a little circle in the middle, and take a shilling, and place it in the centre. Then you put your forefinger (two people) upon the shilling, and then the shilling moves from letter to letter, in answer to your questions.

D.'s letter was extremely entertaining. Couldent you force or cajole her into writing again?

We are getting out into the garden, now, after supper, and its ripping fun. The other night, I and another girl went about miauwing and making noises like the wind, and generally startling everyone. Even Mad, we serenaded.

Last Sunday (Easter), all the family came for tea, and we had an Easter egg hunt, and then we had games. These were spiffing. I had a face like a boiled lobster, when we had finished, I ran so much. The next time Olive and I are to introduce rounders. Its really awfully jolly when they all come, as they are all so gay and jolly.

We are having such fun just now. At one of our parties, one of the girls was made to kiss, at forfeits, Teddy, one of the nephews. Since then, she has had no peace. Now, she is going, and she has to say goodbye, every time he comes — he is fourteen, and she seventeen, and a bit soft, but good 'for the piece'.

Much love,
Flora.

Hôtel Cécil
Chexbres
21.4.14

My dear Mother and Daddy,

Just imagine, I, your lazy daughter, am sitting at the open window, writing, and its not yet seven o'clock. Also, I have been up for more than an hour already.

We arrived here yesterday, in time for dinner. The house, from top to bottom, is sweet — so aesthetic; the entrance hall is brown, everything, with basket chairs, etc., just like a real hotel; the staircases are white, so is all the woodwork, and the carpet goes so well with everything. Our bedroom is blue–grey; the paper blue–grey canvas, no carpet, blue–grey table cloth, and a pair of the sweetest and daintiest little blue and gold beds that you ever saw. The bed hangings are pale blue, too, even the guard over the wall before the wash stand, is blue, too. The other rooms are just like ours, only in different colours, some pink, some white, etc., but all so pretty. The middle rooms have got a lovely balcony before their windows. We havent, but have such a broad window that you don't miss it. The view, however, is the thing, its mag–nif–i–cent!! really.

First, are the little white washed, green shuttered and red roofed houses, running down to the lake side. The lake, quite near, is so beautiful, so calm, and blue, and, on the opposite side of the lake, rise the mountains, absolutely out of the water, sheer, in some places. You don't think, at all, how high up they are, as they are so near, until you look at the little white specks which cluster round their feet, which are good sized villages.

Here and there, up the sides, you see little white specs, and little bigger ones which are huge pine trees. Further up, the vegetation stops, and further on, the snow begins. This morning it was wonderful to see the snow glistening pale rose, under the rising sun. (Its given out, sorry! [ink]). Last night, we left the windows wide open, and could see, from our beds, the reflections of the various lights upon the water, and the lights up on the mountain sides.

24.4.14 I had to stop writing on Tuesday morning, as one of the girls came and proposed that we should go for a little walk. We went, and enjoyed ourselves immensely, and all the others were furious. After breakfast, we walked to a high hill where we could get a lovely view of the lake, and, there, we read or wrote — I dident do neither!! The afternoon we spent at home, and after tea we went down to the village. After supper we promenaded again.

Wednesday morning, at half past five my alarum waked me, and I hopped out of bed and dressed. The same girl met me, and off we went again, this time for a much longer walk. We returned at eight. Since then, this girl and I have been forbidden to speak or go near each other.

3.15. Really, I came upstairs full of good intentions for writing, but fate was against me, and, instead, I made a cross of cuckoo flowers, with Hungary, and have only just finished.

Hungary is just having her bath, so I put a holdall in her bed and a pair of shoes at the foot, and beat up the big feather quilt, and then placed my cross at the foot, and Hungary's wreath at the head, and I flatter myself upon the effect. The quilt makes a very good body, and the holdall has a knob which makes a very good nose, also, the flowers are purple...

On Wednesday, we visited several little villages. We are having magnificent weather — so hot.

Yesterday, we were wakened up at half past six, and got the half past eight train to Berne. We arrived at ten, and went and ordered the dinner, then we went visiting. First, we visited the tower clock, which I sent you. It was very interesting, also, to see all the shops under sort of arcades, not that one could stand and look in at the windows, no matter what weather it was. Then we went to see the bears. On the way, we got a magnificent view of the city and the river, etc.. It was so pretty to see the river and the houses between the trees, and the mountains in the distance. The bears were fed with carrots, but the animals were too lazy and too little hungry to be interesting, but it was very funny when they sat up and caught the things in their mouths. After that we went to see the cathedral; this was really worth seeing: all together Gothic, and the principal entrance was beautifully carved.. Then we dined and reposed for a bit, and then set off to order the tea, and then went to the Lower Council Chambers or sort of Parliament House. This was a huge place, and altogether palatial with statues, paintings and magnificent coloured windows, which the sun made more beautiful than ever. In one hall, there were some beautiful symbolic paintings upon the roof: little cherubs carrying loaves of bread, anvils, etc., and beautiful girls representing corn, wine, etc.. in the middle, there was a specially interesting picture, that of a woman sitting upon a wall before a battle field with a tiny baby upon her knee, and a little boy of about three with tangled golden curls and large blue eyes, full of terror, as he regarded his father and brother lying, the boy dead, and, ghastly, the father dying but holding up, with his last drop of strength, the flag of liberty. The thing fascinated us, and three of us returned to have another peep at it. Suddenly we heard the door bang, and found ourselves locked in. We rushed to the door, and knocked and rattled but nobody heard us. (Even in this hour of distress, I remembered to remove my gloves, for fear of spoiling them when I battered the door.) On and on, we battered till my hands ached, sometimes someone passed by but dident seem to have the sense to relieve us. We were most highly amused at the whole affair. At last, a guttural German voice jabbered something which seemed to have meant that he would go for a key, which he did. We sailed out and met the others coming calmly out of some place or other. They hadent worried, not they! One even said, "Oh, I thought you were locked in, but I dident say anything; I just wanted to see what would happen."!!!

Next, we visited the museum, which was very interesting. We saw old furniture, old means of travelling, old arms, etc.. The building itself was very interesting and queer. Then we had tea. Bye this time, we were nearly dead. I had horribly sore feet.

We took the train to Fribourg, also an interesting town. In the train, I had the rotten luck to sit in someone else's seat, and this someone else returned all too soon, and, (I supposed!! — as it jabbered German), demanded its seat, again! I gaped miserably at it, not knowing what to say. Then, all at once, the inspiration came, and I gasped out, "Er — ah, ich verstehen zi nicht!!" Fortunately, it was intelligible enough to be understood, and the German was instantly replaced by French!

Upon arriving at Fribourg, we walked miles and miles, first visiting the cathedral, also Gothic, and altogether Catholic with its candles and saints and Holy Sepulchre, and a' that. Then we walked about the town crossing bridges over lovely valleys, and visiting the older parts of the town. Fribourg is absolutely Catholic – screamingly so; you bumped into preasts (sic) at every step, and, in the train, we passed, first, a band of preasts and, then, a group of monks, bareheaded and sandled (sic), with heavy brown coats. Outside the town, we were continually coming upon a little nitch (sic) in the wall with a little figure in it, or a wooden cross, or a crucifix. At Berne, everyone speaks German, and the shop signs and all that are in German; also, at the museum, everything was ticketed in German, only the, 'Don't touch,' things being in the two languages. At Berne I saw those Swiss cakes that Annie Dieffe sent us once, and we all bought a little one. Berne is the bear town, and everything is 'beared': their statues, their fountains, their public buildings, their shop windows, their cakes, sweets, toys, jewellery and arms, all bears, bears, bears.. Also, I observed how cheap and pretty the wares were. The Swiss embroidery is simply lovely, and, here, so cheap. I shall try to buy a few little articles, just to show you it. Yesterday, we just reposed, after all our efforts of the previous day.

Here, everybody seems to rise early. Only this morning, just as the clock struck seven, a little mite, about a foot and a half high, rushed out of the house opposite, school bag in hand, and scuttled down the road, as hard as its six inch legs could carry it. In front, I saw another atom, also very pressed for time. There is a small difference: with us the kiddies go to school at half past nine, and never sooner than nine; here, at seven!!!

27.4.14.

Yesterday we went for a long walk in the morning, and, in the afternoon, Mad's oldest nephew came. (Hungary is taking a photo of me, just now!). After tea, we went for another long walk. (Lily, for the last five minutes, has been losing, successively, paper, stamps, temper, head and all, the result being that the table has taken the aspect of, 'After the earthquake' or, 'The hurricane', everything being in a most horrible muddle: gloves, boxes, ink, pens, books, pencils, letters, specs, p.c.s, exercise books, sizzors (sic), waste papers, clothes brushes and human arms!!).

Today it is slightly misty, and the mountains loom up faintly through the haze. Lily and I have rare old disputes about these mountains. Lily hates them, thoroughly, and tells them so; she says that there is nothing so pretty as a landscape absolutely flat, with trees and fields etc. I detest, absolutely, flat country. The journey, in the train in England, and in the middle of France, helped to disgust me, whereas the mountains I find incomparable, and stick up for their right, locally. The plains depress me, and the hills make me skittish.

The wild flowers, here, are so pretty, the fields being just covered: cowslips everywhere, cuckoo flowers, forgetmenots, buttercups, dandylions, daisys, cats eyes and a hundred other little plants that are quite new to me. All over the place too are cherry trees, all in bloom. Yesterday, I gathered a great bunch of marsh marigolds.

Last Tuesday, we went to Vevey, by train, visited the town, which is not up to much, and then took the boat to Montreux. This boat was more full of strangers than it was of Swiss or French.

It was: English to left of you,
English to right of you,
Germans behind you (who)
Volleyed and thundered…

Pointed and prim English accents, and guttural, choked German, with, here and there, a sing songey French accent. It kind of bewildered me to hear the English spoken, after such a long a time. The English, you can tell at once, by their air and their clothes, the children, especially. One family struck me specially, the father, tall, big nosed, and broad; suit British cut; the mother – ordinary; children: two girls and a boy, all young – girls, straw hats and scarfs round, ends hanging down the back, little coats and short dresses; boy, little coat and long trousers. The whole family just shrieked their nationality at you. Then two boys, of from eleven to thirteen, came on, with blue and red school blazers and jerseys, and caps with their badges. Here, you never see school uniforms or badges. Well, whilst I was puzzling the matter out, one of them came along, and, in the most awful cockney nasal voice, said, "Oie don' nouwe." You know the sort.

Once again, our little camp is divided into two parts, and, this time, it is Olive who is the disturber. First, of late, she has been spooning up to Mad, and petting her, and always walking with her, and always agreeing with her, etc., and doing, generally, all the things which are against the rules of the school room. Well, we made remarks upon her conduct, before her, and before Mad. Also, she is madly, insanely in love with the eldest nephew, and she has been unmaidenly enough to show it, in his presence, and to tell it to the girls, and to let Mad know, too. She poses, she dreams, she blushes and is just hateful. Well, now we are giving it to her unmercifully, saying the most awful things, before Mad, to her, etc. Don't pity her, as we know what we are doing, and I cant be bothered to give you all the evidence that we have got against her. All the nice girls, yours truly included, are down upon her, and only the riff raff are upon her side — pardon!!! She has Mad upon her side, that's why we are so merciless, also because she doesent care tuppence what we say, or rather, refuses to believe it — all very silly and stupid, but — naturally — its Olive's fault!!

We return to 'Sécheron' or the 'Château Blanc' on Tuesday, by boat, and there we will find a new pupil teacher awaiting us (English) accompanied by Mr Reavell.

Do you know that I received your letter a whole day sooner, this week. Is Gullen so far from Edinburgh, or is it in the G.P.O. that the delay comes? At Xmas the Reavells and I sent off our presents both at the same time, and the Rs' parcel arrived at Alnwick on the 24th, and mine, the 27th; its disgusting.

Have just returned from playing chess — or trying to, as my part in the game was mainly to get my wretched king out of 'mate', which he spent his time in getting into. One by one, my pieces got sacrificed to the rescue of the king, until the game turned into an undignified chase round the board!! I did not offer to play a second game!! — nor, for that matter, did my oponante (sic)!!

Bye the way, I received a birthday present from Kate, the other day; guess what it was: a sweet little boudoir cape!! Unfortunately, I havent the least idea when, how and where to wear it, this branch being not included in our education, here.

We went to the village church today, and it was such a

funny place. Upon one side, all the women sat, and, upon the other, all the men, and, in the middle, were the places for the strangers, as there is a sanatorium and several hotels here.

I expect that we will begin at once, as soon as ever we return, to play tennis, and I am going to take the game very seriously, and try and learn to play at least well enough not to raise the ire and disgust of those others who have the misfortune to be playing with me!!.

The book, that I am reading now, is all about the French Revolution, and gives you heaps of little tips that the history books dont. It gives you the life of a family during this time, and gives real illustrations of how the reforms, etc., affected the common people.

The extremely large town of Chexbres is taking on an air quite busy just now, as there seems to have been a tripper train in today, as people are pouring down from the station.

Really, I havent any more news now, so,
with much love,
yours lovingly,
Flora.

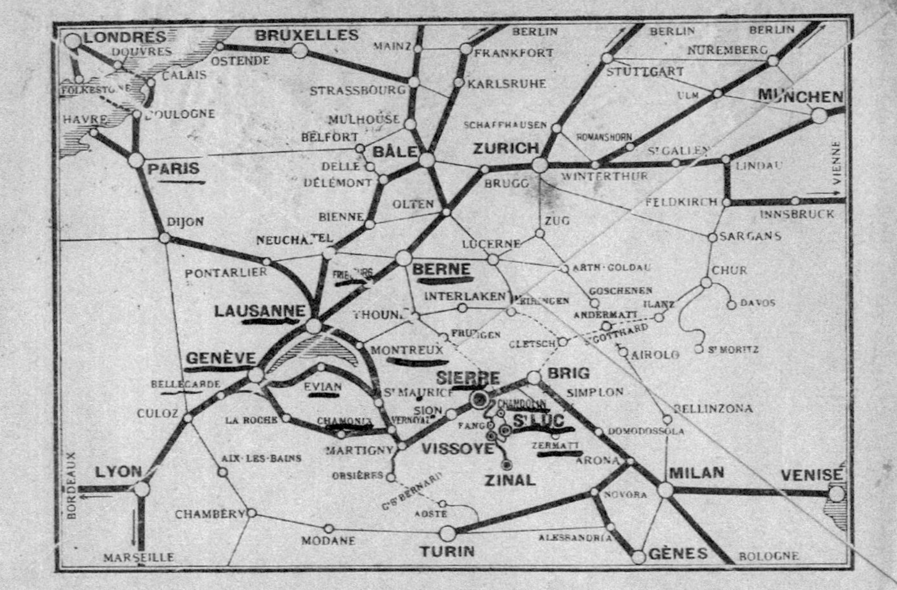
LONDRES
DOUVRES
CALAIS
FOLKESTONE
BOULOGNE
HAVRE
PARIS
DIJON
BRUXELLES
OSTENDE
MAINZ
BERLIN
FRANKFORT
KARLSRUHE
STRASSBOURG
MULHOUSE
BELFORT
DELLE
DÉLÉMONT
BÂLE
BIENNE
OLTEN
NEUCHATEL
PONTARLIER
LAUSANNE
GENÈVE
BELLEGARDE
CULOZ
LYON
BORDEAUX
MARSEILLE
CHAMBÉRY
AIX-LES-BAINS
MODANE
LA ROCHE
EVIAN
CHAMONIX
MARTIGNY
ORSIÈRES
MONTREUX
ST MAURICE
SION
SIERRE
VISSOYE
ZINAL
ST LUC
CHANDOLIN
FANG
ZERMATT
BRIG
SIMPLON
DOMODOSSOLA
ARONA
NOVORA
MILAN
VENISE
TURIN
AOSTE
ALESSANDRIA
GÈNES
BOLOGNE
BELLINZONA
AIROLO
ST GOTTHARD
GLETSCH
FRUTIGEN
THOUNE
INTERLAKEN
BERNE
LUCERNE
ZUG
ARTH-GOLDAU
GOSCHENEN
ANDERMATT
ILANZ
CHUR
DAVOS
ST MORITZ
SARGANS
FELDKIRCH
INNSBRUCK
VIENNE
LINDAU
ST GALLEN
ROMANSHORN
WINTERTHUR
ZURICH
BRUGG
SCHAFFHAUSEN
STUTTGART
ULM
NUREMBERG
MÜNCHEN

Château Blanc, Sécheron.
3.5.14

My dear Daddy and Mother,

Here we are, settled down in our new domaine, and thoroughly enchanted with it. The garden is huge, and crammed with trees; its like being in a forest, some parts. The house smells so nicely of fresh paint, and the wallpapers are really very pretty.

My room is green (pale) with spots. I have a cupboard and two huge shelves, and half of a little cupboard to put my things in. I am, with another new girl, now in my room!! — third, and fifth, altogether. This time it is a Swiss, and she speaks French fluently; she will be a great help to us with her expressions, etc..

Your last letter just caught me as I was starting off for the train, last Tuesday. I was out the house, even.

My dear Mother, I did not forget!! to pack my under clothing; in fact, I was painfully aware of it, but I had no room for it, and Mad let us keep our things in the drawers.

We are fourteen strong, at the moment, and I think I know of four more new girls who are to come.

Its so funny, I am now an old girl, and have to help the new ones. It seems like only the other day that I was a new girl. Never has a year gone bye so quickly, and I hope (at present) that another one never will. I am just beginning to find myself at home, and at my ease, and, pouf! I'll be home again.

My desk is at the window, and I have a most magnificent view. Right in front is a huge tree covered with pale green leaves, and the trunk wrapped round with small ivy. At its feet, the grass grows long, long, nearly two feet high, but beautifully fresh. Behind, the garden stretches on and on, the long grass shaded and shadowed by the sun, and by big trees growing here and there. I have come to the conclusion that its heaps bigger than the field in front of 48 St Albans Road.

We have quite a decent place for tennis, and we have already been playing. The rest has not improved my playing, but at least it hasent worsened it, as that wasent possible!! However, there is already a slight improvement; I can serve overhand, and, twice in ten shots, succeed in getting the ball over the net, and, sometimes, by means of a desperate 'fluke', get the ball into 'in'. Generally, the other eight times, I slash the ball, 1st shot, into the net, and, second, out of bounds. I think cricket or golf would be more in my line, as, when I see a ball coming, I never can resist the temptation to slash out at it with every ounce of my force, and send it miles over the trees. We have already lost four or five balls in four days, sometimes losing five at a time, and finding some others, the next time.

We returned from Chexbres on Tuesday, taking the train to Lausanne, and getting the boat from there. We had tea on the boat, much to the other passengers' amusement, and then amused ourselves as best we could. We played a game called 'Monsieur and Madame' which we are a bit cracked upon just now. Someone goes out, and those in the room choose two people, animals, articles or qualities, one being masculine, and the other feminine, like a girl and her father, coat and skirt, etc.. This game is best played in French, as everything is either mas. or fem. The person outside tries to guess what two things we have chosen, we replying, yes or no.

Well, we were playing this, and shrieking with laughter, and, bye and bye, we had quite a little audience of interested spectators. Amongst them was a gentleman, evidently English, and he started speaking with Olive. He was most interesting; he'd visited China, Japan, India, Africa, England, Scotland, Ireland, Wales, and came from America. He'd been all over Europe too. I tried to speak English too, but only succeeded in making myself ridiculous, as, either I couldent find the words, or, I lapsed off into French, without thinking, so I left it to Olive to entertain him.

It was so funny going to a new house. I got a room on the top storey with Lily, but was brought downstairs the next day. In the morning I started unpacking, and, at first, found it very amusing, but, by tea time, I was thoroughly disgusted with it. Hour after hour I slaved away, and still there was as much disorder as when I began. At last, I became desperate, and jammed things into boxes and cupboards, and at last succeeded in getting at least the semblance of order. Since then I have been busy playing tennis at every spare moment.

My rash is certainly better, but having got to a certain state, refuses to go any further, but always hangs on and on!

At Chexbres, I heard the cuckoo for the first time, and I saw green, purple, yellow, white and brown butterflies.

We have a new English pupil teacher here now, and she can scarcely speak a word of French, so speaks English all the time.

Its so funny, my book is about the French Revolution, and, our History for tomorrow is the history of Prussia, and, in my book, and my lesson, I've come to exactly the same point, the only difference being that my book gives all the awful details of the different battles.

I have just made a discovery in the garden. We have even got a little stream running at the foot of it.

Please, if you are writing to Kate, tell her that I have started her letter, but that I never can get enough time to finish it.

Bye the way, near to us there is a big park where we go now for our promenade. Well, the other day, Melle Albertine was going out, and what should she meet on coming up the avenue but a nurse and baby, etc.. Upon being asked her business, she explained that she thought that this was the Ariana!!! Now, however, we have a big plate upon the gate with 'Pensionnat for Young Ladies' upon it, in shining letters.

With much love,
yours lovingly,
one of the 'Young Ladies'.

To get on with Kate's letter, I took this one and copied it, word for word, nearly, and shall do the same thing next Sunday.

Château Blanc
10.5.14

My dear 'Grandma' and 'Grandpa',

How do you like your new titles? It does sound funny, Daddy a 'grandpa', already, and as for Mother… 'Grandma'?!!!! I expect that Dorothy is altogether unsquashable now, in her new position. Bye the way, when does the employment of commas, etc. come into the education of Dorothy? Her sentences would be a little clearer! if she would only consent to employ one, now and again!!!

It has rained every mortal day this week, and yesterday and today is freezing cold, and the rain just plops down!!

I bet you just wont believe what I am going to relate to you now. Its this: that the girls are all teasing me about my desperate infatuation for my umberstick, as it's a case of, "Everywhere that Flora goes, the umberel' goes too!" But the reason is very simple: my orange hat got a bit wet, once, and the crown went like this  also the straw got marked. Now the marks are all gone and you don't notice the crown, but I havent the least inclination to spend my money upon a new hat, so, as it always looks grey, I always take my umber. Today, I shared mine, for a bit, with another girl, and we walked into a stack of garden chairs!!

I wasent in the least tired after all those promenades; in fact, you would often have seen me flayling down the road after the others, gone with Mad to make a voluntary walk.

We gave Olive such a teasing and a drubbing that, all of a sudden, she declared that she wasent in love any more, and that Maurice was not the person to suit her, at all, at all. She announced that she would have to have a — chic — husband, all brushed and sleek, (and one with no idea not co–inciding exactly with hers, sort of, "Like my new hat, dear?" "Sweet, darling," "No, its horrible," "Yes, darling.") A quarter of five minutes of that would result in either the man or me being out of the window!!

Maurice charMING!!!!! Ask it of the society girl, she'd think you mad. Ask it of any other of us here, and they'd nearly die of laughing. 1st point: he has legs like this; 2nd point: a voice which squeaks and bellows in the same word! 3rd: much too good an opinion, in general, of himself.

Of course, nobody would ever dream of saying that Olive has not her good qualities, as she *has*, and a *lot*, only she spoils them.

Her latest is to buy a hat like this  side,  front view also a costume dark Saxe, which sounds very hard and old. She will have an air very old in it, but that is her ambition. She says that, when she returns, she wants to be, 'Miss Olive Reavell.' Ahem!!

There are two silly new girls coming next Tuesday, and they are to be put in the room opening off ours, and the present inmates are to be shoved out, and, very naturally, we are furious, as they were very nice — both. One, 'Madame Cheval' — Mrs Horse, literally,(from her explination [sic] of what is a mare) is specially killing. She has us nearly rolling on the floor, sometimes. She is little, with a huge mouth, and big teeth, and a turned up nose, and huge rolling eyes. Well, when we tease her, she employs all these features into making the most frightful grimace that ever you could imagine; and the best of it is that, for all that we encourage her and laugh, she never stops being perfectly natural. Also, she pops out, all of a sudden, with the most extraordinary remarks, which just double you up helplessly. The other night, she put on a summer night gown, for the first time, and the other girls called to me to come and see 'Madame,' all in virgin white. I went, and there stood a dazzling vision, gracefully posed by the bedside, with one finger in its mouth, and with an expression of coy modesty upon her sunburnt face. Of course, I went off into convulsions, at once. She is also very generous, *very*. Why, when she found a piece of chocolate under my pillow which I had saved from supper, she only ate one half of it, and handed me the other!

Just the other day, a moth came in bye the window, which mightily offended (sic) and frightened Madame. After flying in all directions, from it, and addressing remarks upon the politeness of a gentleman's coming into a lady's room, etc., she seized my tennis racket and started flourishing it about, and slashing it vigorously at the thing. I was washing at the time, in the little side room, and nearly killed myself laughing. Madame's grimaces alone were a pantomime of the 1st class. Next morning, she informed everyone, in a fearsome voice, that there had been a man in her room the night before.

Today Mad was in a very good mood, so someone called out, "Give us some chocolate, Mlle, please." The rest of us backed her up right loyally, and, in the end, Mad went off and came back with a whole pile of 2d packets, these she distributed round, most amiably.

Do you know, its awful how I am getting fat. My arms are

bursting out of all my sleeves, and my face is nothing more or less but a very good imitation of a full moon, except that its purpully (sic) pink.

Mad says that people will be sending their children here as a cure for anaemia, as she has made and started so many cures. If anyone wont eat – Iron pills; if anyone looks sloppy and wont eat nor nothin' – Scots Emulsion. Also, if you don't help yourself well at meals, she takes your plate and heaps stuff onto it, giving you a good old row to help it down.

Bye the bye, my everyday shoes are really in a very bad way and, you must remember, that they are more than two years old. Do you think that I should buy another pair, or stick on with them till I return?

You know, Mad should get Madame's photo taken as an advertisement for her Pensionnat, as, when she came, she was pale, yellow, thin and ugly. Now she is sunburned and rosy, fat and pretty, and all in one and a half months.

I must really try to finish Kate's letter now.

Much love,
your loving
Flora.

Château Blanc
19.5.14

My dear Pa and Ma,

Its 'chic' at present, or nearly so, if the sun would just only not burn a hole in my back and head. Mariele and I have sneaked a table from one of the bedrooms, and we are writing outside, out of sight of the house and everybody. The only drawback to the position is that the table is anything from being steady.

Horrors!! Don't you start trying to get me into dances, for goodness sake, if you don't want me to die in agonies. The very thought sends cold shivers down my back. Really, the very last thing that you have need to do is to worry that I shall be bored or anything like that, because I shant, and, as for amusements, those who will be amused always find something, and its only the grumps and frumps who find life a bore. I, at present, am living in hopes that I shall be able to earn my pocket money by teaching Dorothy French!!! (Don't faint.)

Its awful here, you are disturbed every minute. All sorts of varieties of animals come onto our papers, and then we have a regular blowing competition. I blow them onto Mariele and she blows them onto me.

Bye the way, Marjorie has been home nearly three weeks, and what do you think she wrote to Olive yesterday?: "I do hope something turns up soon, as I – cant stick it much longer!!" I can sympathise, after Prague, Dresden, etc., etc. and all the gay times she's been having lately.

Yesterday was a very bad day for us all here. 8 o'clock breakfast, and table not finished. Mlle Alb. growls and scolds me like an old monkey with toothache in all its teeth. 9.55 I smash Mlle Marie's tea–glass, to smithereens!! 10.10 Mlle Marie growls because I had done an exercise in an old exercise book, then I couldent answer a question she gave me — so…!!! Then, after tea, Mariele, not to be left behind, smashed the handle of the sliding door where the dishes are passed at dinner!!!… Then, I think that, all included, what with scoldings and letters, six girls out of seventeen cried!! Not bad?

Oh, bye the bye, we have staying with us, for a month or two, the child of an old girl, who was here twenty or so years ago. Also, there are two new girls, in the room off ours. They are very jolly etc., but cant speak much French yet. They brought heaps of chocolate and sweets with them, which they distributed about. Upon first entering their room, you would be struck, and favourably struck too, by the sight of a big family bible lying conspicusly (!!) (sic) upon their table. Upon opening the bible you would find it full of (sweets) of another kind!!

Olive and I are getting our German lessons, at last. I am beginning, altogether, at the beginning again, as Olive has never had any lessons, and I have forgotten heaps. It makes all the difference in the world, a teacher who talks the language herself, to one who takes it as a stranger.

We two have just decided that we have need of something sweet in our mouths, so we have formed the deep plan of sending the society girl off to Mad, to ask her to give us some choc, again, and we others will all troop after her and back her up….. Good luck: Mad gave us the choc, although she was absolutely horrified when she heard that we wanted it at once, and that we wouldent wait till after supper. We aint daft, not we!!!

I. Is the room leading off mine, at Délices, taken one Sunday afternoon. It gives you an idea of what our rooms were like. Even the P.C.s on the wall have come out so well.

II. One frontage of the house, and door which is used upon ordinary occasions, P. taken when the house was empty, still. One window of my room — the other.

III. State entrance, dining room. This shows only a tiny corner of the garden.

IV. Is our old Délices!!

V. Is a group taken upon Easter Sunday. If you look closely, you will see the eggs which we are clutching tightly. The two little girls in front are Mad's two little nieces, and the first to the left, 2nd row, is her eldest one. The complacent and self satisfied individual 2nd from the end, right, back row, is <u>me</u>, smirking with self sufficiency.

I put on a white crêpe blouse, yesterday, and I was nearly strangled by the collar. My white muslin blouse, I let out at the sleeves: muslin blouse sleeves too tight — burst!! Tussore: waist at neck! About all that I've got left, that isent getting skimpy, are my stockings!! Its as well that I'll be at home in three months!

Its awful. In the beginning of July six girls go, and amongst them are some of the new girls, come for a few months, for the big mountain trip, only. 'Madame Cheval', recently annexed but already quite settled, Olive, Mimi (fat lady), Mariele and I will be the last to leave, as Olive, Mimi and Madame go in

August. Mariele is horribly frightened that she will be the last, as she returns for her sister's wedding, and will have to stay a week or so longer, after.

With much love
yours lovingly,
Flora.

Château Blanc
24.5.14

My dear Mother and Daddy,

Its been boiling this week, and we've just roasted alive, more than anything. Today its raining, but at least its cool.

Who have you got as Assembly Guest? And is he nice? How disgusting of Helen to leave you in a fix, like that. Really, I would never have thought it of her. Have you got someone else, now?

You know, its awful, but all my blouses are too tight at the neck, and a bit strained in other parts. I can only hope that I don't get any fatter — or else!!!!

The girls here are rather inclined to regard me as a sort of fabulous monster, I think because I don't make a great fuss about when I shall come home, etc., but I say that I shall be home all in good time, and that it isent worth while wasting time making plans and sighing for the return.

There has just been a small fuss here, after dinner. We were all sitting quietly in the schoolroom, when, all at once, there came a crash! and then a shower and tinkling of falling glass. Naturally, we all rushed out, and, there, before the door, lay a sea of glass, and a huge hole in the glass door, all one huge pane smashed. It was one of the girls, who was coming down stairs, when her foot slipped on the mat, and she took a first prize header into the glass window. Her nose bled a bit and her head is a little cut, but otherwise she had a miraculous escape.

Talking about stairs, our Suèdoise, from Swedenland, is turning out to be a bit of a Tartar. Her pet antic is to put out her foot in front of you as you are coming down stairs. She nearly killed the pupil teacher that way. The intended victim was sauntering down the wide wooden stairs, dreaming sweetly — doubtless — when, all at once, a sturdy leg shot out before her, and it was only by grasping the banisters that she was saved from having her brains dashed out on the hard uncarpeted stairs…

We had strawberries for the first time last Sunday and again today, only, the cream is, very sadly, missing.

Mad's sister had a sale of work, this week, and, accordingly, we all went too. It was very nice, and also very simple. I bought a few things, and brought away many ideas for the next Auxillary (sic) Sale. We had tea with cakes and <u>two</u> mer–er–um (its hopeless, I never can remember how you spell it), is it meringues, or merangues or meringes or what?!! And after that we had ices — coffee. Oh, they were scrumptious, absolutely, and so big. Actually some of the girls stuck, they were so big. (Don't worry, yours truly waded on triumphantly to the — delicious — end. Next day we went there for supper. This also was spiffing, and we had ices again. We supped so well and so little wisely, that most of us were content to sit still afterwards — I, of course, felt nothing!…. I had to embroider a bib for the sale, and you should have seen it when finished!! I did not ask if it had been sold, or not, as I preferred to remain in blissful ignorance on this point.

My Singing Mistress says that I have certainly made some progress, which perhaps does not say much, but my Music Master does not say that I have made even a little progress, which <u>does</u> say much!!

Mariele goes home on Wednesday for her sister's wedding,

and will return in three weeks. Happily she lives just on the borders, a five or six hours journey from here. I guess that she will find Genève much too near when once she is home, as Mad certainly does not lavish too many signs of affection upon her, Mad having a rooted objection to girls who are not altogether like those in the Sunday School Library books, with their odour if sanctity and their glass case vertues (sic).

You know, I wish to goodness you wouldent keep thinking that I am going to come home a model in all things, etc.. as I am less a model than ever, and, as for being a 'Finished' or even a 'Young Lady' — !!!! Cease to connect me and this idea, and build up your hope in Dorothy.

Mollie Reavell will probably come here, so you could send Dorothy at the same time, with Marjorie, again.

Let me tell you, frankly, that the position of pupil teacher is one that it will probably never be my fate to occupy, as I shall *never* be other than 'Pupil' in this world, and, also, I'm sure Mad wouldent have me, as I forget so. Imagine me explaining French Grammar to a lot of girls, I who shine so brilliantly in the lessons of grammar, or, further, think of me trying to explain English Grammar to a group of sarcastic Germans!! No! no, its not for me, that position, I can assure you!

I am now going to write to Aunty Harry — what a miracle?!!

With much love,
yours lovingly,
Flora.

Château Blanc
31.5.14

My dear Daddy and Mother,

I absolutely havent got the strength to write, today, as its (just look at the mess my blotting paper made!!!) so hot and heavy.

I was very pleased to get your letter last week. It seems to me that the Assembly wouldent get along at all without you, as you talk of speaking here, opening there, and going the next place. The Assembly will be nearly over now, is it not; how is Mother bearing up under it, without a maid.

How funny, I dreamt about my nephew, two nights running, and each time he was fair and fat.

You havent got an idea how I long to be inside your car again, when we are dragging along the dusty roads, doing our daily 'promenade'.

At last, I feel inclined to write, so I'll now give you a description of a most ripping day that we spent, last Friday. Well, at 5 o'clock last Friday morning my alarm woke me — to my imence (sic) disgust, etc., but, willy nilly, out I had to come. The other girl was so excited that she kept rushing here and there, in and out, and then, at last, started throwing her bed-room slippers at me — she got them all back, with mine, into the bargain…

We breakfasted at six, and we went off to get the seven o' clock train. At Lausanne, we ate buns and ham, and walked about in the station for a bit. We arrived at Montreux at eleven, and then took a little mountain train, which took us up and up the hillside, winding and twinding round and round. Near to the end of our journey, dident it just begin to rain!!! and, by the time we reached 'Les Avants', it was pouring. Luckily the hotel was near bye, and in we scuttled, as fast as we could. The hotel was a palatial building, full of carpets, corridors and windows, etc.. We dined there in a huge hall full of huge windows and polished floor. We had a table right in the middle of the floor. The dinner was ripping, but, only, I had to sit next to Mlle Albertine, and in front stood a whole row of supercilious staring waiters, and, what with all these things, I dared hardly open my mouth to put the stuff in. After dinner, it still rained, so we waited in the hotel till two, and then we set off. Our intention had been to pick narcissus, with which the fields were covered white, only, with the rain, we couldent pick any at all. Well, we started off on foot, meaning to walk to Montreux, again. After crossing some fields, and following some little paths for a bit, we came into, what were called, the Gorges of Chaudron. It was here that the fun began... As the paths were muddy and narrow, Mad ordered us to turn up our skirts and hold them, thus wise walking in our petticoats. I can tell you it needed some skill to hold up a skirt and an umbrella, and to see that you dident slip more than was absolutely necessary. We slithered down a narrow rocky and muddy path, amongst the trees, beside a little stream. Down and down we clambered, passing little fairy spots, covered with moss and creepers, or crossing little bridges over rattling streams, then passing through deep gorges, the sides of which were planted thickly with trees and plants, of all kinds; now, coming out of the trees into a flower covered field, to plunge again into the trees; now, running along a little mountain path overhung by shadowing cliffs, while, far below, in a deep dark gorge, ran the stream, now descending rapidly, and coming out upon a splendid waterfall, rushing and scrambling over the cliff side to come thundering down into the bed below; again, we would come upon a deep gorge, the sides of which were covered with creepers and plants in flower, and only a muffled roar of the stream could be heard, far below. Then, again, we would cross a bridge, and see a distant waterfall, or a cave overhung with plants. Once, we came out upon an enormous waterfall. It fell from high, high up in the gorge, and fell straight down the perpendicular rock side, nearly 100 feet high – without exaggerating one bit. It was splendid to see the water splashing down the sides, amongst all the trees and plants. I simply cant describe what we saw, as its indescribable. Only just try and imagine for yourselves a walk in a wooded gorge, along a little path which led you down and down, and the more you descended, the more splendid became the cliffs towering up above. The waterfalls, too, were beyond words. The farther we got down, the less it rained, and, by the time that we reached Montreux, again, it had stopped. We got tea in a café, and then made for the boat. On the way, we had a hunt for a bakers shop, and couldent find one, nowhere! After having hunted vainly for about twenty minutes, we at last found one. Bye this time, it was raining again!!

On the boat it was ripping, as it was so fresh and nice. Afterwards we went into the cabin and started giving guesses, etc… Then we went out again, some of us, and played tig!! round the boat. At 9 o'clock we arrived at Genève, some being hardly capable of dragging themselves home. I was quite fresh, still, but I slept heavily and long, that night, and was a little sore next day.

It has just struck me, just now, that it must have been an awfully funny sight to see a Pensionnat, in Indian file, and in white petticoats, all slipping, slithering, running, jumping, dodging the branches, holding up umbrellas, all at the same time.

Last night, the English pupil teacher offered to teach us the hornpipe, and we accordingly accepted the invitation. She placed herself in front of the house, and we arranged ourselves in a long line, in front of her, and the lesson began... It was a pity, I think, that nobody saw us. Just imagine a whole line of girls, kicking their legs about, in a vain attempt to dance the hornpipe. After that, she started with the Reel steps, and this was still more lovely. I think that I shall never forget the vision of Mimi, skirts up, making desperate efforts to imitate the really graceful movements of Miss Lyon — Mimi is neither slim nor graceful, nor do her legs add to her charms, so, to see these stubby, chubby legs, with two fat feet encased in a pair of enormous galoshes, waving wildly about in the air, was altogether too much, even for me, and I collapsed, absolutely. After that we started solemnly to run round the house, once or twice, also to try and do back somersaults on the grass — it being dark by this time.

We are going to have a holiday tomorrow — again — as its Penticost (sic), its what you call — chic. Bye the way, when was 'Victoria Day'? Is it past yet?

Olive, having, to all appearances, got rid of her undesirable 'amour', is beginning to improve. In fact, she is getting quite presentable. She is much more natural, and doesent give herself so many airs etc., and so the peace is restored once more.

Mariele writes enthousiastic (sic) p.c.s of all her doings.

Poor thing, it was always her great worry what she could possibly do with the gentleman that she would get at the wedding, and her last P.C. announced that they were going to give her — two!!!!

We have all been in a great flutter this week, and, very often, the air has been rent by sighs and groans of a most heart rending kind, also, at all the spare moments, girls would be seen scribbling away, and scoring out, and rummidging (sic) wildly in formidable dictionnarys (sic). The reason for all this excitement was that the subject for our monthly composition was 'Friendship'. That, in our native tongues, would be bad enough, but in French!!!

I really must stop now, only, first, one thing: you don't happen to know what my precious nephew (if he, in any way, resembles his father, he <u>will</u> be precious!!) is to be, or is called?

With much love,
yours lovingly. Flora.

Please thank Miss Crease very much for the sweets, if you see her, and tell her that I'm awfully sorry that I havent written, but we have wasted so much time today that I couldent.

Château Blanc
7.6.14

My dear Mother and Daddy,

Its boiling hot today, and sunny. Up till now, since dinner, M.Dunon, brother–in–law, has been taking photos of us and the house, to make into P.C.s. I guess they'll be very pretty.

We are going to Aix–les–bains tomorrow, therefore will have to be up sooner than the lark e.g. 5 o'clock or half past 4! Cant say that I want to go, very much, but then I wasent asked my opinion. Also, we return at 11 p.m.!!!

Mlle Marie is off for her annual holiday, and we poor wretches are left to the tender mercies of Mlle Albertine. If things go on as they've started, there wont be a man jack of us who wont welcome Mlle Marie back again with open arms!! The pupil teacher will take the lessons in her absence.

I told you, dident I, that I got a box of creams coconut, etc. from Miss Crease, made by the Boys Auxilliary. They were ripping, all the girls said so.

One night, after having had a hot game of hide–and–seek, we went to bed ragingly hungry, and, after yelling out of the window to the servants below, to bring us some bread, which they refused to do, I bethought myself of my tablet, and off two of us set downstairs to get it. We arrived safely, and grabbed the box, and fled. Then we went to Mad's room, and told her, and offered her a bit, which, happily, she refused, we having just enough for us four.

Oh, bye the bye, you know that gauzy stuff upon the crown of my crinoline hat, well, the suns and rains of this year have altogether destroyed it, and, on the boat going to Nyon, the wind finished it. Just imagine my mortification upon arriving to find a huge hole in the stuff, and the ends waving wildly in the air. Well, yesterday, I went down town with Mad Albertine, and we bought a piece of satin, blue with yellow roses — big and muddly — for it. It cost about 7 ½ c, and I have still enough to make a collar or something. Well, straight away after supper, I got my hat, and an awfully decent girl arranged it for me, and she did it so quickly too, and so nicely, now my hat looks ever so much smarter than before.

This month's bill is a horror, only, the six weeks expenses for our mountain trip are included: something like £10, I think, probably a little more.

I got a huge letter from Mariele this morning, twelve pages, no less. She is having a spiffing time at home, so gay, with all her brothers, aunts, cousins, friends, etc.. She, too, is tasting the joys of trying on the wedding dress, etc.. I think that the German weddings must be so gay and jolly, and they act there, too. Mariele has to recite in a little play.

We will soon be off to Chamonix — in ten days, but, as we have had so much gadding about this year, we are to stay only four days. We will visit the glaciers, etc…

Last Monday, being the 1st June, was the 100th anniversary of the union of Genève with the Swiss Confederation. Therefore, there were some displays, only, as the schools were still going strong, the real displays were put off, and will be held in July. They have built a huge theatre (temporary) upon the lake side, and here they will represent all the scene which took place a hundred years ago. The boats which held the Swiss Deputies will come sailing in, and there will be songs, etc., etc... At night, after the third day, there will be a most wonderful display of fireworks, and, oh, there will be thousands of interesting things, street banquets and a' that.

Last Monday, 1st, the students had a torchlight procession, all in their uniforms (those in the clubs), and all in officiel (sic) bonnets. First came carriages, covered with flowers, holding the leaders of the different clubs, magnificent in their sashes and banners. Then, other carriages, equally decorated, containing representatives of the foreighn (sic) students: the Germans, resplendent in uniform and shining sabre, walking; then a crowd of them in white trowsers (sic), sashes and white kid gloves and gauntlets, upon horseback – the horses were ripping. We two got separated from the rest, and, after hunting round, found some others in the same condition, and so on, till we got ourselves collected together again. Then, we lost two of us for half an hour, and then found them, smiling happily

Friday night we went to a hall, where a lot of pictures showing the history of Genève, up till the moment when she joined herself to Switzerland, were given. It was very interesting, and we came home in cabs.

Tuesday night, we had a rare old fight about the German students, and their scars. England, Switzerland, Sweden and Hungary against all Germany and Austria. We yelled and shrieked at table, and, in the garden the feeling raged so high that the camp was divided into two, and we nearly had a free fight. Once, I gave a girl such a drubbing into upon this subject that all she could say, when I had finished, was that she saw that I was right, but, as it was a national custom, she had to support it.

Its killing, sometimes, when Olive asks me how you

say a word in English, and when I say it, we both burst out laughing, as its altogether bosh!

With much love,
Flora.

Château Blanc
14.6.14

My dear Daddy and Mother,

Here I am again, and off I must go for dinner, so ta — ta –.

2.o — You should just see us all now, five of us are sprawling upon the grass on waterproofs, cloaks overalls and rugs. I hope that you will be able to read what I write, as I am sprawling full length, face downwards.

We are probably going to Chamonix, this week, but its not quite settled yet. Also, this week, a very tragic event is going to happen, namely, Lilyputin is going home. We all put on long faces, even at the thought of it. She will leave an enormous blank, as she was the youngest, and an awful monkey, into the bargain.

It was simply killing last Friday. Mad took it into her head that some of us were ill, and, accordingly, off she went, with five girls, all equally disgusted and growling and grumping. The doctor gave them all pills and potions, and sent them packing. Two were too regular, another not enough, another had pimples, and thought she was going to die, and another has boils, and burned them so vigorously that she had made them worse. At home was another irregular one, another who felt sick, and I, with that funny sore throat that I get about once a year regularly. Its gone again, now.

On Friday, after dinner, we had some spiffing fun. You know, the grass in the garden had not been cut, as they were waiting until it was ripe. Well, this week they began to cut and stack it, and, on Friday, we started playing in it, as the stacks were knocked down again. Oh, we did have fun. We chased each other with armfuls of it, and buried each other. Miss Lyon, the English pupil teacher, we caught nicely, and whole five of us piled up the hay on top of her, just leaving her head out. She looked just like a snail, and whenever she tried to free herself, we saw to it that her house went with her. Then the men came with rakes and pitchforks and a cart, and began to gather the grass up. For a moment we were grief stricken, but soon we seized rakes, etc., and worked like navvies. Others climbed up into the cart, and arranged the hay that the men and girls threw up to us. Mad hauled us down from there, so we hopped around for a bit, and then, when the wagon was nearly full, two of us climbed up again. Then, when all was finished, we harnessed ourselves to the cart, and drew it down to the stables, shrieking and laughing.

You should have seen our bedroom floor after we were brushed and emptied, as we were crammed with hay.

All this week Mlle Marie has been away, so we have been very gay, at our end of the table, also, at night. But now, alas, returned is she, and we have now so good to be!

You know, its awful, by the middle of July, only five of the original sixteen, who were there at first, will remain: Olive, Mariele, Mimi and I — horrors, its only four, as I had forgotten that Madame was not an old girl.

By the way, I have got a piece of news for you, Daddy. Its this: our history teacher had been talking about Calvin, so, after the lesson, I went out to her, and asked her if she knew where Calvin was buried. She said that he was buried at the Cathedral of Saint Pierre, but that his original resting place was in the cemetery of Plain–Palais, and that the tree was still there, she thought. Now that we know where it is, couldent we visit it, if you come to fetch me? You would be able to see it for yourself.

I got such a nice letter from Aunty Harrie, this week, also one from Phyllis, asking me what was up, that I hadent written. But, you know, the time passes so quickly here, that I never realise that I havent written for a long time.

It seems to me that I have encamped right on top of an ants' nest, judging by the number of visitors of this species I am receiving.

Do you know that, at long last, I have made half an inch of progress at tennis. Yesterday, I was six games to my partner's three, but I needent boast, as the other girl is about as brilliant as I, in tennis.

We are getting heaps of cherries now, and strawberries too, but they arent up to much without cream.

You know, I've come to the conclusion that, if ever I go to Hell, they'll make me darn stockings all day long, and during the night too, as every Friday afternoon, I sit and darn, darn, and strengthen, strengthen, until I go nearly mad, and then, before I wear the stockings two days, they're all holes again. And the worst of it is that I don't object to a real downright hole, but the strengthen strengthen, all the time, is simply atrocious, and its that that I do nearly all the time. Mad said that I darned pretty well – should think I ought, with all the practice I've had – I've two pairs at the wash – holey; three in the cupboard – caved; and one on, still whole.

With much love, yours lovingly, Flora.

Send me some monish soon, as I am stony broke, and frightfully in debt. Told Mad about the mistake, and she gave me the £1.

Hôtel Beau Site, Chamonix
21.6.14

Dear Mother and Daddy,

I'm writing before breakfast, so as to get on with my correspondence. We arrived here on Friday, at midday, after three or four hours on the train. We were up at five to finish packing. We all got into a huge omnibus and rolled through the town, much to the passers–by's amusement. In the train, I had the luck to be in a compartment where no elders were allowed. There wasent much of a view, at first, and soon we got hungry, so they gave us buns. I yelled out, "Hurry up there, I'm hungry!" so a girl took a bun out of the bag, and chucked it at me. I missed it, and under the seat it went. I fished it out, and, in trying to clean it, dropped it again. This time I just popped it into the bag, and took another… – Wonder who got that dirty one? – . Then I take down a guide book, which was hanging on a rack, and open it, – Whirrr! – out flies a huge horrible moth, down goes that book, and out by the door go I, followed by several others, and general panic reigned until some practical individual put her foot upon it.

Soon the scenary (sic) became pretty. We entered into a little valley with huge hills on either side, covered with pines and little chalets. Then, we began to get glimpses of snow behind the clouds, and to see lovely waterfalls and feathery cascades. Then, we saw deep deep gorges and more mountains. Chamonix is just wedged in between two mountains, and seems to be composed mainly of hotels. The hotel is very nice and homely, and our rooms are right on top, and we have a landing all to ourselves. We unpacked at once, and got into sporting rig. Making acquaintance with the Chamois locks: the cupboard key, you put in upside down, and then turn it round and round, as hard as you can go, giving little tugs between times, just to see if it isent feeling inclined to open yet. With the chest of drawers, its still better: you can turn the key round and round, in both directions, for half an hour, before it'll open.

After a splendid dinner, we trudged off for the Glacier of Boissons, which we see from here. Once started, it had to go and rain, and, therefore, we had to go and get our big coats; all the time it rained, off and on, but we dident worry. The walk up was awful. I was nearly dead by the time we reached the little inn. But, a cup of tea, strong, strong, which flavoured of pines and I don't know what, and one or two little biscuits — we were perfectly refreshed again. Then off we started for the glacier. Before going onto the glacier, we visited a grotto or cave which ran along all under the ice. We entered, and were conducted all through. The roof was vaulted, and, every here and there, candles burned. It was most beautiful to see the pale green walls and roof, in the faint light. Just imagine walking under a glacier, in a tunnel formed out of sheer ice. It was cold, naturally, but very interesting. Sometimes we would come upon a little stream or waterfall coming out of the ice. After this we went on deck. There were all sorts of little hills and valleys, and places where the guides had to make holes for us to get down. We had huge mountaineering boots with nails, etc., so we walked very easily and never slipped. We got ourselves photoed upon the ice, and the photos are very pretty. I took to the glacier like a duck to the water, and got over in fine style. The mountains up above were covered by the clouds, mostly. We were really on a bit of the Mt Blanc, if you like, or, at least, at the foot of it. Once over, we raced down and down, through woods and dales, till we reached the foot, and made for the hotel. We did eat for supper that night. Now, there is another Pensionnat here too, but such a crowd of little Mummy's darlings, never did I see. They are so – oh! so polite to one another, they hardly smile, and speak in whispers. They don't wear nailed boots, and they don't visit glaciers.

Oh! Oh! Oh! Its only half past seven, now, and we breakfast at nine! and I'm so hungry.

At night, all the clouds cleared away, and we saw all the mountain tops splendidly; they were beautiful.

Next morning, I waked up to see Millette at the window gaping upwards. When she heard me moving, she shrieked at me to come quick. I hopped quickly out of bed, and raced over to her. She pointed up, but I, only half awake, could see nothing for the sun on the snow, so, by the time that I could look, there was nothing more to see, as the clouds had closed again.

We got a ripping breakfast, rolls and honey – real, *and* butter, and started off for an all day excurtion (sic). We walked and walked, in the hot sun, and the paths mounted steeply all the time. Oh! the walk of the day before was nothing in comparison. We climbed and climbed, never stopping to rest. At last, we were allowed to rest for five minutes. I dropped down, and I was so tired that I cried, the tears just came, and how thirsty we were. My throat was glued together. After an all too short rest, we trudged off again. This time it was worse than before, and I got a fearful headache. I can tell you nothing of what I saw, or anything, except that, in one place, rocks, pines and all were lying in confusion, having been knocked over by a tremendous storm. At last, we arrived, and, to quench our thirst, we got ham sandwitches (sic), hard boiled eggs and dry bread…! At the end, we got a little drop of strong black tea, but it was but a drop in the bucket. Here, the scenery was worth looking at: snow, snow, and, before and behind, he peaks, jagged and broken, stretching up into the sky. I never saw anything so grand in my life before, and, beneath, the glacier winded (sic) down, like a river; it is called, 'The Sea of Ice'. The bit where we crossed was very unexciting indeed, quite flat, and only a few crevasses to jump over. We walked on between rocks etc., for a bit, and then camped for dinner. Here, we were allowed to drink, but not the pure water: either with wine or sugar. We gathered flowers, and continued. We passed heaps of lovely waterfalls. Bye and bye, we came to a place where there is a path cut out of the rock; this we took, holding onto the railing, on the safe side. Mad yelled behind us, "Don't you dare look down, or above, *or* let go of the railing!" I found it not so very dangerous, and looked down *and* up, and, sometimes, did let go of the railing. Then, we arrived at a pretty little inn, where we got milk and biscuits. Just at this stage, one of the girls, Grete, found that she had lost her purse… Do you know, she had been silly enough to take her purse, with *all* the money she possessed — 7 – 8 francs, and all her keys, and to put it in her jacket pocket. It had fallen out once before, and Mad had told her not to put it in her jacket pocket, but to give it to the guide, if she dident have another place for it, but the silly just put it back into her pocket, and buttoned it up. The jacket she had slung onto her back. Well, Mad sent the guide back to look for it. You know, we felt so sorry for the poor man, having to trudge away up there again, even though it was only to the camping place. Well, we descended, and took the train back, as it was all flat road now. Grete got her purse back. I think an Englishman had found it, and given it to the guide, or something like that. She gave him 2/–, or, at least, Mad told her that she had to. I think she lost a silver pencil too, another silly thing, taking a silver pencil upon a mountain trip. I took five pence in my spectacle case, and kept feeling, always, to see if it was there. I have green specs for the mountain, and I shall wear them at Genève too, on sunny days, as the sun dazzles me hopelessly, and I cant hardly open my eyes.

Its awful, really, its not nearly time for a break yet, and I'm getting ravenous.

You pronounce Aix, ééex, with the x.

We go to Chamonix for three or four days, just to see the Mt Blanc and the glaciers, I think.

Last night, at supper, we had an Italian who played at the window, but the waiter drove him away.

Here, you come upon the typical country scenes. Yesterday, we met heaps of cows, all with bells round their necks, and, the day before, we came across some cows in a little wood, and the boys leaning against the trees, watching them.

There are such a lot of English and Americans here, just swimming everywhere you turn.

We have all got white felt hats, and every girl has her national ribbon on it. It looks so pretty to see all these white hats with the gay ribbons on them.

It really is lovely, the view that we have from our window, pines, streams, gorges, glens, snow and mountain peaks. When I have finished this letter, I am going to copy it out once or twice, and send it round.

At last, we have breakfasted. I ate four rolls!! There are a whole packet of Americans here, and oh! the accent…

We're writing outside in the hotel garden, now; it's such a pretty one, all trees, flowers and arbours.

As there is no Protestant church here, we are staying at home, and getting on with our letters, instead. Its awful, perhaps we'll have to go for some rotten walk, this afternoon, instead of writing.

I must stop now, and copy out this again.

Much love.
your loving
Flora.

I am about the only one whose (sic) brought a clothes brush with her, so my room gets invaded with clamouring individuals.

I hope that you keep all the photos that I send you, as I want to stick them in my album, afterwards!

Château Blanc
26.6.14

My dear Daddy and Mother,

Here we are again, quickly settled down again, at Château Blanc. We returned on Tuesday, at half past six at night.. On Sunday, we wrote letters in the garden, and the afternoon we went for a walk. We went to gather rodedendrons (sic) — once arrived, it began to pelt! — so took shelter under an overhanging rock till it stopped. Then we separated, and clambered about the hill, gathering the wild rodies. Afterwards, we took tea under the trees, at a little inn, and had just finished when the rain came on again. In we rushed, and waited nearly an hour during a thunder storm, and then returned.

Monday, we were to have climbed up to a cabin high up on the mountain side. Well, off we started, in spite of the protests of the hotel master, and all the waiters. After having walked for half an hour or so, blump comes the rain, and it rains in earnest, this time. Happily we had our umbrellas, having been ordered back to get them, some time before, but they dident protect us much. Then, just as we had to pass a bit without trees or anywhere to shelter us, it hailed as well as rained. We rushed on, trying to get to the cabin before we were altogether drowned, but there wasent much of us left, by the time we arrived, dripping. We invaded the cabin, and demanded some tea, we providing the provisions. We had to ear all the things that we had brought for two or three meals, all at the same time, and the tea!!!! She brought a little tea pot which held enough for two, three inch, cups at a time, and, in between, she had to make fresh. You can imagine how long it was before we were all served. Then she gave us the bill of £1.15, for 34 cup, at 1 franc each. Mlle Albertine looked at the bill, then at the woman, and said, "Is that all?" Then she asked us all how many cups we'd had, and that, all added together, only made 24. Also, Mlle A. refused to pay more than 5c for each cup. Imagine, at P.J.s you get a pot for 1/–, and that serves for three or four cups, but she, she charged us by cup. After we had finished, we had to wait two hours or more, before the storm went off. Then, we made off, as fast as possible, for the hotel.

The next day, we returned, after an exciting packing up. We got chocolate, rolls and cherries in the train.

The day after, Mariele returned — and the row, too!!!

We are having splendid weather, now, so warm and sunny. We only hope that it'll last, as the Centenary is very near, now, next Saturday, it begins. Already, the streets are beginning to be decorated, with pillars, flags and greenery. We have got our places booked, long ago, and, also, windows to see the display of fireworks, which will be splendid.

It's awful, but, Thursday next is our last lesson day, and, after that, holidays. After the eighth, we go to Zermatt, and then to St Luc in the Alps, for four weeks.

Couldent you weigh some of this paper, and an envelope, and see how many one can send for 2 ½ c, as I don't know, and am really very sorry that you have to pay for the overweight.

My room sounds so pretty, now, so high–art, with rugs, etc… I always have longed for a room for myself, and a pretty one, too.

I think that I shall be the last, or the second last, of the old band, to leave, as three more go this week, and still more the week after. Olive leaves in August, as third last, I think. Mariele will have to pay for her gaddingds by staying till late in September. Mad Alb. goes to England, London, to her brother, for summer, so, perhaps she wont be back — cant say that that will worry me much, as we don't get on extra well! Mutual affection!!

Mad has visitors in today, and, of course, it was I who had to be sitting beside her, so I got the full dose of them, in front of me, and beside me!!

Have you settled your holiday destination, yet?

We live quite near to the theatre, erected for the great day, and, at night, we can hear them singing, or the orchestra playing. It's so pretty to hear the music coming faintly up.

Everybody here finds that I'm getting very fat — except me!! But Mad told me that I'd get thinner, at once, whenever I got home. Let us hope so…

Mad has just been talking to me, and she says that she'd be very much obliged if you'd only recommend her school to other English girls. You can assure everybody that there are not many Pensionnats where you are so free, and, at the same time, under control, and we're the only Pens. at Genève, where you go for excurtions (sic) etc., so much, and Mad's horribly careful of your health: if you turn up your nose at your food — Iron Pills, Malt, etc… If you're pimply, pills and purges, and there's no escaping her, either.

With much love,
your loving
Flora.

REPUBLIQUE FRANÇAISE
25c
POSTES
Mrs Ewing.
48 St. Alban's Road.
Edinburgh.
Scotland.
Ecosse.

Château Blanc
5.7.14

My dear Mother and Daddy,

This has been a very exciting week for us, what with the Centenaire, etc…

On Tuesday we went for an excurtion (sic) upon the lake, and took supper outside at a little inn, and arrived back at Genève at nine.

On Wednesday, an awfully nice girl left, then, that afternoon, another received a telegram telling her to come home at once, as her mother was ill. Her mother is a lonely widow, and Mad was sure that there wasent any danger, only nervousness, but the girl was in an awful state. Once calmed down a bit, she held up wonderfully. She really was awfully brave; her face was white and pitiful, but she never shed a tear. The girl, who was beside her at table, said that sometimes her whole body shook and quaked, but her face never moved a muscle. She went at seven the next morning, and, since then, we have had no news.

That night we went to the lake baths for the first time this season. It was spiffing, and the water was as warm as warm. Then, after supper, we trooped across the road to the school opposite, which was the dressing room for the actors, the theatre being quite near to us. Well, we went into the courtyard to see the actors passing. The court was full of funny–costumed men, women and children. There were men dressed in bear skins and sandals; Roman soldiers; old Swiss costumes: the round hat, full cloak with slashed sleeves, and long stockings. There were little boys in white trowsers (sic) and green or red blouses, with white turbans; little girls in Turkish costumes; men in coloured trowsers and tailed coats, fancy waistcoats, and queer tiled hats; girls in low cut, high waisted, frilled dresses, or long trains, and tight waists; and all the different old uniforms for the soldiers. Those in mail coats were too funny. They shrieked with laughter at each other, and did gymnastics, to see how much they could move about. They were awfully tickled with their tin shoes, and tried treading upon each other's toes, etc... They had fine helmets, with red and yellow ostrich feathers in them. These, they amused themselves with, in putting them onto, or rather, putting small boys into them, and then shutting them so that they couldent get out.

Sometimes, two men would come across each other, and, simultaneously, they would begin to titter and to mock. The different trades of Switzerland were all represented: the clock makers etc... The former had huge baggy trowsers, and one man, as he came out, took them up in his hands, like a dress, and held them out, and then, just doubled up with laughter. Oh, bye the bye, I must not forget, you know, that Napoleon visited Genève too. Well, he was represented, too, and, if it wasent Napoleon himself, risen from the grave, it was a decendant (sic), as like him as could be possible. Whenever I saw him, I knew who it was supposed to be. It was a little burly man, with a fat heavy face, big nose and forehead, slightly bald in front, and perfectly clean shaven. The only difference between him and the original was that he looked much too good natured, but probably he will harden up his expression, for the occasion. There were also some girls and boys dressed in floating grey gauze, with only a little grey combination sort of affair beneath. Guess they must have felt cold enough in going down to the theatre. These dance and sing, representing the shadowy hours of the night. The theatre is enormous, and built for the occasion, by the lake side.

On Friday, it rained all day, and everybody thought that we were going to be drowned for the Centenaire, but, on Saturday, it brightened up again. In the morning, we visited the town to see the decorations. Really, it was touching how they had worked. Every little close and shop, every little corner and garret, had something. Sometimes the decorations were home made and gaudy, sometimes as fine as the finest shops could supply, but I think that the poor little papers and flags were more splendid than all, as it showed how everyone, down to the very poorest, was willing to do all he could to beautify the town, even if they had to make a sacrifice of something to provide the means. Lots of proprietors let out heaps of stuff to decorate the streets and houses with. Every house had its windows festooned and flagged, rows of little pennons hanging from one window across to the other. In town, garlands of greenery hung from the windows to the lamp posts, and huge flags hung about, some in the middle of the street. Sometimes, one house would have one huge flag, red and yellow for Genève; and another, equally big, red with a white cross in the middle, side by side; and, at all the other windows, a flag representing each 'canton' of Switzerland. You can imagine what a gay effect the red and yellow, and red and white had. In the old part of the town, where the streets were narrow, you saw one mass of colours, a regular wall–forest of flags and garlands. Never, never have I seen anything to compare to it. They had even rebuilt the old town gates, in wood and canvas, where they originally stood. In short, not one place, where a flag could, or <u>couldent</u> be stuck, was left undecorated. The hotels had flags of every nation at every window, and their balconies were swathed with red and yellow, and red and white cloth. The road by the lake was turned into a princely avenue, with triumphal arches every hundred yards. These consisted of two huge white pillars, with garlands of greenery upon them, and on top, joining them, all joined together, were two Swiss flags, with a Genèvian one in the middle. The foot of the pillars were covered with greenery. All the town seemed to have brought out its old Christmas trees, and put them in front of their doors, and decorated them with paper flowers and flags. Even the garden hedges, in some places, were covered in red, yellow and white paper roses. On the lake, the steamers that were to go and pick up the President and the Council at Nyon, were beautifully festooned with the flags of every part of Switzerland. Oh, you cant describe the sight of the town, and on a sunny day, too, you could only look, and wonder, and then respect the patriotisme (sic) of this independent little people. Upon the principal bridges, there were huge, real arches, with welcoming inscriptions to the Deputies, etc., printed in letters of gold, upon them.

Then, we returned for dinner, and, here again, a wondrous sight awaited us. Some of the girls had preferred to stay at home to decorate the table, whilst we gallivanted about town, and they had worked well, I can assure you. This is how the dining room looked: in the middle of the table there were five vases, in the middle, one covered with red and yellow paper, with red and yellow flowers in it – Genève; and, surrounding it, were four others, smaller, covered with red and white paper, with red and white flowers in them — Switzerland, and the five were attached together with two long ribbons, one red and yellow, the other red and white. Then, all the serviettes were wonderfully folded, and, upon each, was a little round of red and yellow folded paper; at each place, too, there was a tiny vase of flowers, Genève et Swiss, alternating, tied with red or yellow paper. Then, above, there was a huge chandelabra, and this was beautifully decorated, too: each candle was accompanied by a flag, Swiss, Genève, or those of the Centenaire, whilst, coming from the top, and going from one end of the room to the other, as a long festoon, one half was red and yellow, the other red and white, the colours went link by link, alternating. These chains, the girls had had to cut and gum together, themselves

The whole was really wonderful. The Mads[1] were so enchanted that they couldent thank or praise enough, and Mad Albertine photographed us as we sat. We got an extra good dinner, with a red and white ice, at the end, and red and white cherries, too; also, red and white wine, and red and yellow potatoes. We set off again in the afternoon, and wandered about till tea time, and then tea–ed in town. At five, we went to a house where we had taken windows to see the procession. We had three windows, just at a corner, where we could see splendidly. First, came the guides, on horseback; then a band; then a regiment, the old Grenadiers; at the very end of this section, there came three huge stalwart men, one being specially so, with grey moustache and all. Well, these three passed, stalking gravely along, and then, just behind the biggest of

---

1 Mesdemoiselles

them all, you saw a little speck, which bobbed along. Upon minute examination, this speck turned out to be a little boy, all trigged out in an exact same uniform as his father, huge busby and all. The wee soul, he *did* march bravely too, and turned the corner so neatly, keeping the same distance behind his father, or grandfather, all the time. He was so sweet and so funny, toddling along there behind this gigantic soldier. The crowd cheered him lustily. Then came a group in sky blue and black uniforms; then a lot of others, not very interesting; then a crowd of men in plain clothes, having, at the head of every division, a man in a coloured robe, the robe being made of the colours of the canton that each man belonged to; then some naval officers, and some more plain clothed objects; then some old soldiers; then a group of men from Berne, all in old world costumes, the two first leading or being led by two spiky–collared bull dogs; then some more men in the ancient costume of Bâle; and then, and then, and then came a crowd of men, plain clothed, but who were cheered and cheered all along the road, and who were very gay. When they began to pass under our windows we clapped and waved too, and they looked up, and started waving and cheering to us too, taking off their hats. As they came on, those behind got more and more enthousiaste (sic), and soon we had the whole band who looked only at our side, and at our window. Some of the gentlemen had fans which they waved to us and they threw us kisses by the hundreds. One man stopped beneath us, and flung out his arms in a despairing gesture to us, and then kissed his hands wildly to us. We had the whole band to ourselves, as they never looked at the other people on the other side at all. We have decided that the inhabitants of the canton of Zurich are very nice people indeed. Then came students, all bra' in their Sunday best uniforms, with their banners, scarves, flowers and all. Of course, we became vociferous again, and waved our dainty hankies, etc... They stopped and sang right under our windows, so we had time to admire them properly. Then came some gymnastic clubs, all dressed in white; and then the cadets. I never saw a more miserable looking lot than these. First, their uniforms were very ugly, and not a bit smart, and the boys' faces were so drab too, also they had been forbidden to look around them, and were mortally shy. This last vertue (sic) gave to their already ugly faces a finishing touch. That was the end of the procession, which lasted more than an hour. For supper, we got patriotic tarts: one, Genevois, with the coat of arms (key and half eagle); the other, Swiss: red and white cross. Then we sang patriotic songs — at half past nine, and were bundled off to bed at ten.

Tonight we are going to see the firework exhibition. We have a balcony or something in the hotel of Russia. It begins at eight or half past, and dures (sic) till half past eleven or later. Tomorrow we go to the theatre to see the historical play. Bye the way, I don't believe that you understand what all this fuss is about, so I shall explain. You see, Genève was, until 1814, a little town which belonged to nobody but itself, but which had to keep up a continual fight against the surrounding powers, who wanted to annex her, la Savoie being the most dangerous. Well, time after time, Genève asked to be let into the Swiss confederation, but the Catholique Cantons always made objections, and she had to give it up. Then, Napoleon, in 1798 or 1799, whilst running about picking up kingdoms and contenants (sic), bagged Genève, and made it a French Canton, much to the Genevois' disgust. For the moment they were conquered, and it seemed as if it was all up with their independence, but they were not beaten yet, and, all the fifteen years that they were under the French, the Genevois never ceased to plot and plan, and hope and pray for better days. This came, eventually, with the fall of Napoleon and the coming of Bubena with the Austrians. Once again, Genève was free, but she had had enough by this time, and saw that she wasent strong enough to fight all alone any longer so she renewed her prayers to the Swiss Council, and, at last, obtained their consent to enter into their Confederation, and, the 1st June 1814, the Swiss came in boats, like yesterday, and the Genevois went to meet them, like yesterday, and they drew up the document, etc., and Genève was declared, from that moment and for ever more — Swiss... Today, they are trying to repeat again, all the scenes which took place a hundred years ago.

Then, Friday next, we are off to the mountains to repose from all our pleasures and excitements.

Today, at tea, again, we had patriotic cakes, which were excellent, I can assure you.

Do you know that I, your imperfect and disorderly daughter, have taken it upon my proper self to correct and to chastise the inmates of my bed chamber, for the self same faults as I have the habit of practising, myself, namely, if Milette dares to leave a dress or skirt or anything which ought not to be there upon the pegs in the bedroom, I pounce upon it, and arrange it nicely upon her bed, together with various other articles, like gloves, handbags, etc., which happen to be lying about, and then disappear. Sometimes, I tell her that she'll find something in her room, if she goes and looks. She understands, at once, and flies. Once, she left the chair in the middle of the floor, so

I hung it onto the bed, too. Also, Milette and the two infants, in the other room, have got the very bad habit of speaking German whenever they are together, so I offered to come and whack them every time they spoke. They consented… I'm kept very busy! Also, its very inconvenient when, in the middle of washing your teeth, you have to fly to thump some guilty sinner. Sometimes, when I spank them, they don't remember what its for, and they turn round upon me, and I have to fly!

With much love,
your loving Flora.

You can give away these photos to someone, if you like, as I have copies of them in my album.

Our address in the mountains is: Hôtel Bella Tola, St Luc sur Sièrre, Valais, Suisse.

Rev. Dr Ewing.
48 St. Alban's Rd.
Edinburgh.
Scotland.

GENEVE
29.VI.14.VIII
EXP. LETTR.

Hôtel du Cervin
12.7.14

My dear Daddy and Mother,

Oh, I feel more inclined to sleep than to write, as I have just devoured two or three pounds of fruit: cherries, pears, apricots and peaches. Mariele, Mimi and I each bought a pound of fruit; the other two, more than one, and we sat and shared and shared, alike, in the garden, after. The last apricot took a good lot of swallowing and forcing, before it got down. We are at Zermatt for four days, on our way up to St Luc, and its perfect; but, first, I must tell you of what we have been doing at Genève this week.

Well, on Sunday night, we hired a balcony in 'l'Hôtel de Russie', and were lucky enough to have one right on the top landing. All the lake was covered with little boats, with red or yellow Chinese lanterns. They looked like glow worms, in the distance. Some boats were decorated with lanterns so as to represent different things: some were butterflies, some flags, some the big pillar erected in memory of the Union, and one represented the post card drawn specially for the Centenaire — man at the lake side with flag in hand. All the street lights were put in red paper bags, and all the numberless bridges, which compose the centre of the town, were hung with red and yellow lanterns. Underneath us, the streets were thronged with people, and the principal bridge was one huge mass of heads. The fireworks were magnificent, and how they did roar and crack, in the darkness. You thought that the rockets shot out of the water itself.

The fire continued for more than half an hour, without one stop; then, after ten minutes rest, they started again, harder than ever, it was lovely to see the reflection upon the waters. Then, all the piers and breakwaters lit up with huge Vesuvius, red and yellow, which flared and shone, and then went with a frightful report. Then there came a chain of white fire, which broadened out, and flared wonderfully. Then, the piers lighted up again, with red and purple and green and yellow lights. The reflection upon the water was lovely, and it threw up the dark boats from which the fireworks came.

Then, to finish up, one of the boats lit up, and showed the national monument. Then the whole thing flew up into the air, in every imaginable colour, with a roar and a crack, whilst thousands of rockets shot up after. It was splendid. (I cant write lucidly, now, as Mariele and Mimi are writing their letters together, and, in consequence, they giggle more than they write, and I have to thump them, also, the pupil teacher comes along every five minutes to scold us, and, as her French is rocky, she makes us rock too. And, once I discovered there was a pump behind me, and got up, and made as if I was going to squirt the water onto them — we were in the garden, surrounded on all sides by balconies and family groups — well, Mariele got up to fly, and caught her foot upon the chair leg, and fell, all her length onto the ground. It was awful, and the people laughed dreadfully.)

After the rockets had stopped, the town lighted up with Bengal fires, and then we went home all in the crowd, at midnight. Next day, at nine o'clock, it rained, but we took umbrellas, galoshes and coats, and slipped down by the performers' door to the theatre. The inside was enormous, and packed.

Our seats were in the 2600, and there were about a hundred rows behind us, still. The stage was Grecien (sic), with pillars and alcoves etc… First, you saw a watchman, then a bell ringer, and these two talk together about Genève. Then the watchman says that he hears and sees the ancients of Genève, some time. The bell ringer wont believe him, so the w.m. tells him that he'll see these things tonight. Then a weird, mournful whistle sounds out, and a curtain rises, and there glides down the wide staircase a group of girls all clothed in floating Grecien dresses, all grey purple, with bare arms and feet. More and more of these came on, boys and girls all dressed alike. These were there all the first act, and had mock fights and sang, and played games, just like fairys, and so, so graceful; some were bell ringers, and, when the bells rang, they did the actions of ringing a bell, lifting their arms up into the air, and then pulling, and bending down, so gracefully. Also they hailed or showed their disapprobation of the tableaux, as they came. The tableaux were shown behind a veil of gauze which gave them the look of old pictures, so quaint and faint. They were shown by means of electric light, turned on at the beginning and end. I saw the Romans, the ancients, the Savoyards, the man from Berne who drove the latter away, Julius Caesar, l'Escalade, Jean Jacques Rousseau. 2nd Act: Genève the 31st December, when the French go away, after the fall of Napoleon. This gave a very good impression of the life and people of that time. 3rd Act: Shows the rejoicings of the people at their delivery, and girls dance and sing, and children play pretty games, and the soldiers come in, and the children dance around them. 4th Act: The curtain behind the scenes rises up, and you see the lake lying a few feet away. In fact, the frontage of the theatre was built upon the water. Then, in come hundreds of soldiers and children, as well as crowds of quaintly dressed men and women. Two lines of soldiers, in ancient uniforms, came down the hall, and onto the stage, creating quite a sensation. Then, one of the hours, in grey, recites something about the lake, and a woman begins too, awful accent, unfortunately. She began in a very melodramatic tone, with, "Oh, Lake!" etc., etc… since it's very à la mode to yell, "Oh, Lake!" in the most 'pig in love being killed' voice, all over the place. It was so pretty and so original to have real scenery, and the rain had just stopped, and there was a tiny gleam of sunshine. You saw the country side, and the hills, and a steam boat passed, also a sail boat. Then, the boat came gliding into sight, full of men in blue uniforms, and a band played. The bridge was full of gaily dressed women. Then the soldier band on the stage began playing a beautiful Swiss song. After the firs line, the first band stopped, and then there came the echo from the other band on board, and so on, all the time, until the boat landed. Then there was a hand–shaking, and an excitement. In the middle of all this fuss, the watchman comes in, and tells them that his work is over, Geneva being now Swiss. He then congratulates them all, and kisses the Swiss flag, and then the national Anthem is sung. While it is being sung, eight young boys, clad in flannels, wide open at the neck, bounded up the alleys, waving the flag Genevois. They looked so graceful, and they leapt up the stairs, and bounded lightly around. The colours upon that stage were magnificent: the reds and blues, the yellows and reds, the whites and purples, and all the different shades of these colours. There were at least 150 people upon the stage, with room for half as many more. We would all have loved to have seen it again. It's very exciting here now, as it's raining, and we three are under an umbrella tent, and now the rain is coming in by the holes, and each one tries to shelter herself, at her neighbour's expense, from the drops. I only hope that the tent wont tumble off.

Since Monday, I have been mending and darning all day long. Friday I began to pack, it was awful, but I think I've got everything in the end. On Saturday, we caught the quarter to eleven train, and arrived here at 6.15. The latter part of the journey was lovely. The Valais is a canton composed of two ranges of mountains, with only a little narrow valley where the train passes, and arrives too.. We're at a big hotel, and have to dress at night for dinner, but our rooms are in an annex, not in the real hotel. My Swiss girl has gone on a visit, so I was left mateless, and there are three girls in Mariele's room, so we two had hoped, without much hope, that Mad, in a generous moment, would put us together. In the train, we sent Mimi, our self confident 'grandmother', to ask. At first, we heard a decided, "No," come, and then, Mimi arguing lustily. After some time, we were sent for, and made to promise that we'd be very, very good, etc., etc., etc... Well, we promised, and here we are, all alone on the top flat, but, unfortunately, just above Mad.

The view from our window is splendid; the Matterhorn rises up from behind a hill, white and superb. Then, nearer, the hillside is scattered with boulders and pines and little chalets.

Yesterday, Sunday, we went for a lovely walk in the fields, scented heavily with the myriads of pretty flowers which covered it. We also passed through a deep gorge, by a little railed path, built out of the rock. Underneath, the torrent roared and thundered, and dashed itself against the rocks. It was really awesome when you saw yourself enclosed in by steep rocky walls, with only a frail wooden path between you and the torrent beneath.

In the afternoon, we wrote in the garden, or tried to, as you will have observed. We had tea on the veranda, and, as it rained, were spared another walk. At night, coming out from supper, I saw an English picture, and called Olive's attention to it. As we looked at it, a gentleman stepped forward, and asked if we would like a little pamphlet in German — I think he took us for Germans, at first. Then, he invited us to come to a little meeting that they were holding in a dependency of the hotel. As it was in English, we jumped at the offer, and searched for Mad, who told us to bring him up. After some confab in which Mad displayed her best English, she consented to take us. We went, and it was very nice and simple. It was a band of sixty people who had come to Switzerland for 'camp'.

This morning we were up at half past five, and down at half past six, and in the train at seven. We took the train right up to the mountain top, and then climbed onto a little hillock to see the view. We were right up in the snow, and, before and behind and on all sides, were snow capped mountains, the Matterhorn solitary and imposing, and, to the left, the Brithorn or Brighthorn, the twins or Castor and Pollux, Ly something, and the Mt Rosa. Beneath us stretched a huge glacier, and the mountains, sloping gradually up, were white and thick with snow. We walked down again, from 3140 or something metres, not feet. My neck, behind, is all red with the sun, and my face too, and what numberless flowers we gathered, flowers that we'd never seen before.

Wednesday, we go on to St Luc, where we rest till August.

Thank Dorothy for her letter, and tell her that I shall write as soon as I have time — she writes killing letters.

With much love,
your loving
Flora.

Coat of Arms of Bern

-6.VIII.14.-3

SUCC. RUE DU RHÔNE

HELVETIA 25

Mrs Ewing.

48 St. Albans Rd.

Edinburgh.

Scottland.

Ecosse.

Hôtel Bella Talla
19.7.14
I have underlined all the places, upon
the envelope, that I have visited.

Dear Mother and Daddy,

Here we are, quite settled down, now, at our mountain residence. The hotel is surprisingly big and civilized, but, fortunately, very simple – delightfully so, after Zermatt with its toilettes, its bands and its swank. St Luc is a tiny village perched upon the mountain side, with a most splendid view. The village opens up at the two ends, and at one end you see the snow capped peaks of the Matterhorn, etc., and at the other, the valley opens out wide, wide, showing long stretches of forests and fields, with little yellow ribbons flowing here and there which are the roads. Then, higher up, the snow begins again. Beneath us, down in the valley, a river runs, and along the sides are groups of little brown villages and forests.

On Tuesday last, we climbed up to another mountain hotel. It was a frightfully hot day, and, in about an hour, I was finished. Mad saw it, and, as one of the girls was on mule back, she made her get off, and put me on, instead. Oh, how thankful I was! After that, I pulled along all right enough. After dinner at the hotel, we went outside, and sprawled about, admiring the view. We were just at the foot of the Matterhorn. I went for a roam, and managed to find two tiny bits of Edelweiss. We then decided to pack up; that went quick enough, anyhow. I'm getting quite expert in packing up, I can assure you. I can get about two tons of things of all sorts and sizes into my little handbag. I generally have to sit on it before it'll shut, but that's a mere detail. On Wednesday we set off for St Luc. At Viège we changed the train, and sat in the station and ate sandwiches and cherries, to the onlookers' great amusement. Then we remounted, and went on to Sierre.

Here we got out, and went up to a beautiful old château, turned into an hotel. Here we read, and dined, and played patience, till three o'clock, when we went into the courtyard where four dog carts were awaiting us. We mounted, and off we went, in Indian file. The road was very wild, with big mountains on either side, and lakes and streams. Fortunately, it dident slope much, but winded round and round the mountain side. Once, we had to get out and walk, but, otherwise, all went well. Sometimes, we passed along the edge of a precipice, and the cart rocked so much that we thought that our last hour had come. Farther along, the path was hewn out of the rock, and there were tunnels, and all sorts of interesting things. Then, we called a halt at an inn, and provisions were handed round. Then it started to rain, and up went the umbrellas, mine, of course, had got torn away from two of its spokes, but, nothing daunted, I held the whole side where Mad could see it, and the other where she couldent. We arrived at the village at last, from which we had to walk. We sheltered in an old barn till the worst was passed, and then set off again.. About half way up, the rain came on again, and this time it rained in earnest, then it started to thunder, and the rain fell in bucket fulls. On and on we struggled bravely, getting soaked and soakeder every minute. Never was I out in such weather; it seemed as if the skys had opened up, and the water was rushing out. The little mountain path became a rushing stream, in which we had to wade. The water rushed off in streams from our umbrellas, and the girls without their coats were soaked to the skin, and our skirts could have been rung (sic) out, and our feet squelched out the water in our boots. On the way up, we passed a broken tree, and I thought it looked rather newly fallen. Then we met some peasants, taking shelter, who seemed to be very excited. These told us, with many gestures, that the lightening had struck down an enormous tree, just a little while ago. Just think: if we hadent been delayed in the old barn, we might have got the tree upon our crowns. At long last, we got to the hotel, and Mad said that we were all to go straight off to bed, and get a hot drink, but the landlady said that supper was just ready, etc., etc., etc... so we took some hot soup and tea and pudding, and scuttled off to bed. Next morning, we breakfasted at nine or half past, and then unpacked. In some rooms, there were only two drawers, and two nails upon the walls, and only one cupboard in all the six rooms.

We dident do much the first day, only moutching (sic) around a bit. We have a room where we can sit all undisturbed, and here we always have tea. It's so funny: Mad has a spirit lamp, and she boiled the water for the tea, and we had milk and dry bread and chocolates. Afterwards, we went for a walk, till supper time. Since then, we have done nothing special, only walking, reading aloud, and doing fancy work. Tomorrow we are probably going for a long excurtion (sic) up to an hotel perched upon criegl, the neighbouring peaks, and from there we are to gather Eidelweise.

Sometimes it's frightfully cold, here, and sometimes frightfully hot. At night, all the girls complain of the cold, and demand huge eiderdowns, etc., but I feel the cold only when

I wake up in the night, and have to fish for the blankets etc., which repose in a heap upon the floor.

I was awfully sorry to hear about the fire at Greenfield, that lovely house; is it reparable at all, the damage? Is the cause or the fire known yet, and Maud and her trousseau.

It was awfully good of Mr McPherson to give you a watch bracelet, and, still more so, that he has remembered us too. Ought I to write, or would it do if you thanked him for me, as I hardly know him at all, and spoke once in my life to him, and don't think he even knew who he was speaking to. Are you going to the sea side or to the country, this time? You will notice that I have still put your Edinburgh address upon the envelope, but Dorothy had written your address as Peebles, and I wasent sure if it wasent Peebles or not, so I wait for your next letter to be sure. Is Daddy going with you, again, or is he going to lead the simple life again, with cream and fruits again?

We went to the Catholique Church today, only for the sermon, not for the Mess (sic).it was very queer and funny, but the people all looked so reverent. After church, there was a procession of all the congregation, a lot of the women being in white overalls, the men being in white overalls too. Behind these, came the ordinary people.

Poor Phyllis, she has her birthday tomorrow, and her letter isent finished yet. I must run.

With much love,
your loving
Flora.

Hôtel Bella Tola
26.7.14

My dear Daddy and Mother,

It's a case of, 'Germans to right of me, Germans to left of me, Germans behind me, who volley and thunder.', and it's awful. The hotel is half full of Germans, with four solitary English, not counting our Pens. My scrawl is, perhaps, more scrawlish than ever, today, as I'm writing upon my knee, in the verandah.

Every day is very excited, just now, as the news has just come that war is declared between Austria and Serbia. If there's one country that I detest, and thoroughly too, it's Austria: nasty, horrid, bossy, greedy, quarrelsome, priggish place. We've just been having the Balkan war in history, and there it was that my love for Austria grew. Since then, it is progressing rapidly. The best of it is, that the nation, for the most part is thoroughly disgusted with its government. Our Autrichien waxes eloquent with richous (sic)!!! wrath upon the subject.

The people at the hotel are so interesting, and, for the most part, very nice. There are four Germans, two couples, who are very interesting. One man is big, broad, walks with a swank worthy of a negro chief, or highland chieftain, with a huge head, covered with tightly curling fair hair. When he came, he was promptly nicknamed William Tell by some people who had seen the play, and found that he resembled the character. Then, another person came, who titled him 'Parsifal'. we discussed him together and were sure that he was nothing less than a great actor or singer, with his poses and sure manner, and accustomed to admiration, etc. walk. We thought that he was travelling incognito, and that his wife was a great pianist, as we heard her playing, often. Well, upon looking into the visitors' book, we found that his occupation was that of a 'School Master'!!! What a downfall for us – and for him. His wife is very nice too. Only the other day, whilst Mariela was playing the piano in the drawing room, who should come in but 'Madame Parsifal', as we call her, with a bundle of music, and said that she could have it to play, if she liked. She also offered to play for us when we wanted to dance, anytime. Just had an agreeable diversion, but must first describe the three–man, who glories in the nickname of, 'The Dentist', as he wears a white lounge jacket in the house. Well, we were less taken with him than with the others, as he dident show any signs of high art, etc., but, all the same, he had very nice merry little eyes, and a fat, jovial face, and round, well stuffed body. Well, yesterday, we went for an all day excurtion, so about half a dozen got left behind, and these wiled away the shining hours, in conversation with the four Germans. When we returned, we found them all raving over the 'Deutches'. The Dentist, especially, charmed them, he proving himself to be quite accomplished, speaking English with the English, and German with the Germans, and French for fun.

Today, we were sitting in the verandah, one or two of us, and the Dentist began talking. I was writing quietly, when, suddenly, someone behind me said, "Edinburgh is one of the finest cities that I have ever seen." Naturally, I pricked up my ears, and turned round. It was the Dentist, and he was speaking to me. I stammered out, "Oui, oui! N'est–ce pas?" or something similar, and it was quite a minute before it dawned upon me that I'd better reply in English. Of course, I spoke very slowly and difficultly, but I was comforted by a nice compliment. He said, "You speak so beautifully clearly that I understand everything that you say, perfectly." I said that that was because you had to articulate very clearly, in French, and that had helped my English, as I was always blamed for speaking indistinctly, at home; also, it's English which is practically a foreign language for me now. Well, we chatted away for a bit, till we had to go upstairs for the service, there being no Protestant church, here. After the service, Mad read us a bit about the ultimatum that Austria had chucked at poor little Serbia, and I have invented a few more very explicite (sic) and polite adjectives about dear, good Austria. Well, to continue about the Dentist, when we descended again, he was still there, and we spoke a bit, in between the writing of letters.. After a bit, he departed, and then came back to the window, and made signs for us to open it. I opened it, and he shoved in three packets of chocolate, and then fled. We yelled, "Thank you very much," and, " Wielen danke," after his disappearing form, and then settled down to dispose of it. It divided out equally, there being half a packet for each one. I, like a silly, ate mine at once, and am now waiting the results, as I'd been feeling a little sick in the morning, and was just feeling better — you see: I'm just as caracterless (sic) as ever.

There are two school teachers who <u>are</u> just the real type, one is fair, quiet, prim and proper, with a face as placid as a summer sea; the other is dark, plump, nearly gay, and very sweet, with a great respect for her evidently intelligent compagnon (sic). There is a typically French family too: Father, who screams his nationality, long faced, pointed beard, thin, and with a face absolutely void of expression. The mother looks very nice, walks badly, and has an untidy coiffure; another, the aunt, probably, is a tiny wee bit thing, with beautiful black hair, looks tired and fussy, possesses a silly little dog, which she orders about in a most ridiculous manner; a grandmother, who resembles all other grandmothers; and two children, a girl and boy, perfect French types, with their yellow skins, dark eyes and hair. They are very nice, both, and we talk sometimes; as to their ages, I am in the dark: the girl might have twelve to fifteen, the boy, fourteen to sixteen. You cant judge here, French children's ages. There is another funny couple too, the man, sour, tall and glum, the woman, tall, thin, ugly and dull, with a weakness for green blouses. You see them hanging round the grounds, or setting off sourly for a walk, but never do you see them laugh together, and they seem to have also realised that silence is golden, as they keep it studiously when together. But, at table, the scene is changed: all of a sudden, a tremendous bellow causes us all to jump and to turn round, and there we see our taciturn sour face hee–hawing and haw–haw–in at some joke of his own invention, whilst, all around, the ladies tee–he, in a chorus. Madame sour–face, however, does not share her husband's gaiety. Probably, she is trying to calculate how her boring and uninteresting husband becomes so brilliant and so witty as soon as he is out of her immediate clutches. There is also another man, that we call the 'black man', as he has black hair, black piercing eyes, a hooked nose and black beard, from whom we fly at top speed whenever he comes our way. He lives on the same flat as us, and so we are kept running all the time. Oh, there are heaps that would be worth describing but I guess that doesent interest you much.

On Monday, we climbed to the Weisshorn hotel, placed upon a hill, nearby. It was a two hours climb, but the road was very good, so we weren't much tired. We had to walk along the mountain top for two hours after arriving. Then, Mad wanted to descend about a mile for milk and butter, and then reascend again. One half of us wanted to go down, the other, not. Suddenly, Mad saw a whole herd of cows grazing peaceably below. Instantaneously, she said, "Er — er, it really isent worth while going down there," and fled. Ever after that, we keep yelling, when we don't want to go anywhere, "Mademoiselle, theres a cow, there!" We dined at ten, and returned to the hotel, and teaed at two.

Next day, we reposed, and the next, it was a girl's birthday, so we three others in her room got up at five and went out to pick flowers. We brought in heaps, and decorated a table most beautifully, with pines roses and cornflowers. I made the garlands, that being my forte. We made a very pretty one for her plate at table. At tea, we had a big cake, which Mad provides for the birthdays. We took tea out in the fields, under an old mill roof, as it came on rain. It was so romantic, all sitting under an old leaky roof, munching cake and milk, whilst the rain fell in torrents outside. We returned, all in the rain. Next day, it was a little boy's birthday, and, at dinner, we found on our table a lovely huge cake, and a plate of smaller cakes, besides. These were from the little boy, by his own desire, as he had received such a lot of cakes and sweets. After dinner, we collected the children, ourselves included, into the salon, shoved tables, chairs, etc. out of the road, and we played musical chairs; winking; hunt the thimble; find the ring etc., etc.. We did have fun, and then we had cakes for tea, again. At night, after supper, three of us collected all the youth available, and played snap or beggar my neighbour, the latter game lasted all the evening, as, as soon as one had no more cards, another shoved some under the table, and so the game went on. It was so funny when something had to be explained, as there were two German boys who understood nothing else, a French girl and boy, and two English girls. Now, Miss Lyon dictated her ideas to me in English, and I struggled bravely to translate them into a French a little comprehensible to the Frenchies, and then we were stuck, as my German does not allow explications of any volubility. Happily, we found a little boy, who spoke both French and German equally, and he translated into German for me — and there we went. Next day, we hung round a bit, reading and embroidering, in the morning, and nothing special afterwards, except that we went to bed at nine.

Next day, at four in the morning, my alarm went off — brrrrrrrrrrrr! until out of my sweet slumbers I came. Then Milette woke up, and shoved the beastly thing under the bed–clothes, but nothing could dampen — or deaden — the ardeur (sic) of the alarm, and, at last, it dawned upon Milette's waking brain that she was being wakened with a definite purpose, and out she hauled the clock, again, still screeching gaily. Then, the porter came, and banged upon the door, and we, to show how good we were, yelled out, "Merci!" before he'd hardly touched the door. Then I said, "Milette, get up! or you'll never be ready." Milette grunted; a bit later: "Milette, are you asleep? Get up, will you!" Milette: "Get up, yourself, etc..." then, I said, "Milette, its half past four!" Milette: "Liar!" (Its French equivalent isent as strong!). Then I said that it was a quarter to five. This startled Milette, considerably. At last, I got them out of bed, after half an hour. I stayed for an extra ten minutes, so was ten or a quarter of an hour late for breakfast. At five or half past, we started off for the Bella Tola, a five hours walk — on and on we trudged, in the fresh morning air. After about an hour, we rested, and there we met a little lame lady, who was making for the same place as we. She, in spite of her nearly useless leg, arrived on top before us. We marched through water, marshes bogs, fields, streams, snow and flowers, oh, such lovely flowers: blues, yellows, purples, whites, reds, greens, browns, all mixed together. In spite of the fact that they had to nearly haul me the last bit, we arrived in four hours and one half. Arrived on top, we had to walk along the top to the highest summit, and, for once, arrived on top, there was a valley below, on the other side, where we saw the Rhône, and above, a long chain of mountains, the Jungfrau, etc…., and, on the other side, we saw the Mt Blanc. The one drawback to the situation was the cold. It was freezing cold up there, and there was a very strong wind, too. We were surrounded by snow, on all sides. Well, we all snuggled down in a heap, with our capes etc., and ate a bite or two, and then descended as quickly as possible, absolutely frozen, in spite of our thick capes. Some of them had their hands frozen and useless.

Once down a bit lower, we found a place a bit sheltered, and took our dinner, and then reposed. I placed myself upon my back in the sun. Then, M. Bernoud, a gentleman who always comes with us everywhere, and who is <u>most</u> amusing, he proposed that we should return by the Weisshorn. Mad refused, plump, but we all made such a fuss that she let us go with him, whilst she returned with one of us. We walked for two and a half hours, and arrived to find the hotel empty, except for one visitor. Poor Milette, her aunt and cousin and friends had been there, and she had hoped to meet them again, but they were gone, just that morning. We emptied three or four jam pots for five girls – not bad? And three times we had to call for hot water and bread. I drank six cups of tea. M Bernoud is a caracter (sic), really. He has a knock out word for every occasion, and makes fun of everybody and everything. Yesterday Mad emptied a whole can of tea into his pocket, and soaked his handky. At tea, he convulsed us with his remarks upon the adventure. Today, at dinner, he informed us that he had washed his handky and ironed it himself. His daughter had been ironing out some blouses, so he thought he'd like to do that too, so he hauled out his handky, and ironed it, himself. He also discussed the fashions with Mad, at table. His opinion was that, as the men were now wearing open necks, the women would wear collars up to the nose; also that, in a few years, the men would be showing their sholders (sic). All together, we walked ten hours, yesterday. When I arrived at the hotel, my face was, without exaggeration, the colour of a boiled beetroot, even that would have looked wishie–washie beside me. I shone, simply, and after a layer of glycerine, I illuminated all my paths. At night at supper, people stared horribly. At night, in bed, Mad came in with some flour, and, after putting on some Vaseline, she floured me all over. In going out she spilt all the flowers onto the floor. This morning, the flour had stuck to my face, and I couldent wash it well, as it was too tender, so I am a beauty, as you can imagine. The supper bell is ringing, so I must fly.

These are the new stamps. I bought them specially for Dorothy. The man is William Tell, the Swiss hero.

With much love,
your loving Flora.

Hôtel Bella Tola
2nd Aug. 1914

My dear Mother and Daddy,

We are in a jolly state of excitement, I can tell you, that's to say, the country and some of the girls – of course, I am not interested in the number. On Friday night, the retreat was sounded all over Switzerland, for the reserves and soldiers to get ready to be called out at any minute, to the frontier. Yesterday afternoon, the men from the village were called down to head-quarters Visoix, and will not return. Also, yesterday, being the first of Aug., the anniversary of the foundation of Switzerland, there are always very high jinks, but, of course, with such an unrest all over, we celebrated it very quietly. In the morning, we stayed at home, and did what we liked – I dident, as I had to write a letter. After dinner, half past three, we all went into the dining room, and helped to decorate it a bit. We arranged flowers all round the table, forming a long wreath of red and white flowers. Then we placed feathery fine branches above all the doors, and hanging from the ceiling. Then M. Bernoud brought some flags, and we placed them in the fruit dishes, and, as the wall paper was red, they put white paper crosses upon it, forming, thus wise, the national flag. altogether it was very pretty. I am getting heaps of ideas for decorations, etc. these days, so perhaps I shall be able to make myself useful in that direction, when I return.

After our efforts, we ascended to dress, putting on our smarts for a bang out supper. Its spiffing sitting next to M. Bernoud at table, as, when there is anything nice for supper, he always serves me twice as much again. At dessert, he takes four or five fruits in his pocket for me, and then I divide them out afterwards, with the others. Yesterday we had ices, and, as they had taken away my plate before he had been served, he said, "Oh, take the bread plate," and he promptly emptied the bread onto the table, put a spoonful of ice onto it, and handed it to me. Naturally, I had no spoon, so he said, "Take a fork." This I did, to the table's amusement. Then he filled his pockets with pears for me, and then forgot one, which he found all squashed up in his pocket this morning. During the supper, three children came round carrying a cushion full of flags, which they distributed amongst the diners, and then handed round a plate for contributions in aide (sic) of a fund to get a clock into the village. They got £3 something. If it hadent been for this beastly war, we would have had bonfires upon all the mountains, and fireworks, and village choirs, and heaps more decorations etc.

Olive has just received a letter from home saying that her father couldent come to bring her home, as all the officers were forbidden to leave the country. Poor kid, since last Christmas she has talked of nothing else than, "When Papa comes." And she had the exact minute that he was to arrive at Genève, months ago, also she had the plan of the voyage that she was going to make, sent her last March, I think, and has talked of nothing else but, "When I shall be at Lucerne," or, "I shall do this or that at Rome," etc., etc…until we were frankly sick of her, her Papa and her beastly voyages. Last week, she received a complete time–table of her voyage: at what time she would arrive at Lucerne, at what time she would leave it, and all. Now, its all paff, of course, and the poor thing is white with emotion. But really, it was silly to plan the whole thing so far in advance, and to get so excited over it all. Mad used to scold her, and tell her that something would crack or happen, if she excited herself so. She says she prefers to wait till all will be quiet again, when her father will be able to come for her. We tell her not to get so down in the mouth, as all isent lost yet, the war not being altogether begun yet, and, too, lots may happen in a month's time. At any rate, we're quite out of any danger, here in Switzerland, as S. is a country which takes nobody's part, only receiving the wounded and fugitives, and preventing the enemies to cross her as a short cut to the attack. Poor little country, things may go hard with her, if the neighbouring countries profit of all the general fuss to annex all the bits coveted for many a long day. They're a good bit nervous of the Italians, who have regarded the Grisons from afar, with an ever increasing interest. Genève will be France's tit–bit, and Bâle etc., will fall to Germany, but this will only happen if the war really does take place — and we are all fairly optimistic, still. In the towns, the excitement is great. People are besieging the shops for provisions, and are laying in stores for months. The trains are stopped, communications cut off, strangers are flying home pell–mell. On Friday, no less than twelve visitors took to their heels, and more fly every day. People, who were to have come, have cancelled their orders. They say that the strangers ae given three days to return home. After that, no one can go in or out of his country. In the village, here, there is no more sugar to be got, nor petrol. Tomorrow, the porter has to go to join his regiment, and the chefs will be called out soon, too. M. Bernoud has offered to clean the shoes, but his offer has not been accepted. If the chefs go, we shall be in a pretty pickle.

We are continually receiving telegrams containing the

latest scares; so much so that we never know what to believe. Tomorrow the French family leave. It's a pity as now I'll have nobody to play cards with, at night, also, they were really very nice, the children.

One lady here is not feeling extra comfy, I can tell you. She had a son at school, in Bordeaux, and when the alarm spread, the school closed, and, since then, the mother has had no news of her boy. She has telephoned and telegramed to Lyon, her home, but can get no reply, as the communication is cut off, now.

The other day, we went for a walk down to visit a most picturesque little village. It was such a funny little place. The little wooden chalets huddled up against each other, looking as if they were supporting one another, and they had good need to be supported, too. They looked as if a push would send them toppling, and the dirt…Oh, they were dirty, and so queer. Mad once made a really good joke upon the villages, only it turned out to be not original, afterwards. She said, "Do you know why the air in the Valais is so much purer and sweeter than elsewhere? – Because the peasants always keep their windows shut!!" That's true, you very rarely find an open window, in your voyages round the villages. We also went inside the village church, to see a very valuable old picture which hangs there.

On Friday, we started at nine, and walked all morning, camped for dinner, and then sprawled about for the rest of the afternoon. I got a little more burned there, and then forgot all about it, and washed my face naturally. The skin is pealing (sic) off again. I was a lovely guy for a time, with my pealing (sic) face, shiny nose and crimson complexion. It's a bit soberer now, but my skin still glistens in the sun or electric light. Talking about lights, yesterday, when the ice came in, all the lights went out, and the ice lit up the room, (not quite) but, in the middle of the plate was a shape in real ice, and in the inside of this there was a candle light of some kind. The shapes were red or white, and looked so pretty in the dark room.

Do tell me a bit how England stands in all this muddle, as the news is all tipsy curvy here, and I cant make head or tail of it.

What an awful shock poor Maud must have got upon finding all her trousseau gone, and a year's work done for nothing, but she seems to be very brave about it, all the same.

Does Daddy stay with you, or with himself, at St Albans Road?

We are having quite decent weather, now, much too hot for gallivanting over the country side, as we have to.

Do you know, nobody ever knows what nation I belong to. Olive, they recognise at first sight, but me...One of the girls said she thought I was a German, at first. Today, I picked up an English lady's spectacle case, or something, and she thanked me in the most excruciating French. It was killing. I'm beginning to be able to recognise the foreign accents of those foreigners who try to speak French, now. I think the English French accent is the funniest.

It appears that the village curé's maid is a bit of a tartar, and that she has a strong aversion for Protestants of all kinds. When they visit the curé she hardly lets them in, and is frightfully rude. Also, when she doesent want him to go anywhere she just doesent let him. M. Bernoud told us some killing stories about her. The latest is, that war has begun between Russia and Germany, but nobody believes it yet. Let's hope that we'll never have cause to believe it.

With much love,
your loving
Flora.

Hôtel Bella Tola
9th Aug. 1914

My dear Daddy and Mother,

It's queer writing a letter when you don't know when it will arrive. They say that letters take fifteen days to come. My last letter probably went gallivanting round Italy, and has got stuck somewhere, so I don't suppose that you've got it yet. I havent got yours yet, at any rate. Perhaps I shall get it today, but I havent great hopes. Olive is in the same pickle, only she was to have returned in about two weeks, and she doesent know what to do at all, they say its impossible to go in or out of England, the same all the other countries, so I don't know how she's going to manage it. I'm jolly glad that you hadent made any arrangements for my return yet because, like that, I hadent got myself excited up just to get squashed again. I sort of feel that I have a long time to wait yet.

The war seems to be getting more and more serius (sic), and the people more and more anxious (however do you spell those words.) it will be an awful thing if this war does come, fancy all Europe up in arms. The girls here are pretty anxious, the Germans specially. Mariele has four brothers and goodness knows how many uncles and cousins, who must all go to fight; just imagine, four brothers under arms, all in different regiments. She says it would be nothing short of a miracle if all four escaped, and its frightfully true, too. Her sister's husband, married last month, must go too, tho' only as a doctor. Nearly all have brothers who must go. If England mobilizes Olive's father must go too. Isent Mr Robbie a reservist, or something?

If so, isent he called out too?

It was last Sunday night that we learned that Russia and Germany were going to war, and that they were already fighting. Monday we learned that Russians had invaded Germany. They also said that the English had bombarded Hamburg and had put the town in flames – this we did not believe. Since then the news has continued to get worse and worse, also nobody has had a letter from home for a week, at least, and some, for a fortnight.

Monday, the village warriors got into their uniforms, and prepared to go down to headquarters. We went to see them when the curé, etc., said farewell, and it was really horrible. Some of the men had their eyes all red and hard, with the tears they were holding back. Others joked and laughed bravely. The women cried a lot, too.

Nearly all the men have had to go, and its just hay making time, so the women have had to turn and do the men's work, too; not that the addition will be very great, as it's the women who do all the dirty or heavy work here, and the men who become fair and fat. I could give you a very good example of this. The other day, coming back through the fields, we met a man and his wife bringing in the hay. Here, there are no roads, only little paths, so they cant bring in the hay in carts, but must carry it. Well, the wife led the way, with an enormous load of hay upon her head, one of the biggest loads I ever saw a woman carrying; she simply disappeared under it. Behind her came Mr Peasant, hopping along, balancing a tiny load of hay upon *his* head. It's the same thing all over.

Yesterday, Mlle Marie went up to the curé, and asked if we couldent help the women a bit, and he mentioned some deserving cases to her. That afternoon, we set off, armed with big wooden rakes, to our destination. On the way, a little girl stopped us and asked us to lend a hand, so we left four of our number, and continued. The walk was pretty stiff, and it was awfully hot. At length, we arrived, and we divided up again. Two went down to help some women in a field below; Mad and another mounted a bit higher; and we three last, found a field further on. We three had the best time, I think, as the work wasent a bit hard, and, after finishing one field, we remounted to go to another. On the way, we passed the woman's house, and she stopped, and brought out some simply spiffing cheese, and let each cut ourselves a slice. It tasted just like slightly soured milk. Then we finished the other field, and came up again. This time, she invited us in, and gave us the hard brown bread that the peasants eat, with some more of the delicious cheese, and also some lovely cold chocolate. Really, I never, never tasted chocolate so good, perfectly cold and sweet. Then we said goodbye and went to find the others. We found them, all working like niggers, but they stopped when we arrived, and we all had tea, bread and cheese — not a patch on ours — and cold water. Then each one told her tale. Mad had helped a poor woman with five little children who had worked all the day before, and had baked her bread all night, and had been in the field all day. They got in all her hay for her, and the poor thing was most awfully grateful. Some of them had even tried to carry the hay upon their heads, like the peasants. Those left behind had had to work on a very sloping hill, and been more on the ground than upon their feet, but they received wine from the peasants and were home long before we were. The village cure was there, and he worked harder than any.

Bye the way, have you kept any of my letters? As there are one or two I would rather have liked to have read, those upon the Centenaire, etc…

I hope you will get this letter in less than fifteen days.

With much love,
your loving,
Flora.

Money is frightfully scarce here, so I enclose this letter. Please put a penny stamp on, and post it. That saves me 2 ½ c, and you 1 ½ d. I do hope it isent too heavy.

ST-LUC
(VALAIS)
STATION SIERRE
SÉJOURS ALPESTRE ET
DE REPOS DE 1ER ORDRE

GRAND HOTEL ET PENSION
BELLA-TOLA
GABRIEL PONT, PROPR.
DOCTEUR ATTACHÉ A L'HOTEL

2.nd Aug. 1914.

My Dear Mother and Daddy.

We are in a jolly state of excitement I can tell you, that's to say the country and some of the girls, of course I am not included in the number. On Friday night the retreat was sounded all over Switzerland, for the reserves and soldiers to get ready to be called out at any minute to the frontier. Yesterday afternoon, the men from the village were called down to headquarters Visoix, and will not return. Also yesterday

Château Blanc
23rd Aug. 1914

My dear Daddy and Mother,

Here I am, writing another 'doubtful' letter. I only wrote a P.C. last time, but decided to risk a letter, this time. It will arrive some day, I suppose. The last letter received from you was dated 2nd Aug. It arrived at about the 14th or 15th. Since then, I have had nothing. The Reavells are in a great state about 'Pa Pa', who, to war, must go. Olive is determined to return, as her mother wants her to, but how she is to do it is a mystery, as there are no trains, no nuffin'. Mad went to the English Consul to see if there weren't any English trying to get back. He said, "What do you want to return for? You are a thousand times better off here; it's only folly to want to return." He said there was a train being organised for English, but, if it happened to be needed for soldiers, then you were liable to be left on the lurch half way between there and back again. Also, from Genève to Paris takes thirty hours, and the crossing, eight or nine. Cant you see me thirty hours in a stuffy French train, or <u>nine</u> hours on board!!!! Well, that was squash no one, but then Mad heard of a gentleman returning to London, so she went to see him, but he said that the voyage would be frightfully dangerous, and he really dident know if he could return, or if he could take the responsibility of a girl upon him. Olive has telegraphed for money, in case she should be able to return. Mad told this to us both, but I said that I thought it better to bide still until I heard from you again as, if I telegraphed, "Send money, can perhaps return," and you had written, "Stay where you are for the moment," everything would be in a muddle. They say too, that, later on, it will be much easier to voyage, and much less expensive. A passport costs 10/–, and that only to Paris, where you have to fork out another 10/–. Then you have to spend several nights en route, and, of course, the voyage itself is twice as dear. Everyone says that its much better to stay where we are, and, in any case, one cant do much else, at present.

We are very well here, in no danger whatever, and are living very quietly and economically. We eat plain food, but get plenty. Mad insists upon our eating properly, so as to be well armed for all that might happen. We discuss politics ardently between us, and nearly don't squabble at all – only with Mad, who is dead against the Germans, and all for the French. This morning, we four started discussing the Alsace Lorraine bisaness (sic). Two of us were Germans, one Swiss, and one Scot — here, I am very Scotch, and everyone makes a great difference between the two nations, the Scots being more liked than the English. Well, Lia, an ardent German, waxed eloquent on why Alsace should belong to Germany, and why it seemed to want to stay French. I learned that, until Louis XIV's time, Alsace belonged to Germany. Then Louis bagged it, and the Germans were not strong enough to retake it. Also, the French said to the Alsaciens, if you will just turn French you can do this that and the next thing, so the A.s said, "Very well, we'll become French, and do this that and the next thing," then they settled down, and found life pleasant, and soon became good Frenchies. Then, in '70, when their motherland hauled them back by the ears, and gave them bread and water diet to bring them back to their senses, they howled and dident want to become German again. They found it much nicer to be French and to be dirty and slack and lazy. Now the French tell them that, if they come back, they can be dirty and lazy to their hearts content again. That's the Germans' version of it, and, I must say that I've great sympathy for the Germans, but also for the Alsacians, as, in two hundred years, one has well the time to forget that ones not what one looks like. Mad is all for the Alacians, of course, and she and Lia have had some high old rows, lately. Hi! I hope I aint a'givin' political news, else my letter wont never arrive to its destination, but will fall into some unfeeling waste paper basket, in the middle of France.

Letters are frightfully scarce here; only the Austrians ever get anything. I only hope that I wont have to wait another three weeks before I shall receive your next letter. We are only nine, now, and next week a cousin is coming to fetch the Austrians. They arent sisters, but they, "All go the same way home." Then, we'll be only six. Mad says that then we'll live all the time in the veranda and little drawing room, just like a little family. At supper we have stopped the meat – to everyone's delight – and we get such nice things instead: sometimes potatoes roasted in their skins, and eaten with butter and cheese. This is scrumptious; you should really try it; other times Welsh rabbit; other times porridge, and, always, stewed fruits, sometimes with rice or semolina, for dessert. Then we go for a walk, to digest it.

Lessons havent begun seriously, yet, but in the morning we have a dictation or translation, and recite prose learned the night before, till eleven or half past. Then, we embroider and read aloud about Italian freak saints, who see stars, or rather, visions, and are altogether impossible, etc., till four, when we tea. Bye the way, I have a wondrous piece of news to tell. In the dictations, Olivette or Mimi were always the first, but this last week I had generally less mistakes than Mimi, even, but not less than Olive, of course, and yesterday, I turned out with three, and Olivette with five. I nearly dropped through the floor. The Dictées are always first sight. But I shouldn't really boast, as both Olive and Mimi are in a pretty excited state these last days. All the same, however, I really have made some real progress in speaking and in pronounciation (sic) this last month, thanks to St Luc, where we were amongst real French people, and were able to talk to them and hear them talking, also we read an awful amount of books, in spite of all the walks, talks and letters we wrote. Now that I've been blowing my own trumpet like that, I shall have to take jolly good care, or else I'll be having my old number of errors again.

Have you heard any more of the newly weds these days, and of how that marvellous son and h'air is doing. We had an awful laugh, the other day, upon that word. We were talking about books, and, somehow, the 'Heir of Redcliffe' came up. Then, Mad, bursting with pride, said, "Oh, yes, I've read it; isent it so sad, this 'Hair of Redcliffe.'" I collapsed behind a chair, whilst Miss Lyon took a fit of convulsions, upon the spot. Then Mad spotted me, and demanded if it was the remembrance of the book that was making me cry!! She's ridiculously proud of her English, and if only she knew what a hash she makes of it! I hear Mad's murmuring soft and low. I wonder if she makes such a hash as Flora does of her spelling!

Oh, I must tell you something: last Tuesday, M Bernoud came to see us, and we wouldent let him go; we held him to his seat when he tried to escape. At last, Mad came and delivered him, and then he invited her and us to tea for Thursday. We yelled with delight, and Mad accepted. Thursday we sallied out in muslins sweet, at 3 o' clock. On arriving, M. Bernoud took us round the garden, and brought us to a stop under a greengage tree. This he shook and poked until the fruit rained down upon us. We gobbled them down at an express rate, and they were good. For quarter of an hour we gobbled, and then went in to tea. Here we ate buns upon buns, and two slices of greengage tarts. After tea, we went straight out and started with more vigour than ever. The last fruit that I ate would hardly, hardly go down, and I hoped desperately that M. Bernoud wouldent offer me any more.

He, Mrs and Miss are coming tonight after supper, and we have had to arrange a programme for them, as usual. Well, last night at supper the girls started yelling that I'd got to sing, too, this time. I refused flat, and continued to do so, in spite of all. Mad was there, but she was writing a P.C., and dident pay any attention to the row. I more'n half guessed as what she dident want to hear. That's why I refused. But in the bed room, Milette began again to make a fuss, so I said, Oh, very well, I'll try something tomorrow, just to see how it goes, and, if Mad asks me, perhaps I'll sing. I've said it flat that I shant open my mouth if Mad doesent ask me to, and I'm pretty certain that she wont, although the girls are going to yell out my name. You see, it is so painful and ridiculous of me to try and sing when Olive is there with her magnificent voice; she makes progress every day, that girl! Everyone who hears her says what a wonderful voice she has. I guess her parents will be delightfully surprised when she returns, as she has changed tremendously. She came, a pigtailed, short skirted flighty school girl, and she returns, a sedate, long skirted, proper pattern, finished 'young lady', in all senses of the word. I s'pose I ought to envy her a bit – but I don't! My mottoe (sic) is 'Your only once young' so be young whilst you *are* young. In consequence, I aint sedate, I aint proper, I aint pattern, I aint finished, and I AINT a young lady!!! I'm just a chrysalis, and a rotten one with that, I guess, as yet. The only thing I have done really here is to get fat! And I have done that, I can tell you!!

I wonder when you will get this letter, its disgusting the time the letters take to come and go.

Do you have to economise too? Its rather fun, except when you cant have butter and jam for tea on Sundays, as usual.

I really must stop now, as I must arrange my coiffure, done very hastily this morning, as we talked politics till quarter past eight, and breakfast was at half past!

With much love,
your loving
Flora.

Flora is a very nice girl, and I am very contend to sleep with her. Excuse me, but I am a very impertinante girl. Milette.

Château Blanc
26th August 1914

My dear Mother and Daddy,

Olive is returning home today, with a lady and family who return too, so I am writing this with the intention of giving it to her to post in London. I was dressing calmly at the window when suddenly Lyon yelled up, "Arent you going to write a letter to your parents and give it to Olive?" I was out of the room and downstairs in two tics, and am now scrawling for all I'm worth. I wonder if you've received all my letters; I've written every week, as usual. I, as yet, have only received your letter of the 2nd Aug, but the other will come soon, I hope.

Bye the way, I have a bit of news for you. Olive's uncle has a personal friend out here, and he wrote him asking him to take Olive with him if he was retuning. Well, he wasent returning yet, but his wife's friend was, so he has arranged everything for Olive, and was so good, running all over the town for her. Well, he said he was returning about the last week in September, so Mad said she had two other English girls who would also like to return, and would he be prepared to take them with him when he went. He consented at once, and said he would do all for us too, also, he's a personal friend of Mr Reavell (uncle) and very, very nice, and trustworthy. Mad is very cross with Olive because she is going now, as its so very uncertain, and risky voyaging these times. She thinks that things will be in a better condition later on.

We are in a most awful condition just now. I, for one, don't know if I'm on my heels or my head, with all the fuss there is about. Yesterday, our three Austrians departed with a cousin come to fetch them. Oh, the scurries and the worries and the bothers until they were once safely off. At the station they were to meet two other girls from another Pensionnat, so they were a gay party, a whole Pensionnat, as they said. After the carriage had gone, we went along the road a bit, till we came to a level crossing, where we awaited the train. Hilde and I got up onto the wall, and when the station mistress wanted us to get down, we just dident!!. The train passed so close, and we saw them splendidly again. I had taken my apron with me to wave, and it acted splendidly. Now we are very quiet and lonely, as we are six, only, in this huge house; at table its so funny. Happily, our room is quite full still, we four having to stick where we are, but all the other rooms are empty, except that of Miss Lyon, who is all alone

We are getting a few lessons each day, but nothing special, also its been impossible to half prepare them with all the fuss we've been having these last few days. One afternoon I shall never forget, as long as I live, I think. We were all in the school room supposed to be doing prep, but we weren't. Lyon, from the back seat, was screeching and yelling at the girls to come and pay for this, that and the other thing, and the girls were refusing and arguing at the top of their voices. Then, in the second seat, Milette was yelling at us to come and tell her what books we wanted. And we were yelling back. I had Lyon yelling at me to pay and to go and get some money from Mad, and Milette yelling at me for my books, and Mimi to write in her album, and, in the middle of all this, I was learning my prose, darning my stockings, hunting up book catalogues, doing my accounts, and racking my brains for something to write in

Mimi's album. All these things I was doing at the same time, with the result that the prose was learned next morning, the accounts arent made up or paid yet, the stocking still gapes, Mimi's album is still empty, and the only thing that I did manage to do was to find the books I wanted for my departure. I asked for 'The Youth of Napoleon', and 'Posthume (I think that's the word) Memories of Napoleon.'

Once Olive is off, we will become a little calmer again, I hope. Did you hear, too, those absurd rumours that Genève was burnt by the French, or that all the Pensionnats shut down, and that the girls were shoved into trains without destination etc... Mad was frightfully indignant, as we are really so quiet and safe here. If you hear anything more like that, just don't believe it.

I am reading such a spiffing book, just now. Its all about the French Revolution and the Royal Family, and gives you, in full detail, all the details that History just mentions. Mad really has some spiffing books.

Do you know, this Mr Leighton, who has offered to bring us home, made a splendid joke the other day. Mad had asked him whether food wasent very scarce in England. "Oh, no," he replied. "You see, we are getting the greater part of our provisions from Germany, at present!!"

Mad Albertine is still prisoner in London, much to our joy!!

After Olive goes, I shall be the one and only 'old girl', the last of the old band. How little we thought, one short month ago, how our plans were to be knocked over. Mariele, who was to be the last to go, was the first. Hedi was to have gone two weeks ago, and went only yesterday, and Olive, who was to have had such a lovely voyage with her father, and a triumphal entry into Alnwick, is going today, with a complete stranger, straight home to a bemoaning household. They havent the least notion whether 'Pa–Pa' is in England or in Belgium or where, and are very anxious.

The train leaves at one thirty, but Olive has to be at the station at eleven, so as to get a place; she will have to stand for two hours, waiting.

I hope you'll get this letter, at least, all right.

With much love,
your loving
Flora.

Please say what you think of Mr Leighton's plan. I think it really is the best thing to do. And its so difficult travelling just now. Mr Leighton would accompany us to London, and there he would see me into a train, in a full compartment, of course, and then Daddy could meet me at Newcastle. Lyon and I want to travel 3rd class, to save expenses, but that depends upon Mr Leighton; perhaps he wont want to. Then, if I come alone to Newcastle, that'll save more'n £2 – I'm great upon economising, these days!!

Hedie Mossner

Château Blanc
29th or 30th Aug. 1914

Dear Daddy and Mother,

I got two letters this week, one on Monday, and one this morning, also, I got three packets of D. Sketch, yesterday. Thanks so much. Its so interesting to get an English point of view, and to see how enthusiastic you all are. Here we get the 'Journal de Geneve', a very quiet, sober, reasonable and cautious little paper, and, of course, as Switzerland is neutral, it gives the opinions of both sides, and the telegrams of both sides.

Often its so ridiculous to get the French and German opinions together, as French telegram says, 'French victory, many Germans left upon the field.' and the German telegram says, 'Great German victory, French completely routed, army still pursuing them, great losses, German losses insignificant etc etc... but there's things to say for the French, that their telegrams are always much more moderate than the Germans'. they often say, 'Army pushed back by Germans, but rallied again, gained success over Germans.' Then, of course, the Russians write, 'Brilliant successes all along the line; Germans sustain heavy losses, etc.' and, of course, the Germans write, 'Russians routed, big losses.' I must say, that tho' the 'Journal de Genève' is supposed to be strictly neutral, he no' jest awful on for the Germans!! It gives both sides of the question very fairly, naturally, but, all the same, the naughtinesses of the Germans are always greater than those of the French, and I must say that I believe the paper, as I think that the German soldier, once his blood is up, must be an awful brute. I always imagine the French soldier as very polite and chivalrous, all along the line, although I guess as what even he even forgets to say 'pardon', sometimes, when he tramps upon his neighbours toes, in battle. Also, the Germans seem to be so stupid and thick. Three times they have fired upon their own soldiers, and the frightful things that they do in Belgium are enough to turn your blood cold.

It seems as if fate were against me ever finishing my letter today, as this morning I had to read your letter, then, this afternoon, I tried to advance with my newspapers a bit, as I'm very behind. Well, I read till two o'clock, and then entered to get my writing instruments. Of course, I had to go and meet Mad, who collared me and said I was to read the Journal de Genève instead of those English ones, and shoved the thing upon me, so there was nothing for it but to read it.. I read the important things, and thought that, at last, I could begin, but no! three of Mad's nieces came, and we all started talking politics at a fine old pace; we jabbered on till tea time, after which I fled, grabbed my paper and pen, and came here, where, at last, I made a beginning. But, alas, peace reigned but for a short space of time, and the nieces discovered me, and, together with Milette, we were soon off again, as hard as ever. They're gone now, and let's hope this time I'll get finished.

The Germans are detested in French Switzerland, and the French are detested in German Switzerland, but, in spite of that, the little country is quite united.

Its very difficult to imagine that all Europe's flying at each other's throats, when, here, we are so quiet and gay. We go for long walks, we play tennis, we were up at Châtelaine the Reymond's house for tea last Thursday, and, as they have a ripping huge garden, we played at all sorts of nice games, having tea under a huge oak tree, whose branches swept the ground, and had the appearance of a huge leafy pavillon (sic). Next day we went to thank M. Bernoud for the plums he sent us, and, there, we ate still more. Yesterday, M.Bernoud came to tea, and we went to the baths, after — not M. Bernoud, of course!! Here, Mad said we were not to swim on our backs, or anyfink, only to swim soberly about, which was most disagreeable of her, as my special pleasure exists in making a weard (sic) attempt of a dive into the water, and then to swim wildly for about half a minute under the water, as I think, until I imagine that I must be nearly half way across the baths. Then I take my face out of the water!! and make the humiliating discovery that I have been swimming, half the time, with my legs out of the water, with only my face under the water, also, I generally find myself within a yard or two from where I started!

Tomorrow, lessons begin in earnest, and I am specially looking forward to the history lesson, as I'm sure that Madame Ubersaxe will give us lectures upon the war. Its so funny being only five, but its not at all funny during the grammar lesson, where you are liable to be questioned every two or three minutes!!

Bye the bye, I aint the least little bit afraid that the Germans will ever get so far as Edinburo' town, as not even they have the slightest hopes of squashing our navy, and they and everyone say that they will never get as far as Britain. Also, nobody except the Germans themselves, and then not all of them, is at all sure that, in spite of their splendid army etc., the Germans could possibly win. In any case, I'm jolly certain that Europe will be a happier place if we win than if the Germans win, with their forced service and a' that.

You know, I am all in a muddle in my head, with all the different arguments that I hear upon every side. I get one opinion from you, and I explain it to the Germans, who thereupon give me their very reasonable verdict upon this same subject, and then I get stranded; or else it's the Germans who argy–bargy about one thing until I'm about certain that they're right. Then I see the same thing taken from an English point of view, and then I'm in muddle no. 2.!! I've decided to give them all reason, and to make private comments thereupon for myself.

For example, you say, it's the Kaiser who'se to blame for all this. Well, here, even Mad says that he had nothing to do with it, and that he did all he could to help keep the peace, as long as it was possible, and that he could not go against the 'people.' Also, they've got a whole string of very plausible arguments about the Russian affair, which all sound very nice and truthful, but at this moment I appear to have forgotten the most important ones, as I'm as against their part as ever.

They tell such funny stories from Alsace, too, how the people detest the Germans, and what tricks they play. They say that, once, a German officer had been in a café lording it over, and a' that. Then, when he went out, an Alsatien (sic) came and deliberately <u>disinfected</u> the chair and place. Wasent it delightful? Of course, the man was put in prison after. They say, too, that, once, the French arranged all their capes and coats upon the field, and then retired, and the Germans fired furiously on those poor capes for goodness knows how long.

They say, too, that in '70 the Germans bagged all sorts of spoil, including myriads of clocks of all kinds. Well, the French say that the Germans took away so many clocks that the hour of vengeance has not been able to strike!!, but I guess they've been manufacturing a good many clocks these last rimes.

Yesterday, when I told Mad that you all said how much better off I am here, and that Daddy had said that I must stay here for the present, Mad exclaimed, "Ah, there is a reasonable Papa, at last!"

Bye the way, have you remarked that, next Wednesday, I shall have been away from home exactly one year. I simply cant imagine it, and the time has flown so quickly, too. I am the only one of the old band who has completed her whole year.

You know, being here, as I am, in a neutral country, and living amongst members of nearly every country now at war, I have the opinion of everybody. And, too, one always takes more interest when you have known some of its inhabitants, and learnt their customs and habits.

They say that there are lots of British at Berlin, who refuse to come home, and who say they don't know why we fight the Germans, who are so like us in every way.

Its really so silly to see how every ruler is thanking and praising his respective soldiers for the brilliant victories they've gained, and of how they send telegrams congratulating each of them. Poor old François Joseph, I guess they keep him entirely in the dark as to anything but the brilliant victories gained by his side, judging by the enthousiastic (sic) telegrams he sends to William. The Austrians expect him to die any minute, but all say that, if he did, his family would embalm him quickly, and shove him into a cellar, and leave him there till the war was over, when the nation would be told, and not a moment before.

The Germans here are sure that their crown prince will

be dead before the war's end, as he is so frightfully rash and reckless, dashing into all sorts of danger. At any rate, the Kaiser sets a good example to his people, giving six sons to the army.

Just before I stop, can you tell me where our kings William II and III have gone to? There's William of Orange, who is William I, isent he? And then comes William IV. Can you explain this mystery to me?

With much love to all,
your loving
Flora.

If ever the Germans do come to Edinbro' town, be sure and let me know, as I would not miss seeing the fun for anything.

Château Blanc
6th Sept. 1914

My dear Mother and Daddy,

Thank you so very much for all the 'Sketches' you sent; they were so interesting, as all the girls could tell you. Its always a cause for great excitement when its reported that I've got some newspapers again, as even the Germans read them, and when they find themselves attacked, they either swallow it with an unbelieving smile, or, if they're very hard hit, they defend themselves. Hilde is very reasonable and not at all difficult, but Lia is patriotic before all, and resents very much when anything is said against the dear 'Vaterland.' They all say, with one accord, that Britain has been hankering after war with Germany for years, and that the Belgian affair is only an excuse. They say that if it had been France who had violated the treaty, we would suddenly have found ourselves in a condition not at all fit for war, and would have laid low. I, in return, informed them that it was current in Britain that Germany's dearest ambition, for many years, had been to have a slash at us, and try to squash us flat. Of course, we don't agree and never will, for that matter, but we're very good friends, for all that. I was awfully vexed, the other day, when they got hold of the 'John Bull' you sent me. They said nothing at the time, but afterwards they said, "Well, you can say nothing more against us for having printed that menu card, with the different allies as the meats, and our regiments as the sauce, after that thing that's in your 'John Bull'. I tried to explain, but in vain, that those things were very bad class, etc.. and that I dident approve them, nor did many of us, but, alas! the deed is did!!

Bye the way, did you think of me Wednesday last, 2nd, and on Friday 6th? I thought of you a lot, and of last year. What a difference there is between the two!

Have just returned from church, where I heard the most splendid sermon I think I ever heard in my life. Victoria Hall is reopened again, and this was the first Sunday since July. I dunno one bit what his text was, or anything. All I know is that he spoke upon the war. Now, Mr Thomas is a very fine speaker, but never, never did he speak as he did today. He just let himself go, and thundered at the people, the words rushing in torrents from his lips. Oh, if only those whose fault this war is could have heard the scathing, despising, disgusted way in which he spoke of the lies which had begun the war, and the lies which were still going on; of how he spoke of the men who were at last beginning to see what a wrongful cause they were fighting for, and who were suiciding for shame. (The Germans, I suppose, although he never never mentioned, in the remotest way, any special government.) His flow of language was simply magnificent, and several times he made people jump by bringing up a very personal subject. My word, how he stormed against those who were hiding stores of money in their houses. He said, "Where are those thousands? If you have got them, stop being mean, stop robbing the poor and needy, and give it back again." He spoke so well that lots of people cried, old ladies especially, and even a lot of men.

I have just received your letter of the 24th; it takes only ten days for the letters to come now. I got one last Sunday, too. How frightfully down on the Germans you are, to be sure! Up till today, I really dident put too much faith in all the stories of

German cruelty and sin, etc… Also, I thought that there was much to say on both sides. You see, living with Germans, you get both sides of the question! Only today, when Mr Thomas thundered against the acts of cruelty committed in the war, and of civilians shot, and women and children put before the army to shield it, etc… then, even my sluggish blood began to boil. But, for all that, I don't, cant, and wont hate the Germans; poor things, its those beastly, priggish officers' fault, all this, not the people's, who are <u>not</u> so frightfully keen. The German officer is, generally, a beast, pure and simple. If a German officer enters a café, out all the common soldiers must go. Also, the Germans themselves make fun of the officers. For example, if a boy fails in his big exams, his parents shove him double quick into the army, where he becomes officer and can bully, right and left, the common soldiers, often twice or three times older than himself; and woe betide any misguided one who dares to reply: its, at once, a case of black hole or cellar, with bread and water, when thought necessary. It was Mariele who remarked, when told that Hilde's brother, a boy of seventeen or eighteen, was a lieutenant, "Oh, that says everything; me no like bruvver!!!" Mariele is a good German, but it was she who told me stories of the officers, whom she detests. Her brothers, two of whom had the misfortune to be in the hands of a — brute, a real true brute, for their military service, tell pretty stories. One was goaded to reply twice, and was most inhumanly punished!

Everyone is suffering from heat — or animal — spots, preferably the former, and its <u>awful</u>. Every time you come across a girl, she's sure to be rubbing her legs or back. I, during lessons, vigorously scrubb (sic) my elbows. I am the best of the lot, as yet, as only my ankles and a little bit of my legs are spotty — at night is a real comedy!

Bye the way, I am <u>so</u> glad that you have kept all my letters, as I had hoped upon hoped that you had, but remembering your hatred of lumber, etc. I hadent much hope.

Mr Leighton came to tea on Friday, and said that, for the moment, he too was stuck, and dident know when he could return, so salvation from that quarter seems to be a bit off, for the moment.

Bye the way, if any of my anxious inquirers attempts to commiserate me with 'poor dears' etc… just you tell 'em that being 'Prisoner of War' isent half bad. First, I shall probably learn a little more French; second, I'm learning how and where to be examomical; third, being in Switzerland, I get opinions of all the world, quite impersonal. Also, in a few days, we'll be getting soldiers' bread instead of white bread, as bakers havent any more white flour, or must save it. Couldent you send us along a little of your plenty? Now, please don't go away with the impression that, bye and bye, we are going to starve: not at all, at present there's no danger of that.

Your letters have never arrived to me open, but, lately, I have been leaving them open.

Bye the bye, yours truly is trying to knit stockings, but isent showing herself too brilliant in that direction. Twice or thrice, I knitted the same wire twice, which resulted in an inch being pulled down. Then, I had to learn the Swiss method of knitting, as mine was so ackward (sic)!! Dark thoughts and purposes surged up in my infant brain, but, happily, I learnt the method before I'd done anything desperate.

The harassing tails (sic) of war and strife which surround

me havent in the least interfered with my appetite, nor, for that matter, with that of any of us. We eat like young horses. The other day, I ate a piece of bread as thick as the space between these lines, and as long as three quarters of this page (broad wise), in addition to two other inch thick pieces. Naturally, Mad wasent there that day!!

Last Thursday, we were invited out to one of Mad's friends house to tea, and, later, were given permission to wander all over the farm, at our will. We visited the cows, the horses, the barns, weighed the milk cans, climbed the loft ladders, and then went out into the fields. Here we wandered about climbing into the carts, trying to crack the whips, and, at last, found a place covered with tiny pears, fallen from the 'lift'. We ate the pears!!. Then the lady brought out her dogs and her goat, which follow her all over, and they teased each other, the goat butting the dogs, and the dogs chasing the goat. Then, on parting, we received two basketsful of pears.

These last days, we've been helping the gardener a bit, weeding and raking, also helping to take in his hay, and gather up the fallen fruit — don't like the last job: cruelty to animals when you arent allowed to eat 'em !!

Our voyagers to Bohemia have been having fine times — you know: our five girls and a cousin. First: two stepped out to get a cup of coffee, and the train went off and left them!! They rejoined their party at the next station, however. The next day, in train, they found they'd forgotten half the baggage at hotel. This too was rectified hastily. Then, at certain station, they meet two moters (sic) in one of them's father's employ, by accident, and finish voyage in auto! Once, during a thunderstorm, the motors got separated, and one reached hotel, and other <u>dident</u> — till next morning, to first driver's dismay. Then Mimi, the slim one, was hauled out, only just in time, from under a motor's wheels, by a gallent (sic) 'so'jer laddie' — pardon: an officer.

With much love,
your loving Flora.

Château Blanc
13th September 1914

My dear Daddy and Mother,

Your letter and card were very startling, this morning, but, nonetheless, welcome, as were also the 'Sketches.' I received your card the same time as your letter, and the two, today, Sunday, as usual. I always get your letters Sunday, now. Mad has just informed me that I mustent be alarmed if I don't receive any more letters for a bit, as all the Channel's boats are to be occupied transporting troops — thing I dont see is how they cant take letters and men upon the same boat!

Mr Leighton came to see us the other day, and he said that, for the moment, he could do nothing either, but he is still willing to take us when he does go. Miss Lyon received telephone from the Consul, telling her to come and see them, so she is going at once, tomorrow morning; perhaps she will hear something definite. At any rate, I'm jolly well not going to stay here any longer than is necessary, if what you said about Daddy is true. When I read it, I thought Daddy wanted to go and fight, and felt a bit blue. However, I recovered a bit when I read in the 'News' that he would probably only go as chaplin (sic). Do chaplins have to fight, or run into danger too? What happens to the family and Church when the Lord and Master to war doth go? What I vote is that we finish off this beastly war double quick, and that we don't go in for any more, never. When I think of how at school they used to speak of Germany's ambition, and how they assured us that the war wasent at all likely to come, in our time, at any rate. At any rate, as its come in our generation, it cant come in the next, which is one comfort.

These last days, the German Agency has sent no more telegrams, we have only received the French news. The French always seem to say when they have been defeated, which is more than the Germans appear to do, judging by Mariele's letter. I'm going to get it, and quote scraps, they're so funny. First, she says her youngest brother has been called for and has gone to the front. This isent funny, by the way, and her poor mother felt that this was nearly the last drop. Joseph, the eldest, is fighting hard in France for some time now: sixteen days not out of his clothes. Fritz, the second, has not been heard of since the 2nd Aug., when he announced his intention of returning at once from Africa, by a cruser (sic) or by China; now they don't know what to think of him, if he's dead, or what. Mariele said, "Perhaps he's even prisoner of the British, mon Dieu, poor boy!" which just showed her ignorance, dident it? The third is not fighting yet, nor the fourth. She has already learnt of the death of one of her cousins, and I guess they're all just waiting for another blow. It's practically impossible that all four sons could come back, and they know it.

Now I'll tell you the funny bits. She said it was awful to bring up your boys just to send them to be shot down, and all because of the jealousy and envy of the other nations, specially that of England. "It's Britain who's to blame for it all," she wailed. "It's Britain who wants to make poor little Germany disappear altogether from the map, and wants to destroy her etc." Here she goes off into a song of praise of the bravour (sic) and unity of Germany, adding that, if there is justice in the world, the war must finish in their favour, if only it dident cost them so many, many lives. There are hundreds of wounded at Freibourg, already, French and German, who are treated exactly alike. She says that the Germans in France are frightfully treated, some even had their eyes put out. She then said, "Have you heard of our continual victories? I suppose not." (I hadent!!) "Its very sad that people don't say the truth, all over. I find it unthinkable to make the people believe such false news as they do at Paris. One day the truth will come out, and then that will be so much the worse for the French." She then remarked that she hated England the most of all, and thirsted for vengeance. In Germany, all English and French words were being ostracised, and those who let one slip out put a halfpenny in a little box, for the Red X, I suppose. Also, they're going to invent a German mode, so as to be perfectly independent. She and her friends have little social gatherings in which they knit for the soldiers. Now comes the funniest bit of all. She scolds against us for having attacked a German vessel in neutral waters; she says its most low. Here I quote again, "You know the Germans would never do such a thing; tell me one dishonest action they ever did. There, you don't know any, and look how they treat us. We are much too good–natured, and let them do all they like with us."...Evidently the invasion of Belgium has not yet penetrated Freibourg, the German Government not finding fit to tell the German populace this little exploit. However, everyone here says that the Kaiser wasent to blame for the war, as it was those beastly officers who kicked up such a row, and behaved like a lot of school children escaped from the nursery, until the Kaiser gave in, at last. I quoted from Mariele's letter, as I thought you would be interested to get a little bit of a German point of view. I do wish you could read my reply. I barged off into a four or five page phylosophical (sic) discours (sic) defending my country, the French, admiring the German soldiers' prowess, and getting a most lovely little bit in about the German boat. I told her that she couldent complain too much, as it was the Germans themselves who had shown us that 'neutrality' was only a vain term in this war, and that all countries and all waters were likely to be invaded. We had learned that in Belgium, and wont forget it either!! She was frank with me, so I was frank with her, but I don't think she'll be cross; she's a good sort — despite her nationality.

Lessons are in full swing again, only I am not taking any more piano or singing lessons. Also, M. Porret, the litterature master, being considered a bit too high brow for our limited intelligences, Mme Ubersaxe has been commissioned to give us Litt. as well as Hist. lessons. She signalled her succession by ordering us to read one of Corneille's plays, 'The Cid,' and then give a written account of it — very brief. It was much less terrible than we thought, however. Lyon, whose French is as yet very limited, wrote a very funny one. In one place, she announced that 'Chimène' sent an 'ultimatum' to her father's murderer, Rodrigues. The year is evidently working upon her nerves.

The other day, Milette and I were talking about a book I was recommending her to read. I said, "Its all about Marie Antoinette and the Royal Family, etc." Milette: "Marie Antoinette? Who on earth was she?" I, flabbergasted and breathless, "You mean to tell me that you don't know who was M. Ant.?" M., "No; who?" I asked her whose wife she thought she was, and, after reflecting, she said, "Was it Louis XIII?" I replied that it wasent. I then asked her if she knew what illness she died from, saying that it was very infexious (sic) at the time. Lia had to tell her that. But even knowing that she had been beheaded in the F. Rev., that dident aide (sic) her memory. She was sure that M.A. was the wife of Louis XIV or XV, and was a wee bit doubtful as to whether it wasent Louis XVIII!!. We told her, at last, and she <u>was</u> surprised. Then Lyon entered, and, just for a joke, I informed her that Milette thought that M.A. was the wife of Louis XIII, and asked her who <u>she</u> thought M.A. was. Now Lyon is very intelligent in her own language, so what was my stupefaction when she doubtfully asked if it wasent Louis IV!!! That was <u>the</u> bit, that an educated girl of 24, so much read as Lyon, should not know who was the heroine of the Revl., shocked me greatly.

We were up at Châtelaine again this week. We played in the garden. I guess that we're all getting cracked here; at night we behave like a troup of escaped lunatics. The other night we kicked up such an infernal row that it's a nine day wonder that Mad dident pay us a visit, with the broom stick. — not that she has the habit of using a broom stick on us, only, it's the time of revolutions, just now. What we were so gay about was that I was sitting upon my bed when, suddenly, someone smothered me up in my eiderdown. I shook the thing off, and, carrying it with me, set off in search of vengeance. Lia, however, grabbed her sponge, soaking wet, and squirted the water at me. I sought refuge under the eiderown, and flung her pillow at her. She flung it back, and I grabbed another sponge, soaked it, and started baptising her. I, driven back into my own domains, found that Milette had basely pinched my pilly. I strode up to her bedside, and, sponge in air, demanded my property. She, rashly, refused to reply, so, grasping the bed clothes firmly,

I squeezed the sponge. You should have heard the yells she emitted, pig being killed wasent in it. She dident tell me where my pilly was, but I soaked hers for her, at any rate. The pillow was found in a cupboard nearby. Once, Mad caught us talking after ten o'clock, and ordered us ten lines apiece. I learnt the smallest ten lines I could find, and still continue to talk, but not to learn.

We often get lessons in the garden, now, and are nearly always outside. Every other day we go to the baths. Wednesday we set out, and on came the rain, in torrents, and the wind in volumes. Our umbrellas were nearly turned outside in, but we refused to turn back. We arrived, and hurried into the water, which was so warm. Fancy bathing with a pouring sharp rain falling upon you — chic!!

If Lyon learns anything definite at the Consuls, I'll send you a card. Its her brother who is making inquiries about her.

We had plum cakes for tea today, not plum cakes in the ordinary sense of the word, but an immense round of pastry, very short, filled I with slightly cooked plums; its spiffing. We ate two huge slices, and when Mad said she would bring us another slice, we murmured, behind her back, why not two. After having disposed of this slice, Mad said, "You don't want another slice, do you? I think you've had sufficient." Nobody replied, and Mad, shocked, exclaimed, "What! You will eat another slice…Impossible!" We got it!

We, too, are knitting for the Swiss soldiers. My stocking, needless to say, is of growth extremely stunted!

With much love to you all,
your loving Flora.

Château Blanc
19th Sept. 1914

My dear Mother and Daddy,

Today, Mr Leighton returns and, with him, Lyon, and I rest here; that's the tragic part of the affair.

I received your letter on Sunday, and, on Monday, Mr Leighton announces that he departs on Wednesday. I then knew that it was hopeless to expect deliverance from that quarter, and so said nothing. However, in my room afterwards the storm broke. Lyon and the two others literally fell upon me, calling me blockhead, ass, idiot, and many more desirable epithets. They told me that it was my last chance, that it was my duty to take it, and finally ordered me off to the front – otherwise, to Mad. I told them that I hadent any money, and that Mad was sure to refuse, etc., but they were inexorable. I went and told Mad that you had written, telling me to return with Mr Leighton. She replied that it was a good idea, only I hadent any money, and neither Mr Leighton nor she could lend me any, etc. etc... Of course, I let myself be talked over, but at dinner I brought up the subject again, and this time she said that it was perfectly impossible. After dinner she took me into the veranda and spoke so nicely to me. She said, "You understand, don't you, why I refuse to let you go? You see, your mother has always written, up till now, that you were to stay here for the present, and, also, I have received no letter from her saying anything about your departure. Altogether, I think it is better that you stay here; also, I cant let you go like this, can I?" (Five lines of crossings out).

Please turn over, have got all mixed up.

Well, Mad said that she was sure that there would be lots of British subjects only waiting until things became a little straighter, and that she would speak to the Consulate, and he would be on the look out for someone for me. Naturally, Mad would be very very careful in her choice. She would visit the people, and examine their birth certificates, etc. (I don't think!). If you agree to this plan, you are to send off, at once, sufficient money, telegraphically (sic), and, upon receiving it, Mad will at once begin her investigations. Let me warn you to send more than you think necessary, also for my fees, as I shall have to buy a passport for 15/– or so – a mere trifle. Also, if we get kicked out of the train once or twice, a little cash would always come in handy. Also, you have to take your own provisions on the train, as there are no more dining cars. Altogether, it's a franticly (sic) expensive job, this getting home, but, if I stay here, I'm always running on a bill with Mad.

Mad allowed Lyon to depart, as she had her money, and as she is entirely independent, but, poor thing, if she reached England safe and sound, it would be a miracle, as she's even more irresponsible than this yer 'umble servitor – if that's possible!!

Please send off money as soon as you get this, so as I can send Mad off to the consulate at once.

Hip, hip, I be home soon, in spite of her!

With much love,
your loving
Flora.

Tell that Daddy of mine that its as much as his life'll be worth if he goes off before I return!

(At the back of the envelope):

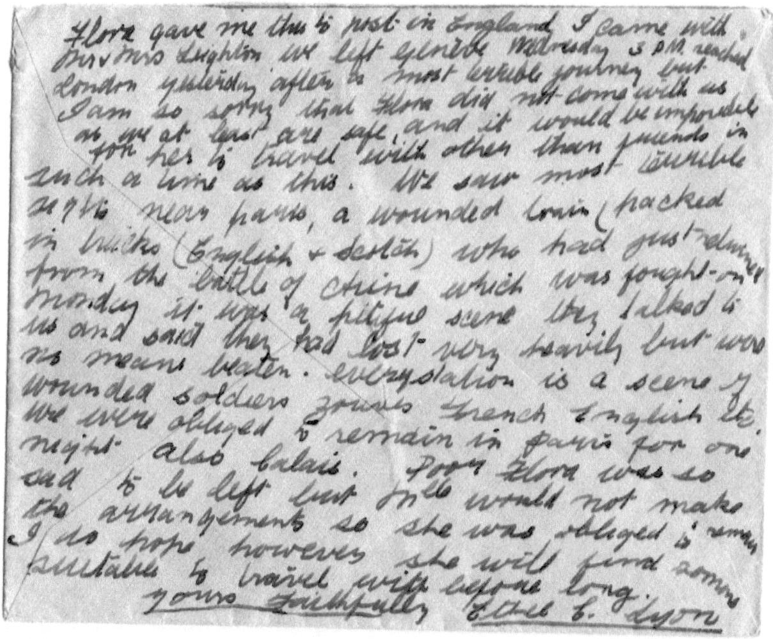

Flora gave me this to post in England. I came with Mr and Mrs Leighton. We left Geneva Wednesday 3 pm, reached London yesterday, after a most terrible journey, but I am so sorry that Flora did not come with us, as, yet, at least we're safe, and it would be impossible for her to travel with other than friends in such a time as this. We saw most terrible sights near Paris: a wounded convoy packed in trucks (English and Scotch), who had just returned from the battle of Chine, which was fought on Monday. It was a pitiful scene; they talked to us, and said they had lost very heavily, but were no means beaten. Every station is a scene of wounded soldiers, zouaves, French,

English, etc.. We were obliged to remain in Paris one night, also Calais. Poor Flora was so sad to be left, but Mlle would not make the arrangements, so she was obliged to remain. I do hope, however, she will find someone suitable to travel with, before long.

Yours faithfully, Ethel C. Lyon.

Château Blanc
19th Sept. 1914

My dear Mother and Daddy,

I got your last letter and card, together again, on Thursday. They come quicker now, you see: one on Sunday and one on Thursday.

This afternoon, we're going down to Cooks to get my money. Mad has just received notice; wonder wot she'll do now…

Lyon is gone, but wont be in England for a bit yet, I suppose, as she announced that, if her baggage stuck in Paris, she's stuck there too! even if she had to sleep in the waiting room. She rather fancied herself sleeping on the hard cushions of a dirty French waiting room – so romantic, and she has a decided taste for the stage.

20th Sept. Have been to Cooks and got the money. Thanks awfully. I really would like to know what Mad will do now.

Its so funny being only four, only you have to do everything. As there are just four, two have to lay the table one week, and clear away the next. Then those who lay the table ought to dust the schoolroom – but they don't – only before the lesson someone remarks how dusty Mad's desk is, and flies for the duster. Also, the cook has been dismissed, or got another place, so now its Mad and the housemaid who do the cooking. Mad surveys and orders, and the housemaid, a real jewel, so clean and thorough, does the cooking. I can assure you that never have we eaten so well as now: no more hard potatoes, no more uncooked, singed fried ones, no more tasteless soups, or uncooked meats. Once, she nearly poisoned us, the cook.

She burned a whole huge pot of stewed plums, and we had to eat them; it was awful! Then, Andrée, the scullery maid, who by rights should wait at table, is shy!! So we do the waiting, the one nearest the 'pass' served up the dishes.

Mad is great on economics. Her last is to do without an English teacher, and who d'ye think teaches English to the girls?... ME!!!... I started with Milette, who has special lessons, and solemnly made her read and pronounce, and translate, gave her some exercises, phrases to learn, and 'I remember, I remember,' to learn for poetry. Then I took Hilde et Lia, and gave them a dictation, and made them read. They've got 'Little Women'. It was so funny to hear them reading the first chapter; every word was familiar, and when they read the parts Jo or Beth or Amy or Meg said, I heard again how we all said them; Eileen as Jo, so vigorous and boyish; Phyllis as Beth, so sweet and mousy. The girl who took Amy's part was a real true Amy, made for the part.

I give four lessons a week, 'to occupy me a little,' was Mad's remark, and I slave and slave doing lessons far in advance, just to try and get a little leasure (sic). However, I don't grumble, as I enjoy myself immensely giving these lessons, and jumped at Mad's proposal. Lyon simply wasent capable of giving them lessons; she had no method, and they dident respect her. With me, they are perfectly nice, as I am one of them. Its so queer, ever since I can remember, Milette has groaned, "Oh Flora! If only <u>you</u> gave the English lesson, I should learn fifty times as well; lets ask Mad, do!" I replied that I'd love to give the lesson. I intend to make them work and get on a bit, at any rate. Also, Lyon had a very <u>English</u> accent, so English that the girls could not understand her at all, but they say they understand quite well when I talk, which is a blessing! At any rate, I intend being most methodical and strict. (He! he! don't you see me?!)

Do you know, one thing is rather funny, at first, and half way over, I always used to sigh and say, "I do wish I could return at the end of September, not the beginning, as Edinburgh looks so deserted and dead, and everybody is away then. My wish is being a little too well fulfilled, don't you think?

Last Thursday M. Bernoud asked us to come and see his works. He provides the water for one half of the town. Well, we set off, and half way there were met by M. Bernoud, and what do you think the dear old man had stuffed his pockets with? — Apples! We each got a huge big rosy one, and then and there, in the middle of the road, began to munch them, to the passers by's amusement. The works were most interesting. He showed us a spring of the most deliciously fresh clear cold water, and gave us to drink of it. He took us into the engine room, and down, down, down into the earth, far below the river, to see a spring that he had discovered. The spring was walled in, and he let down an electric lamp to let us see how clear and deep the water was. Naturally, everything was horribly oily and dirty, and we blacked our hands beautifully. We came home a different way, through woods and dales, and were most frightfully content to tumble into a car, the town once reached.

We have just received a budget of letters from Ollola, Mimi and Hedi; each one had written to each girl separately. Hedi and Mimi are Austrians from a little town near Prague. There they are very quiet, but are preparing for the wounded.

Today, the whole jolly crowd of sisters, brothers, nephews and nieces are coming, with an adopted child into the bargain, for tea. We feel like swearing, as we want to write and read. Madame Raymond has, in all, seven children of her own; at present, the two eldest, Maurice and Olivier, are away guarding the frontiers. Well, Madame Raymond, hearing that the wife of one of her friends in France, now in his regiment, had died, she offered to take charge of the three children till peace time. Fortunately, an aunt took two, leaving her the eldest. 'To (she) who hath shall be given (them)?"

Its most frightfully cold today; I had to go and hunt a warm dress out of my trunk.. I disinfected it so well with naphthalene that you can smell me a mile off, now.

Bye the way, is Daddy serving like any other soldier, now, or is he only chaplin (sic)? I never quite understand. Also, all the 'Sketches' beg, pray and command every able bodied young man to offer his services, so is anyone we know going? There are several strapping youths in the church, I think. I hear Jackie Robbie's going — the poor mother!

Have just decided that I want to come right from London to Edinburgh alone; it isent at all necessary that anyone come to meet me at Newcastle. I'll get into a packed full carriage, if you like, or anything.

Hope shant have need to write many more letters, now.

Much love,
Your loving Flora.

Château Blanc
26th Sept.1914

Dear Kid!,

Guess as what I 'd better write to you, at least once, before I return, otherwise the infant might be a little disagreeable.

First and foremost, I must really apologize most profoundly for my intentions of returning home; it really is most inconsiderate of me, I know, but what will you when one has been selfish all one's life, its very difficult to change in one's old age. Of course, I understand how exceedingly annoying it is, after having been, for more than a year, the daughter of the house, to be suddenly bombarded with an object in the shape of an elder sister, fresh from a boarding, all blooming with surprising and newly acquired vertues (sic). However, I shall try to efface myself as much as my shining aureole and winsome charms will permit, and you can soothe your ruffled feelings in thinking of the glorious and triumphant day when you, too, shall 'return from boarding school'. Upon that day, I, not knowing where to hide my diminished head, shall probably commit suicide, but you, of course, still in youth's charming blush, must not think of such stringent and nefast measures.

Bye the bye, I hear that all civil quarrels have been patched up, and that a general 'pax' reigns throughout all the Empire. I'm interested to know if you and Marjory have laid down your arms — or your feet!! You should, you know, for there's nothing like these little petty quarrels for undermining a nation's power. Let past differences leave you. Come, be patriotic, and go kiss and be friends. Get Cathie to draw up the document, and let the peace be signed, and then, buy a bottle of champagne cold, and drink each other's healths, whilst munching 'jube jubes' or 'sherbert (sic) dabs'. What heavens of delightchousness (sic) those words open up before mine eyes.

I suppose you'll be going back to school again soon. Just you wait till I get back, and I'll make you learn your French lessons, you'll see. I may even, if the fancy takes me, take your other lessons on too — except arithmetic. I think it would perhaps be better if I refrain from trying to teach you this mighty science. I'm great on teaching, these days. I have two different English classes twice a week, and prepare the History with the girls, and scold them when they don't attend.

Bye the bye, did your kinder spiel not come off this year, after all, or are they still rehearsing it?!! I am coming home more keen than ever on theatricals, so we really must get up something to celebrate the signing of the peace, after the war will be over.

On my way to Paris, if it isent dark, I shall probably see lots of trains full of soldiers and wounded. I'm going to take a Union Jack with me, in case, and shall wave it frantically from the window when we pass them.

Now, my deah, before I cease, just one more word, and its this: when I come home I want peace, so, if you leave me alone, I'll, most gladly, leave you alone. You can have the end seat, and everything — except — the permission to lend my books to anybody, not even your Ritchie, Pitchy, Ditchy, or whatever her name is, girl. There, that's all.

Forgive me and forget my sins, and I shall remain for ever and ever amen, your obedient and humble sister, Flora.

Dear Mother, Mad thanks you very much for the telegram

which she has duly received, and bids me say she is already making the necessary inquiries.

Dorothy and friend

Château Blanc
26th Sept. 1914

My dear Daddy and Mother,

At last, I think I have some nearly definite news for you. Mad received your telegram and has been making inquiries for a 'chaperon.' well, she has heard of a lady who must go to England soon, having a daughter at York whom she must fetch, or something. Mad knows her by name, she having been in her sister's class at school. (The lady in Mad's sister's class!) She is of English extraction tho' born and brought up in Genève, and has attained the sober and reasonable age of forty. Mad will visit her and make definite enquiries about the date of her departure, which is about the 14th or 15th of October; she too, it appears, is only attending the events. This would be a splendid opportunity, as at London she would still be there to help me; she would get out at York, and I would continue. I shall write to Olive to come to Newcastle station, and so will be all right. At London, straight away upon arriving, I shall send a wire with the hour the train will arrive at Edinburgh. If you don't receive it at night, you will certainly get it first thing in the morning. That should be enough time to put my room in order, surely. Then, if this lady fails us, there's another with three daughters who returns, also, in October, who is quite willing to take charge of me.

Now, please do, do, do, do me this favour, it's a very little thing, only this: don't tell anyone when I'm coming home, when you get the wire, don't tell a soul, and bribe or threaten Dorothy into silence, as it will be such fun taking everyone by surprise, like that. You could even not tell D. when you get the wire, only when she comes to the station. Oh, please, please, please do keep it a secret. You, Mother, if people ask, say, "Soon, soon," anything, but don't say when. I know you don't see the sense in secrets and surprises, but do let me have my surprise, this time. If you will, I shall be a model daughter ever after, you'll see. I shant bully my little sister, or forget to practise, or go to the wrong garden with the right gardener's money, any more.

Yesterday Mad was out and a visitor came. Now Katerine, the maid, though a model maid for cleanliness and order, is not at all, unfortunately gifted with intelligence, nor does she understand too much French, being a 'Deutches Schweizerin', so she came into the schoolroom in much confusion, with the news that 'Eine Engliche Dame' wanted to see Mad. Well, as Mad wasent in, this was impossible, so I went and spoke to her. It appeared that she was staying in Geneva for a short time, and wanted to find a nice Pensionnat to send her two girls to, later on. She was enchanted with the grounds and house – the outside, at least, as I most politely forgot to invite her in, and left her in the porch. After a bit, she turned round on me and said, "You speak English very well, but you are not English?" I replied with a most vigorous "Oui," and then corrected myself. Then she demanded if I was a girl or a teacher. I replied, "Oh, a girl." When I told her that we had had a lot of Germans and Austrians, but that they were nearly all gone, she said, "Um, um! Good riddens (sic), isent it? You don't like to have those sort of people about, in these times, do you?" I dident dare to tell her that I regretted greatly that they were gone, but its as well, all the same, as we might have quarrelled. Just before parting, she gave me her name, and said it was a very difficult one for anyone not English to remember! I gaped at her simply. Then she said, "Are you Scotch, Irish, or what?" I replied, "Scotch." (Yes, I are, Ma, so don't contradic.) "Ah!" she said, "I knew you weren't pure English."!! Mad told me today, after the lady had departed, after having inspected the interior of the house, that she had said it was <u>extraordinary</u> what a strong French accent I had. M. Leighton said the same thing. Isent it funny?

On Thursday, we went upon the lake again, but, as it had been so frightfully cold this last week, we all went — literally — into our trunks, and emerged, flushed and dusty, bearing, triumphantly, winter costumes, flannel blouses and woolen vests. You could have traced us a mile off by the odour of naphthalene that trailed behind us all through the town. We got on the boat, which was surprisingly full for these days, and departed. Behind us there were four women, all fine in white shoes, light skirts and dark jackets, sisters, I think, as they were all so tall and resembled each other. They were a decided puzzle, as they were as vulgar as vulgar, and, still, they dident jarr on you. They sat there, they flirted there, they started knitting stockings and stopped, they flirted with the gentlemen, and, finally, fussed off the boat.

Arrived at Coppet, we ordered the tea, and then went to visit the old château belonging to the famous Madame de Staël, daughter of Necker, Louis XVI' s minister. The outside was disappointing, as are all the so called châteaux, but inside it was splendid. You entered into a large hall, having on the walls the family trees, etc. of the family, also several portraits and old pictures. To the right was a huge superb statue of Necker in white marble, a book case and some tables, all ancient. We then entered into the library, a long narrow hall, and with most beautifully bound books, the books were modern; an old hand made globe of the world, very primitive; old papers; and furniture. By a disguised door, we entered into Mme de Staël's bedroom, a little square room, queerly papered, with an old, old valuable carpet on the floor. The bed was immense and covered with a magnificent crimson satin counterpain (sic), all flowered in silver, also there were lovely curtains at the head of the bed. Many interesting pictures covered the walls, and, of course, all the furniture, as 'all over' was of M. de S's time. The little room leading off this on was all pale green, pale green silk bed curtains; pale green (crisp and old) sofa; wall papers, and all to match. Then we mounted the old stone staircase, and entered her sort of bureau affair. Upon the walls were a set of pictures representing the war between the Chinese and the Tartars, engraved specially for her by missionarys (sic), and which are simply priceless, no one knows how much their value. For my part, I found them very ugly, but then, my opinion wasent asked. We next entered into the famous salons. These were upholstered in carmen (sic) and white, with queer old tapestries on the walls. The furniture was older than all the rest, as it had been in Paris with Necker. In one corner stood a chest of drawers inlaid completely with red rosy, real tortoise shell, and mother–of–pearl and gold — just splendid. Mad raved over it for nearly half an hour. There were also many interesting portraits and statues. We next visited the huge park, and then descended for tea. Madame de Staël was reported to have been nearly bored to death in her beautiful country house.

In the inn courtyard were a row of tables along the wall overlooking the lake, so we installed ourselves there, and had tea — or chocolate, and cakes.

In the boat coming home, we met our four sisters again, and, much to our amusement, they made friends with an old American who couldent speak a word of French. It was killing to watch them; he spoke by signs, and they always nodded their heads vigorously and giggled, whether they understood or not..

Thanks awfully for the newspapers you sent. They are so interesting. Hilde and Lia too receive newspapers, and I often think how funny it is that we three, reading the papers at the same time, read such different things: they, "Down with 'Perfidious Albion'" as they call us, and how their "gallent (sic) troops are surging along the easy road to victory." I, of course, read exactly the contrary, and am sore puzzled to know <u>really</u> who is right. D'ye know the Germans are frightfully bitter against us for coming in. they never dreamt we should, and now call us traitors; yes, really. They say it was low and dishonourable of us to enter, and that we're just green jealous of them. I said to Lia, the other day, "Now, my dear, I want to ask you a question, but please, <u>please don't</u> answer it. Its this: how on earth have you managed to come to the conclusion that Britain is a traitor?" she opened her mouth to reply, but I implored her not to reply, knowing that we should never agree. I, while I'm here, keep, as much as possible, an armed neutrality; otherwise, I believe nothing or everything in the papers, and judge no man. (Ahem!) You, mother, who are so ardently patriotic, you will be frightfully shocked by some of my opinions. I foresee future lectures.

Have just received your letter and fragment, thanks awfully. I'm cutting bits out of the 'Sketches', and will make a book of them afterwards. At first, I was going to cart the whole bundle home with me, but, on seeing the dimensions, and feeling the weight of the said bundle, I changed ideas. (Mother who here exclaims — "What an escape!").

It is, indeed, high time I came home, as I get fatter every day. My brown skirt hardly fastens now. I'm aching to see my room now, although it will be painfully empty and quiet after la chambre 'dégoutante', as we call our room. I shall tell you the history of that name when I return. We've had such luck, we four; all the other rooms gradually emptied, but ours always remained intact. I shall be the first break.

Upon entering from church, whom should we find waiting for us but Melle Albertine, returned suddenly from London. She says its perfectly easy voyaging; in some places its quite as usual, except for the slow speed of the trains: twelve hours from Lyon to Paris!! It looks quite as if I could pass alright, but please, please don't tell anyone.

We're perhaps going to M. Bernoud's again this week, to eat apples, this time.

Your next batch of newspapers I shall probably keep to read in the train, whilst waiting four or five hours in the different stations.

With much love,
and please don't split,
your loving
Flora.

It wont be nice now that Mlle A's here; the two will fight all day long.

Château Blanc
4th Oct. 1914

My dear Mother and Daddy,

I have still got no definite news for you, the possible lady not yet having replied to Mad, directly. We have heard that she goes, probably, about the 15th, but it isent sure, as yet. I'm looking forward very much to the journey, which will be, I am sure, very interesting.

I expect I'll have a lovely old skelter to get ready when the time comes, as I havent started to pack one thing yet, nor even to put my things in order so as to be easily got at. The only thing I do do occasionally, is to mend an object which has gaped for many a long day, preparatory to running the gauntlet before your piercing eye.

Have just received your card. Did I not say I'd received all your telegrams and money and messages? I thought I had. It appears now that I may have to wait till the end of the month before I can return, with this Mrs Watter, or something.

We have been on the lake twice this week; on Thursday, we went to Nyon, bought some cakes, had tea on board — spiffing cakes, return and learn prose after dinner, next day!

Then, yesterday, we went for a whole day excursion right to Montreux. As neither Milette nor Lia would come, Hilde and I went alone with Mad, taking books and knitting.. The lake was hung over with a heat mist, which hid the mountains. Mad bought a newspaper and so did Hilde, the 'Figaro.' It was tuppence, but she paid it gladly when she saw some of the articles. There was one upon the 'Kronprintz', which amused her mightily. Poor Kptz; they did go for him with a vengeance: among other things, they called him cowardly, but that, I am sure, and know, is rats! He may be all and everything but he's not a coward.

We were all the morning on the boat, from nine to half past one or two. We dined on board, upon spiffing sandwitches (sic), and rolls, pears, cakes and a bar of milk chocolate, to finish up. The scenery, in some places, was lovely, specially at Thonon, et Evian. At Thonon was an old, old château, and the heroine, of a book I was reading, happened just to have lived there. We also saw an old tower with a tree top peeping out from the top. On arriving at Montreux, we decided to stick in the boat till Territet, a little bit further on. Here we got out and took the tram to Chillon, which we visited, even finding an old tower that Mad had never been in. We climbed up and up for ages, by little narrow wooden ladders, really, by which we reached a sort of look–out tower. From here we had a lovely view.

In the prison, Mad showed us the places where Byron, Burke, Victor Hugo and many others, had engraved their names. That of Byron is nearly effaced, but that of Burke is as clear as ever. Just below the castle wall, the lake is a most magnificent blue, which comes from the fact that the depth, at that point, is 300 metres, not feet. Think of it!

We then took the tram back to Montreux, bought some cakes and buns for tea, and wandered round a bit, till the boat came. We had tea at once on board, and Mad was decidedly anxious as she watched the jammy, icy, sugary cakes slipping one after the other down our throats. I told her that she hadent need to be worried as she had brought the right two for the cakes. The two others might have suffered from all the cakes we ate, but we two…never! After tea I read and knitted, like an old Granny, whilst Hilde strode up and down the boat, or tryed (sic) desperately to read. My sock looks like a sock, now, as I'm doing the foot, at last!! Mad did the heel for me. It was so nice the return journey. The mist cleared away, and we saw all the mountains, and the sun went down in a blaze of red and gold, leaving a shining path upon the water; then the moon rose, to the other side, sending a long stream of silver across the dark waters. It was the full moon, and, as there were hardly any stars, it looked more brilliant than ever. Here and there, along the coast, you saw clusters of lights, which denoted little villages, or stray cottages. I had my big cloak, and, at night, when it got cold, I wrapped myself up into it. Mad went into the salon, and told us to come in too, but it smelt so hot and stuffy in there that we preferred to stay outside. We two, barring a stray gentleman who came wandering round, were the only people on the first class deck. Bye and bye, the lights of Genève came into view, so pretty, away in the distance, those round the harbour making a shining crescent. We arrived home at about half past eight, tired and sleepy, but even that dident prevent us from talking till quarter to eleven, when Mad came in and caught us. Regularly, these last Sundays, Mad has given us penny lectures at breakfast. We're prepared now, and always try to be down very punctually for breakfast, so as not to add to her indignation. I don't really think its necessary to bother Uncle Fred to cone and fetch me, as the lady is bound to depart one day, although it would be ripping, all the same, if he did come. If he does, then warn me weeks ahead, as, two nights I dreamt that I had left, and had left my books in my desk, and various other articles.

I got a letter from Mariele this week, and I'm feeling sore, still, from the dressing I got for daring to say that I thought it nearly imposs. that Germany could win against such fearful odds. Ow, I did get it hot! She informed me that I had only to come to Germany, and I would see if they would be beaten. Every man, woman and child is determined to win, and will fight to the last drop till they do. Seems to me as what it'll be a case of the one whose (sic) got the biggest number of 'drops' that'll win. Do you know, I saw one whopper in the Scotsman, a real good one. It said that, in Germany, they were already taking and drilling the old white haired men for the army, and that every man able to carry a rifle had been called up. That's nuffin' but fibs. First, there are heaps and heaps of reserves in Germany, yet, all young men; not even Hilde et Lia know why they're still idle — Hilde's youngest brother, and Mariele's two youngest ones are still exercising and waiting. Then, lots of men, still young, but who are lawyers or such like, have not inlisted (sic), also the landsturm is not yet called up, Lia's father being a member, nor is the Landurer, I think. Oh, no, there'll be many a hard struggle to go through before Germany will be beaten, as they, too, are determined to fight on until hope, men, money and all are gone for ever. They don't exactly put it that way, as they're perfectly sure they'll win, and publish their great victories and successes regularly!!

Bye the way, do you know that several letters addressed to — Belgium, have had 'Belgium' scored out, and — ahem! — 'Nord Deutschland '!!!! written across. German presumption isent the word, especially as Belgium isent yet conquered. We do so admire their magnificent king, here. I think him splendid, so noble and so loyal to his people, sleeping along the roadside with his men after three battle. The shops are crammed with his photos — such a noble, beautiful face. I only hope he doesent get killed in the battle. He seems to lead his men right into battle, and fight as hard as any.

I guess this war is a good enough thing, in its own way, as we were all getting so slothful and cock sure that we forgot to be patriotic. I, for one, never dreamt that I could ever feel as I do sometimes, when I read the things in the papers of how the men rush to join the colours, etc... who knows, perhaps even I shall at length awaken up to find myself patriotic.

With much love to all,
your loving
Flora.

Ask D. if she'll take turn about with the end of the seat!!!

Château Blanc
10th Oct. 1914

My dear Daddy and Mother,

Please excuse me, but I have just found the letter I wrote last week in my block. I got the biggest shock I ever got in my life, I think, when I found it. I cant think how I came to do such a very careless thing. I think I'm getting worse and worse, instead if better and better. I'm most awfully sorry, really, especially as the letters take so long to come, as it is. I understand now how it happened. I hadent finished my letters when stopping time came, last Sunday, and, as I had to lay the table, I first rammed everything into my block, and fled. In the morning, I finished off another letter quickly before lessons, and cleared away my things, thinking blissfully that I had already given your letter to be posted. At any rate, I got the most lovely fright when I saw it. Happily, there was nothing important in it – otherwise…!!!

It is now settled that I leave on the 15th or the 25th; the 15th is very near, and we have heard no more at present. At any rate, I'm getting things in order a bit, so as to be a little prepared. I'm getting sceptical, now, and don't worry any more, I've been put off so many times. At any rate, the journey, when it comes, will be very interesting. Are you going to keep my secret, or not?. I don't deserve it after this week's escapade, do I?

I just heard, yesterday, that Mrs Watter is likely to leave the 26th, although it might be sooner. This looks like definite; let's hope it is. She asked if I had been vaccinated, as one was liable to catch something on the journey. <u>That'll</u> be lovely if they go an' want to vaccinate me!! She also asked me to go and see her, Thursday next, but we've been invited up to Châtelaine for tea that day. This is to be a great fête, it seems, as Olivier, the second son, has got ten days holidays from his regiment. It does seem hard, doesent it, that the poor little Switzerland who has nothing whatever to do with the war, should also suffer. She pays one million a day for her army, and all her sons are away guarding the frontiers. Maurice, the oldest nephew, is high away up in the mountains, where it snows and blows awful. Even the most ardent soldiers amongst them are getting fed up with the affair, as now the college terms are beginning, and this will throw them back awfully. They say, if we could only fight, it would be alright, but just to wait, wait, wait is wretched. Now, each regiment, in turn, is to get a holiday, and you can imagine what joy there is in the different homes, when the soldier lad comes home bronzed, straight and obedient. Think of it: for two months most of them have never slept in a bed, nor seen their friends. I do think it unjust that, because the big nations come to blows, the little ones must suffer, also. I always think of those poor women up at St Luc, still waiting for their husbands, brothers, and sons, who never come. Poor deluded things, the good half of them still imagine that their men are at the war. When the men departed, there was still some hope of things straightening out, so the curé told the women that they'd be back the week after, but that 'week' is beginning to get very, very long.

There isent, however, contrary to first expectations, any danger of Switzerland being short of food, as, this last week, she has received trains and trains full of corn, etc…

Have just received your card this morning. I do hope

I havent put cold water upon your hopes in my last letters. At any rate, I think its pretty well settled now: Mrs Watter is apparently quite determined to stay no later than the 26th. In this case, allowing about double the ordinary time for the journey, I ought to arrive about the 31st, I think. If we started a little sooner, I might possibly arrive as a birthday present for Dorothy – poor kid, what a shame to spoil her birthday like that. I must really try not to arrive so inopportunely, and leave her this last day of peace.

I can tell you one thing, this, that I am <u>not</u> looking forward to my packing up. How ever am I going to get all my things into my trunk. Happily, I had to buy a nice little basket for the mountains, so all my books will go in there.

With much love – perhaps for
the second last time here,
your loving
Flora.

Château Blanc
11th Oct. 1914

Dear Daddy,

Many, many happy returns of the day. I am very sorry that I cant be home in time, nor am I sure, with these uncertain times, that my letter will arrive in time. It seems impossible that its already a year ago since I last wrote you a birthday letter, doesent it? That was one thing, at least, that I never dreamt I would do here again, and what an awful lot of things have happened since then.

This time, unfortunately, its quite out of the question, sending you a present, but.....

Do you know that I find it an awful, beastly swank that youre going out as chaplin (sic). At any rate, please don't go till I return — or else!!!

Will you have to stay out till the end of the war? Because, here, everyone is certain that it will be a very very long business, and they arent all so very sure that the Allies will win. The Germans, of course, don't even dream that they could possibly be beaten. They think the cause half won, now that they've nabbed Antwerp, but, at any rate, if they do get us, they'll pay it dearly. In the French speaking part of Switzerland, the sympathies tend, in spite of neutrality, towards the Allies; and in German Switzerland, the sympathies go to the Germans. But, at any rate, in both parts, theres no nation on the face of the earth so admired, respected and generally popular, as the British. The British fair play and broad mindedness is sung abroad; even the Germans like us as a people, although they hate us like poison as a nation. Ow, you should just hear them upon Belgium. They think it was mean low and dirty of us to have sided against them there. They say, if the French had violated the treaty, we wouldent have fought against them, and that we had been jealous of them for years, and were only too thankful to take Belgium as a gaudy cover to get a smack at them. At any rate, it'll be poor us if Germany gets her way.

M. Bernoud invited us up to his house the other day, and, when we arrived, he took us straight out into the garden and started stuffing us with apples and walnuts. After we'd eaten as many as we dared, the question was, how to smuggle some home. Hilde, the lucky one, had a pocket, and so managed to hide four. Milette, too, managed to put away four, but poor Lia and I had no such practical objects, and so, only managed to hide three. Lia stuck one into her blouse, and left her jacket open, and, on the way home, it got so cold, but she couldent shut her jacket because of the huge apple.

That night, in the dusky silence, you heard from all the beds a series of scrunches and spizz, etc…

Then again, today, please don't be shocked, we met M.B. just coming out of church, and he hauled out of his coat tails — two apples…

Are you still expecting a prim, orderly, thoughtful young lady to be returned to you? Please don't; its best not to.

With best wishes,
your loving
Flora.

Château Blanc
16th Oct. 1914

Dear Mother and Daddy,

Mad is sending you her usual U.O.I, and has graciously permitted me to put in a little word. So much the better for — me, and so much the worse for the translation still patiently waiting to be copied. First and foremost: I see that Mad, in her letter, has been stuffing you with a whole lot of flag, to the effect that your 'dear daughter' is progressing satisfactorily, and being sweet, obedient, and helpful, etc.. which, naturally, if not said, was understood, and a whole lot of fibs to that effect.

Secondly, when you send the money to Mad, send it telegraphicly (sic), as its safest like that. That would be alright, the way you sent mine, only, send it straight here, not to Cooks. Then Mad found that £20 was piles too much for my journey, and extracted £4 for the bill, leaving me about 300 francs, after paying passport, maids, and other odds and ends. She wanted to limit me to 250 francs (£10), but I protested, as I want to have enough for any immergency (sic). At present, I have 340 francs for my journey, and the rest of my time here, but when passport, etc. etc. will be paid, there'll be about 300 for tickets, hotels, etc. I think its sure to be enough, as the fare from Genève to London is somewhat less than 100 francs. Then theres hotels and the fare to Edinburgh, and provisions.

I've to go and be shown off to Mrs Watter next Thursday, and I suppose I'll have to try and be witty or something, as she asked Mad if I was a tiresome, boring sort of girl.

With the £6 I paid for some things in the bill, making it thus wise less terrifying. It appears that I have been quite economical this time, only spending £1.10 or so for pocket money, since June. In fact, we all have. At St Luc, I dident buy any post cards, which was rather a pity, I think, and now, nobody buys any chocolate. The other night, Mad said that, as we hadent had any chocolate for a long time, we could buy some if we liked, and, would you believe it, not one voice was lifted, and not one penny was spent. Mad hasent got over it yet, and proclaims it all over the town.

Now I really must go and copy my poor translation, and, after that, practise. By the way, I'm taking no more special lessons, like piano and singing, but I always have to practise, all the same. Now, there's one thing there that I find most unjust. As you know, I hate practising, and yet never manage to escape. Mad always finds me out, and hauls me to the piano by the hair of my head, and when I try to get off after half an hour, she packs me off back again; now, I like practising my singing, but, as I always do it at night, nearly every time, something comes in the road, and I cant do it; its rotten. Now this time I really am stopping, and shall do it at once, before I get going again.

With much love,
your loving
Flora.

Tell D. to profit well in the time that's left with the end of the seat, as I'm doing gym every night to strengthen my muscles for the struggle to come. — there I am again, tut, tut!

Château Blanc
17th Oct. 1914

My dear Daddy and Mother,

If all goes well, this should be my last letter. Don't be shocked, but I may have to leave, Sunday next. I do wish Mrs Watter would hurry up and decide, only, you see, she's waiting for a letter from England. I've to be presented to her, Thursday next!!! I wonder what sort of impression I shall make? She asked Mad if I was a tiresome, boresome sort of girl, and Mad replied that I was right enough, only a bit brainless or thoughtless, but she said I had one very big fault: I hated talking. I guess the poor thing isent feeling just too reassured, so I shall put on my sweetest smile, my most fascinating airs, and shall be most interested in all the whims of the weather. Perhaps I shall even talk politics, or even stocks and shares in the rubber market, all these subjects being vastly interesting and profitable.

Once well embarked upon our voyage, however, I shall basely desert her, and disappear behind my book, only coming out to eat and sleep. If she does chuck me out of the window in the end, my end would be quick, and she would be hanged, thus 'vengeance' being 'mine.' Um… I guess I'd better become a little more practical, and stop fooling or else you will be thinking that it's a mild, or unmild, lunatic that's being returned to you, instead of the finished young lady?!

So as to have less baggage, I shall send on in advance my little basket with my books and other odds and ends. I shall try to get it ready as soon as possible, as it takes three weeks to arrive at Edinburgh, which is three weeks too long when one is dying to see one's nice books all arranged upon a brand new bookshelf. I have got some such pretty ones: Nelson 1/–, white with golden lettering upon the cover, nice paper and coloured front picture; I have several, all in this edition: three from the girls upon my birthday, one at Christmas, two as a parting present, and two as reading books. I shall have a very pretty and interesting book case when once all have been arranged.

The Germans are all so elated over the fall of Antwerp; they say its the beginning of the end!!! What rejoices them most of all is the fact that there were also English soldiers in the town. They say, "Let us get to Ostend, and then we will show them blighters what Deutschland can and will do." Naturally, 'justice' is upon their side, so their cause is sure — ahem!

They've begun to heat the house, at last, which is very agreeable, in spite of the fact that its gone and come in warmer. Its just ripping now, as we have a hot air mouth in our room — which works!! At Délices, we had one that dident work, and we also had, into the bargain, the coldest room in the house...

Last night we had some ripping fun. Lia and I dressed up. Lia draped up her night gown and made a lovely Turkish loose smock, with the loose trowsers (sic), just exactly the thing, with a broad loose sash round her waist. I took my bath towel, wrapped it round my waist, letting the point trail out behind me, and draped a dress cover over my shoulders. Thusly arrayed, the 'operetic (sic) tragedy' began, I the heartless fine lady, she the passionate lover. I scorned all his bows, and sailed about in haughty disdain, and then, when the knight, broken hearted, turns his back, I open the door and start making signs to another lover. The spurned knight discovers me, and, in a fit of jealous rage, stabs me, and then, himself, and falls dead over my lifeless body. The plot was really better than that, only, the haughty dame, in her eagerness to see her lover, forgot a whole scene, and got scolded by her murderer, once he came to life again. However, the 'operetic tragedy' was a great success, even tho' Milette nearly took an apopletic (sic) fit when we did the killing part with the door wide open. Our engagement cards are full now, and we are to play ever night.

I suppose, as I'm the daughter home from school, and a bit of a novelty, I shall get it all my own way for a little, wont I? well, I'm going to profit well, and am beginning my demands now, right away. Do you think you could manage to have a nice cheery fire in the dining room at night, when I come, as I do so hope to see a really good fire again. I havent seen one since I left, as its all hot air contraptions here. I was going to ask you for one or two other things too, but I shant, as it sounds so greedy, and I mustent start giving you a bad impression of me before you even see me. Its awfully good of you, as it is, to agree to tell no one of my return. I know I am horribly greedy and selfish, but it is my nature true. Thank you so much, and you have all my sympathies for having such an ungrateful daughter. Mad may say and write, as often as she likes, that your 'dear daughter' is becoming more practical and more angelic. It isent true. I'm myself, and my old self, and ever will be.

Mrs Watter has to do something at Paris, and must stay the day, I think. What luck if she'll only take me about with her. I only hope to goodness that none of them there 'taubes' will be on the spree that day, as I shouldn't like to die before seeing you and Bonny Scotland again.

I've just been informed, for the don't know how many time

this morning, that I'm in a very bad temper today... Quite possible, as I've been interrupted ten times, if once, with my letter, and that Milette has a tongue from here to Musselburgh, and disturbs me every minute. Oh, yes! I'm in a very bad temper, so I'd better go and get ready for church, and perhaps that'll calm me.

M. Bernoud came again, this week, with his pockets full of apples and walnuts. He's invited us to tea next week, some time, which will be very nice. He's so good to us, you know.

Madame Reymond wasent very well last week, so we couldent go to tea, which was a great pity, but Mad took us to the museum instead, and then gave us tea in town.

Bye the way, do you know what my new profession is? No, you don't, as I'm dancing teacher! Yes, your clumsy, stiff, ackward (sic), graceless daughter has taken it upon herself to teach the Scotch Reel and Schottisch to her charmed companions. They know four steps already, and are beginning to be quite agile. We also do Gymnastic every night, and, once, Mad opened the door and found us all sprawling about on the floor. She told us that it was very good of us to clean the floor so.

I do wish I could hear definitely when I start. At any rate, I shall send you a P.C. as soon as ever I get word. I shall also send a telegram from London.

Remember and don't say anything about it when it comes, to D., as I fear her wagging tongue.

I am going cracked, I think. I cant write a simple letter without making a dozen mistakes, and putting down my sentences in such a way as to change the sense altogether. Here goes again. Lets hope for better luck.

I am having a rare old time mending and darning to get my things in good order for when you shall see them.

I suppose that all the schools have taken up again. Is D. still proving to be the family's hope and pride?

Have you not heard from Jack lately? You never say anything in your letters. Do you know I simply cant believe that I've been away fourteen months, now. The time passes so quickly. We never seem to have a minute free now: lessons and practising in the morning; promenade and prep in the afternoon; prep again at night; and, after supper, we knit and try to read, at least I do, but Mad and the others start squabbling every two minutes, and shout like mad. I bravely try to read and knit at the same time, but, generally, my patience gives out, and I chuck away my sock, put my elbows on the table with a resolute bump, shut my ears, and read, but Mad has such a voice that its impossible to shut it out.

I'm now going to write a P.C. to Miss Johnston.

With much love.
your loving
Flora.

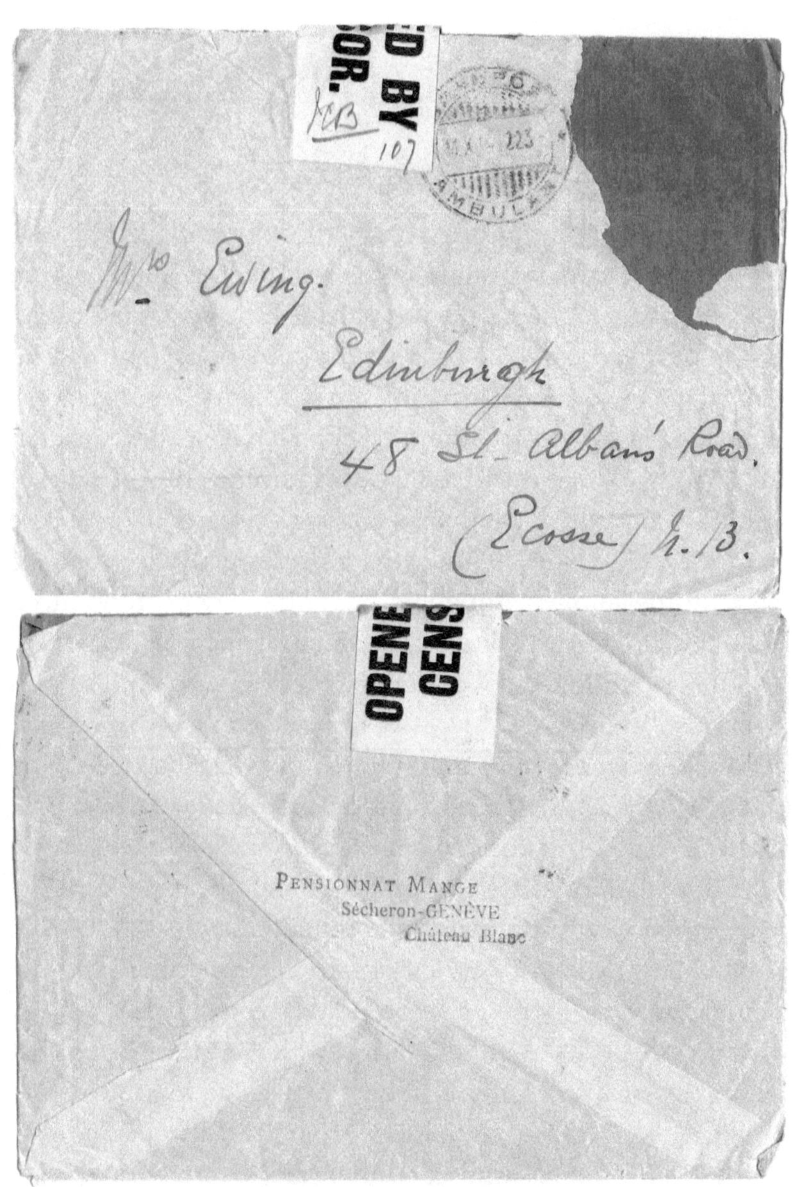

The letter was opened by a censor

Château Blanc
22nd Oct. 1914

My dear Mother and Daddy,

"I'm coming, I'm coming, for my time is ending slow." Yes, I am, at last. I take the quarter to three train on Sunday next, the 25th, and should, if all's well, arrive on Wednesday night. We should arrive at half past seven on Monday morning, at Paris, stay the day and sleep there, go by Dieppe — Folkestone, arrive at London, sleep at the West British Hotel, Southampton Rd, London W6, and catch the next morning train. That is if nothing extraordinary happens. Of course, its quite probable that we should be kicked out of the train, once or twice, to make room for the soldiers. I'm going with Mrs Vatter (pronounced Watter), who looks very nice: little quaint and old fashioned. It will be ripping if she would only speak French with me, all the time.

Mrs Cochrane wrote, and I wrote too, twice. She is leaving tomorrow, the 23rd, which left me only two days to pack up in, and then Mrs Vatter decided at last to leave, so I go with her.

I have already started to pack up, and oh, its awful! You can see by my writing that I'm absolutely flattened out; I can hardly hold myself up, my cheeks are like beetroots, and my hair stands, literally up on my head. I have my basket full up with my books. Its awful the number I have: all those I got at Christmas, and upon my birthday, as well as my music and lesson books. I had an awful time trying to pack 'flat,' and to stuff up all the holes and corners. I had several old pairs of gloves knocking about; these were all employed, as well as small boxes etc. At first, I was sure all wouldent go in, but by dint of squeezing, squashing and shoving, all is in. I only hope some of the books won't get spoilt. The worry is that its nearly twice too heavy, so I'll have to send it by post, which is cheaper but takes three weeks; poor me, I shall have to wait two weeks before I can arrange my pretty books. By the way, I hope you get this letter before you get me, as I doubt it muchly. At any rate, I hope you'll get my telegramme from London. It is always possible that I mayent arrive, except on Thursday, you know. That brat of a Milette has been and gone and catched a good cold, and she seems now to be endeavouring to ladle it round. I'm horribly sure that I've got a dose too; I feel it.

Today begins the packing up, and I know that I'll never have enough place for all my things. When we removed, I had a drawer with all my underclothing, two dresses and a big bath towel; a skirt and shoes in another girl's trunk, and my hats in a paper bag. Woe is me, now, when all those things must go in my poor trunk. I'm most alarmed for the hats, which come on top.

It seems as if I were coming very much indeed for Dorothy's birthday, poor kid.

Are you frightfully shocked that I am starting on a Sunday? At any rate, we are going to church before.

Do you know that dear old M. Bernoud says he's coming down to the train to see me off, bringing a packet of apples. Isent he good. We were to tea with him the other day, and we ate and ate his apples, and helped to gather them and put them into baskets, and carry them to the cave where he has stored, literally, tons and tons of them. I never saw so many before. At tea, we had some most ripping apple tart, and when we left we had hidden upon our persons, between us, about twenty six or twenty eight apples, together with heaps of walnuts; not bad for four people, hein?

I must really stop and go and put things a bit straight.

Much love,
your loving
Flora.

I may as well get my 2 ½d worth out of this letter, so I am cramming it with odds and ends; the French calander (sic) might interest D.

25 25
HELVETIA
GENÈVE 1
9-10
18 · X
1914
EXP LETTR
Rev. Dr. Ewing,
48 St Alban's Road,
Edinburgh.
Scotland.

Appendix

Mariele

München 23
Mainzer Strasse 70
1 April 1936

Ma bien chère Flora!

J'ai l'occasion de donner cette lettre à un ami de mon mari qui part à ces jours à Palestine, et j'espère qu'elle t'arrivera ansi plutôt.

Je suis heureuse de pouvoir te donner aujourd'hui des meilleures nouvelles que les dernières. Je suis retrouvée chez mon mari et mon fils dès du dernier mois de mai et tu peux te penser comment je suis soulagée. Je suis très très heureuse de ce changement de sort, ma chère Flora. Nous avons un très joli logement moderne, mais pas grand, à quatre chambres. Je travaille toute seule sans une domestique. Le travail de ménage m'occupe toute la journée, mais je m'y trouve très bien. Le garçon me fait beaucoup de plaisir, ainsi beaucoup de travail, mais je suis contente d'être unie avec lui. Mon mari est occupé aussi toute la journée et nous sommes contents ensemble.

De nouveau nous sommes enthousiasmés des derniers évènements politiqueus et de notre Führer. Tout l'Allemagne est enchanté de cet homme et de son énergie.

Chère Flora! J'espère que tu te trouves à bonne santé, toi et toute ta famille. J'aimerai tellement de te revoire une fois, après ces longues années. Nous nous aurions beaucoup à raconter. N'est–ce–pas possible que tu partiras une fois pour l'Ecosse et que tu passeras à cette occasion Munic? Je n'ai rien entendu de Genève dès la guerre malheureuse, ni d'aucune des camarades de notre année, ni de Mademoiselle Marie. Je ne sais plus si je t'ai racontée que nous avons perdu deux frères à la guerre. Mes autres frères se rejouissent de bonne santé à Freiburg, l'un avec 4 enfants, l'autre revenant de l'Amerique avec un fils. Ma soeur à Hamburg avec 4 grand enfants se trouve aussi très bien. Ma chère mère est aussi toujours la même.

Est–ce–que tes parents se rejouissent encore de bonne santé? Si ta soeur à Bèrne aimera une fois de venir à Munic, je serais ravie de la voir chez moi. Quelle est la profession de ton mari? J'ai encore tant d'interêt de ton sort. Depuis ces longues années dès la guerre je souhaitais d'entendre de toi. Nous étions donc des amies tellement tendres, est–ce–que tu te rappelles encore? Envoie moi bientôt plus de nouvelles de toi, je me rejouirais tellement. Beaucoup de salutations à ta famille et beaucoup d'amitiés encore toujours pour toi, ton amie Mariele.

Katamon
Jerusalem
21 February 1937

My dear Joan[1],

...I remember escaping out of the gym class in Geneva and running into a little shop and feverishly buying some chocolate, with one or two other kindred sinners. It was rotten sandy chocolate, but as it was the bread — or chocolate — of freedom, we thought it tasted 'delish!' We, however, had to account for every penny of our doled out pocket money, in a weekly 'audit,' so that orgy took some cooking up, after.

I remember that gym class. We walked to a funny kind of gymnasium where we met 'les demoiselles' from Geneva's other Pensionnats — all fair and flaxen little German maïdchens. The mistress was small and intense — and German, and adored a certain German girl who was very good at gym. This girl was always being asked to show how good she was. She was always being picked out as doing an exercise marvellously, *and* she could touch her toes, not a usual accomplishment for a Teutonic figure, I may say. Well! suddenly, I discovered that I could touch my toes too — put my hands flat on the floor, even — and with my whole soul I yearned to be noticed for my trick... Do you think she ever glanced my way! That mean–souled woman skidded past my elevated bo–hind and purple straining face and said, "Ach, Trude, schoen — zer schoen!" I ate the bread of bitterness that day. After that I used to watch for her — for I was very good at gym: whatever Trude did I burst myself to do as well — and I did — but, to this day, I've never had a word of praise... An unjust world! But at least I did have the sweeties!...

1 Flora's eldest daughter at school in Scotland

Flora (about 2 years old)

Flora

Flora's parents

Flora's Father

LETTERS FROM A GENEVA PENSIONNAT
BY FLORA EWING

Very personal, sometimes romantic and naive, the letters will take you through feelings, worries, excitement and emotions with great humour and unimaginable details from a hundred year ago life. The original letters have been kept in the family for one hundred years and carefully transferred to an electronic format by Judith David.

Design and photo scanning by Dotos Limited.
Dotos Books™ is a trademark of Dotos Limited.

ISBN 978-1-910717-00-4

Published by
Dotos Books
www.dbooks.co.uk
LONDON, 2015

www.ingramcontent.com/pod-product-compliance
Lightning Source LLC
Chambersburg PA
CBHW050955210726
48287CB00004B/1239

* 9 7 8 1 9 1 0 7 1 7 0 0 4 *